TEN CAMELS FOR MY WIFE

by

JOHN MEADOWS

John Meadows

Published under license from Andrews UK

First Edition

Acknowledgements

Special thanks to Richard Ayres for his in-depth appraisal of my manuscript. His valuable advice and constructive suggestions were greatly appreciated.

Also, thank you to my friends Bill Lyon, Janette Lyon and Bill Fryer for their continued help and encouragement.

I would like to express my appreciation to my agent, Darin Jewell (Managing Director of the Inspira Literary Agency Group) for his guidance, advice and conscientious hard work on my behalf.

Dedicated to my wife Norma,

for being with me every step of the way.

Worth every single camel.

To Bill,

remember when you drove us to London and dropped us off at the bus stop? This is what happened next......

CONTENTS

Last Tango in Argentina

Flying Down to Rio

Blame it in The Bossa Nova

Chapter One

The Magical History Tour Begins

"Norma, they're taking the car away, come and say goodbye." We stood at the front door and watched our beloved Mini Cooper, our first-ever car, being driven off down the road. We went back into our empty, curtain less, carpet-less, furniture-less council house in Runcorn and surveyed our meagre possessions.

A solitary television, two deck chairs and two sleeping bags are not a lot to show after two years of marriage," I observed, ruefully. Our sparse surroundings suggested a burglary, an eviction, or perhaps a visit by Court Bailiffs. Our eyes met across an un-crowded room as we shed a few tears … tears of joy. We burst out laughing and could not have been happier. We had resigned from our jobs and sold all our worldly goods.

The television was the last to go, so that I could watch the Montreal Olympics. Our laughter went on to another level when David Coleman's athletic commentary reverberated around the room; "The Cuban, Alberto Juantarena has opened his legs and shown his class."

It was the famously hot summer of 1976, and we were about to embark on an adventure of a lifetime: overland to Kathmandu by Magic Bus, and then on to the Far East and Australia. Our plan was to find jobs in Australia, before continuing our journey to New Zealand, the South Pacific and South America.

In addition to sea travel, overland travel and air travel, we will be adding an extra dimension: Time-travel. Occasionally, I will interrupt our space-time continuum and take out my flux capacitor. (The same one I used in my first book on my Greyhound Bus odyssey around America). It hasn't done much mileage, and besides, it isn't illegal to turn back the clock on a time-machine. I will explain more in the future, (or possibly the past).

We arrived in London and made our way to Earl's Court to pick up the bus. A small crowd had congregated on the pavement, and we approached a group of people who were loading-up the bus. The first thing we noticed was the predominance of Australian and New Zealand accents, and, amidst the clamour, it was difficult to identify who was actually leaving, and who was waving goodbye. A small, dishevelled, weather-beaten man with a tangle of dark curly hair and a Zapata moustache, was ticking off names on his clipboard, so I approached him.

"Excuse me, is this the bus to Kathmandu?" I asked nonchalantly, as if I had been at Wigan Bus Station inquiring about the next bus to St. Helens.

"G'day mate," he replied, cheerily, in an unmistakable Aussie accent. He ticked off our names and welcomed us aboard.

As the bus filled up with our new travelling companions, it was difficult to work out who were together and who was travelling alone.

To our surprise, there was very little bonhomie at first, as people just nodded brief acknowledgements to each other and sat down. Everyone seemed lost in their own individual thoughts, as if they were daily commuters on their way to work.

"This is going to be a laugh-a-minute for the next five months," I whispered to Norma, but she pointed out that it was a sad time for many of them, as she noticed the number of tearful goodbyes. The two drivers were last on board, and introduced themselves as Mick, the Australian, and a tall red-haired Scotsman called Dave. We set off for Dover.

In the bar on the Cross-Channel Ferry to Calais, everyone started to intermingle and chat, and the group seemed to have quite an interesting demographic. On the bus, en-route to Paris, Mick invited each of us in the party to come to the front for a light-hearted, introductory interview over the microphone. This was an excellent way to break the ice, and it became apparent that we had some interesting characters on board. Over subsequent months, and in some cases years, some became our close friends.

There was an Australian doctor, Barry, who was about thirty, single and travelling alone. He had been living in London for a while, and he had just achieved membership of the Royal College of Physicians. A couple of English nurses, Angie and Bethan, were also part of the group, so it was reassuring to know that we had our personal medical team on hand, should we become ill or injured in the back of beyond. We met Reg, an Australian, and Colin, an

Englishman who had lived in Sydney for quite a few years. They were travelling separately, but quickly became firm friends since they regarded themselves as professional travellers. Indeed, Colin told us that he worked in insurance, but was proud of the fact that his passport actually stated 'Traveller' as his occupation. (Mine stated: 'Time-traveller', in my imagination, that is).

"So, that's medical and insurance covered," I mused. "All we need now is a motor mechanic and someone who works for American Express to cover all eventualities." Then there was Nick, a tall, laid-back character who spoke in a slow Texas drawl. He had piercing blue eyes, longish hair and a luxuriant beard, and, in his red-check lumberjack shirt, he looked as though he should have been rolling logs on a river, or whittling on the porch of a backwoods cabin. Appearances can be deceptive. He had a very gentle, courteous manner and he told us that he was from the Cayman Islands, where he worked in the family camera shop in Georgetown. There was also Margaret, an antiques dealer, Clarry, a classical guitarist, a young Australian married couple, Peter and Kay, and others, who we would get to know during our adventure.

Mick, the tour leader and co-driver, outlined the day-to-day routine: we were all required to contribute to a food kitty, and participate in a cooking roster, and we would be issued with tents. The itinerary was flexible enough to enable us to either extend or shorten our time at various destinations as required. The majority of our party had toured Europe in the, almost obligatory, VW campervan. Most of them had been to Paris quite recently, and the general consensus was that just a couple of nights would be sufficient. This suited us because we had been to Paris several times.

However, in this book, we cannot just skip over one of the world's great cities, so we *now* have a perfect opportunity to take our first trip into the future. I will set my portable time-machine for the year 1989; the Centenary of the Eiffel Tower...

Are We in Seine?

... I am now Head of Arts at the Deanery High School in Wigan, and we are planning an art trip to Paris. The supervisory staff included art teachers; Janette (who some readers might remember from our American tours in my first book), and Linda, a colleague with an outgoing personality, popular with the children. Also, there was George Minister, the Head of Languages; a most engaging character, with a nice line in wit and comic banter. He had a tremendous classroom presence, and he always had a good rapport with the students. George was in his mid-30s, above average height with a heavy build, jet black hair and dark, bushy eyebrows.

Of course, all school tours require the approval of the Headmaster, and I made an appointment to see Mr. Williams to outline our proposed Paris trip. He was very enthusiastic; so much so, that he asked if he could join us. I told him that he would be very welcome, and my colleagues agreed.

Mr. Williams was in his late 40s, mid to average height, with straight dark hair and a beard flecked with traces of grey. He was a science teacher who also had a genuine interest in art, and he was very supportive of the arts in school. He was as excited as the rest of us to be going to one of the world's greatest galleries: The Louvre. The Headmaster was a Welshman, but, after teaching wave-upon-wave of Wiganers, nearly all traces of a Welsh accent had been beaten into submission. In fact, he was proud to call himself an 'honorary pie-eater', and he was a regular supporter of the Wigan Rugby League Club.

The art trip to Paris proved to be very popular with the pupils, and parental reply-slips flooded in. Not surprisingly, there were numerous forms to fill in: Collective passport, E111 medical forms, contact details and so on. Once the composition of the party had been finalised, we had our first meeting during one morning break time...

"Sir, what's me DOB?"

"Pardon?" I replied, perplexed.

"It says here; 'Your DOB'," stated a year-9 boy, pointing at the form he was attempting to fill in.

"It is, D… O… B," I replied, emphasising each individual letter with a slight air of exasperation. "It means, your date of birth."

This was my first encounter with Shane, whose reputation preceded him, together with his younger brother, Wayne. What a double act. If there was a kerb to trip over, then one of them would inevitably oblige, closely followed by his brother falling on top of him. They would immediately bounce back up, laughing and blaming each other, like a couple of cartoon characters. And we were taking them to Paris.

Wayne and Shane were a picture of concentration; hunched over the table, faces contorted, and tongues out trying to touch the tips of their noses. Occasionally, they paused to chew their pencils while agonising over the next question. They were two lovely-natured lads, and you couldn't help but like them. Wayne had an unruly thatch of dark hair, a freckled complexion and brown eyes that twinkled with mischievous innocence. His brother Shane was exactly the same. They could have been twins, but Wayne was in year 9, and Shane in year 8.

I paused to look over the shoulder of another boy, Andrew Kirkpatrick, to check on his progress. The form in front of him was a visual record of his thought-process; the crossings-out, rubbings-out and alterations. Let me explain: Surname: ~~Kirk~~…, crossed out, then re-written, Kirkpatrick. He realised he had been right first time. First name: Andrew. He managed that first time, no problem. Other names: ~~Kirk…~~, crossed out, ~~Paul~~, crossed out. He *finally* settled for, Kirky.

"What's this, Andrew?" I inquired, pointing at the word Kirky.

"It's my other name, Sir."

"What? Your name is Kirky Kirkpatrick?"

"No," replied Andrew, forcefully, looking up at me as if I was daft, "it's what all me mates call me."

"Andrew," I said, with a touch of unavoidable sarcasm, "the officials at the Passport Office in Liverpool don't really want to know your nickname."

At that point, I sensed a flurry of activity all around me, which sounded suspiciously like frantic rubbing out. Like a boxer at the end of a bout, I was relieved to hear the sound of the bell. Mission accomplished. Just in time.

Time Traveller's Guide to Paris

"John, who are in room 208?" asked Linda during breakfast on our first morning at our Paris hotel. Her body language and general demeanour suggested that she was on the war path, and it seemed as though some of our pupils were in for a rude awakening. I took a piece of paper from my pocket, and ran my finger down the list of rooms.

"What room did you say?"

"208."

"None of our kids are in room 208, they must be other guests."

Linda's body language, facial expression and attitude changed in an instant, as she covered her face with her hands.

"What's happened?" I asked hesitantly, as the rest of the staff at the table stopped eating, anxious to hear her reply.

"Last night, there was one hell of a noise going on; television at full blast and uproarious laughter. I banged on the door with my clenched fist and shouted, 'Turn that telly off and get to bed… NOW!'"

"So what did they do?" asked Janette.

"They turned the television off and went to bed." Once a teacher, always a teacher.

Over breakfast, I ticked off names to make sure that all our party had appeared for breakfast by eight o'clock, as instructed the previous evening. By eight thirty, three of the girls were still missing. Janette was just about to go up to their room, when they appeared in the dining room, looking flustered. I beckoned for them to come over to our table, and asked for an explanation as to their lateness. They apologised profusely, saying that they had simply forgotten to put their clocks forward. I accepted this, and told them to eat their breakfast faster than usual. As they were leaving, one of the girls turned and asked, "Sir, why do we have to put our clocks forward when we come to France?"

"Oh, blame that on the Germans," answered George, with a casual shrug of his shoulders. The three girls looked confused, as did the rest of the staff.

"The Germans?" we asked in unison.

"Yes, it was introduced by The Chancellor in the 1950s... Dr. Adenhauer."

Lace Made of Steel

In 1844, Charles Dickens wrote; 'Paris is the most extraordinary place in the world'. If he was alive today, when the rest of the world is much more accessible, I don't think he would change his mind.

After breakfast we boarded the coach, and headed for the Eiffel Tower. It has been described as 'Looking like lace made of steel'; an iconic emblem of Paris. We made it our first stop to give us an over-view of the city. We were able to identify most of the sights which were on our itinerary: The Louvre, Arc de Triomphe, Notre-Dame Cathedral and the Church of Sacre Coeur, which overlooks the famous Montmartre district. The view from the top of the tower was spectacular, but we could just as easily have been looking at the Cathedral of the Familia Sagrada and Las Ramblas, instead of Notre Dame and the Champs Elysee. At this point, you must be thinking; 'How *high* does the Eiffel Tower need to be to enable us to see as far as Barcelona?' The engineer Gustave Eiffel's plan was originally intended for Barcelona, but the city authorities turned it down as being, quote: 'Strange and expensive'. A rejection which ranks right up there with Dick Rowe, the recording executive who rejected the Beatles following their audition for DECCA, 1962. However, like Brian Epstein, Gustave Eiffel did not give up, and he submitted his plans to the authorities of the Universal Exhibition in Paris. It was accepted, and the Eiffel Tower was built for the 1889 World Fair, to commemorate the centenary of the French Revolution. The storming of the Bastille, on 14th July, 1789, started the revolution by freeing all the prisoners. Guess how many prisoners were actually incarcerated?... The answer is the grand total of *seven*. They were all old men, four forgers and a few lunatics. However, they were all annoyed by the disturbance and were reluctant to leave. There's gratitude for you. Incidentally, the infamous Marquis de Sade, who gave his name to sadism, had been transferred out from the Bastille only ten days earlier. Presumably, he was having far too much fun.

An interesting story is that a skeleton was found in one of the lower dungeons of the Bastille, still chained to the wall. Significantly, the skull was mysteriously encased in an iron mask. This was the origin of the book 'The Man in the Iron Mask' by the French author Alexander Dumas. His name cropped up in the movie 'The Shawshank Redemption', when an inmate in the prison library referred to him as Alexander Dumb Ass. The premise of the novel is that the man in the Iron Mask was none other than the older, identical twin brother of King Louis XIV; and therefore the rightful King. It was meant to be a fictitious, dumb ass theory, but historical research is beginning to suggest that it could be a true story. If so, Louis XIV certainly did have a skeleton in his cupboard.

When the Eiffel Tower opened, it was greeted with condemnation and ridicule in much the same way as the first French Impressionist exhibition was in 1874. How ironic that two of the most famous and enduring achievements of Paris were almost strangled at birth. Indeed, the Eiffel Tower was originally conceived as a temporary structure. It was due to be torn down in 1909, but was reprieved because of its value as a radio telegraph tower. Isn't it amazing how temporary things have a habit of becoming permanent; like Coronation Street and the London Eye. Even Income Tax was first introduced as an emergency *temporary* measure in Britain, to finance the Napoleonic wars. Yes, he certainly has a lot to answer for does *that* Napoleon Bonaparte. Incidentally, the general perception of the Napoleon is that he was a very short, portly chap. In actual fact, he was 5ft 6½ inches tall, which was above average male height in France at the end of the 18th Century. The enduring image of him was the result of propaganda in the British press, in particular the political cartoons of James Gillray and George Cruikshank. Napoleon was actually taller than the 5ft 4 inch Horatio Nelson.

If the Eiffel Tower provided us with a sensational over-view, then, by contrast, a cruise on the Seine took us right into the heart of the city. An instantly recognisable sculpture came into view, but wasn't it in the wrong city? Or even the wrong country? It was the Statue of Liberty, albeit smaller than the more famous one in America. The New York sculpture had been a gift from France. The version situated on an island in the Seine, was presented to the people of France by the American Community in Paris in 1889, three years after her big sister was unveiled in New York. Actually, there is a family of them; a third version stands in Colmar, in northern France. This happens to be the birthplace of one Frederic Bartholdi, the sculptor of the Statue of Liberty. (Gustave Eiffel designed the interior supporting structure). Can we count the one in Las Vegas as part of the family, or is she just a tribute act?

Paris was founded by the Gauls, and later the Romans named it Lutetia. The site of the original settlement, on Ile de la Cité in the Seine, is, today, the most magnificent setting for the Cathedral of Notre-Dame. The huge, rose window in the south-facing façade is one of the most impressive stained-glass windows in the world.

All this history, culture, architecture and art notwithstanding, Notre-Dame also provided the kids with the perfect setting to exchange Quasimodo jokes. Wayne, Shane and Kirky took centre stage, eagerly encouraged by Mr. Minister, aided and abetted by the Headmaster.

Montmartre is a bustling district, which is a microcosm of the essence of Paris. It is similar, in some respects, to Greenwich Village in New York, or the Rocks Centre in Sydney. The area is dominated by the distinctive white domes of the Basilica Sacre-Coeur, and the streets, squares and alleyways are where artists, including Picasso, Van Gogh and Modigliani, once lived and worked. It is still a thriving area for artists and entertainers and several of our pupils sat for portraits and cartoons, as we all enjoyed the café ambiance.

Louvre Doors

The following morning, we set off to visit one of the greatest galleries in the world; the Louvre, which was originally a 13th Century fortress. It became the Royal Palace, and successive French monarchs extended the building and acquired more and more art. Francis I, a contemporary of Henry VIII, is recognized as the founder of this important collection, which today numbers about 400,000 pieces. After Charles I of England lost his head, he also lost his art pieces; Oliver Cromwell sold them to Louis XIV. The French King decided that the Louvre was not grand enough for him, so he moved the entire French court to Versailles. Following the French Revolution, Napoleon decided to transfer the Royal Collections, now property of the Nation, back to the Louvre.

Designed by architect Pierre Lescot, The Louvre is a synthesis of a French Château with an Italian Renaissance Palace. Rich sculptural decoration was added by the finest French sculptor of the16th Century, Jean Gonjon. Following this lavish history, what is the contribution of the 20th Century to the baroque splendour of the Louvre?... A glass pyramid!

Prince Charles famously compared the Clore Gallery extension of the National Gallery in London to, quote: 'A monstrous carbuncle on the face of a much-loved and elegant friend'. I don't know if he has ever commented about the Louvre's glass pyramid, which is just as incongruous. It is another Museum- of-Art carbuncle. (I think I will christen this one a 'Paul Simon'). If Napoleon had been around at the time, I think the Chinese-born, American architect, Ieo Ming Pei, (a name with a Wigan ring to it), would have been introduced to Madame Guillotine.

As we ascended the main staircase, we were greeted by the sight of a 9 feet tall, headless, winged statue, which looked as if it was about to take off in flight. Our group gathered around, and I told them that it was a marble sculpture from Greece, dated about 190 B.C.

"It is called Nike, the Greek Goddess of Victory," I informed the group. "Where have you heard the name Nike before?"

Faces contorted into a quizzical, expressions. Kirky looked at his footwear and a light bulb came on over his head.

"Nike trainers?" he answered, hopefully.

"Correct, well done. The company chose the name because of its association with Victory. Kirky beamed a big smile, and looked around to milk the moment, as if he had just won Mastermind. Then he spoiled his moment of triumph, or victory, by looking back towards the statue and looking down at her feet.

Enigma Variations: You say sfumato, 'I say 'sfumaito'.

The star attraction of the Louvre is Leonardo Da Vinci's 'La Giaconda', a small oil painting on a piece of wood. It is a portrait of Lisa Gherardini; an unremarkable woman, who achieved very little of note during her lifetime. Indeed, even her name derived from that of her husband; Florentine merchant Francesco Giacondo. And yet, she has become one of the most famous people to have ever lived; Mona Lisa. She transcends the world of art, and her face is familiar even to people who have no interest in art, or have never been in a gallery.

The reason for her enduring fame remains a mystery; she is the Mary Celeste of art, the original 'famous-for-being-famous' celeb. Endless research only adds to the intrigue: Was she pregnant? Did she have problems with her teeth? Why does the unidentified, ephemeral, otherworldly, fantasy background not match up on either side of her head? Moreover, it has been suggested that the lady in the picture never existed, and that the painting is an exact mirror image of a Leonardo self-portrait.

As recently as 2015, University research concluded that the secret of the enigmatic smile is hidden in the peripheral vision of the viewer. I have tried this, and I must admit that it is quite intriguing. Do try this at home: look at her face, then look away slightly. The smile broadens to a grin, which disappears when you look back at her. Mona Lisa is playing games with us. We can draw two conclusions from this: Firstly; The genius of Leonardo means that the subtle softening (sfumato) of the lips and cheek bones accentuates the smile when looked at peripherally. Secondly; some post-graduate students have not got enough to do.

Other recent research has suggested that the Mona Lisa in the Louvre is actually a *copy*, albeit by Leonardo himself. The 'original' is kept in a vault in Singapore, and the latest, literally, state-of-the-art technology proves that they were painted by the same hand. This theory could explain why Leonardo kept the Louvre version for the rest of his life, and why it was taken to France. Leonardo went to Paris to work for King Francois, as a military engineer, and his letter of application still exists to this day. In it, the artist listed his professional attributes, and, famously, added as an afterthought, that he also did some drawing and painting. As understatements go, that takes some beating. It is as if Enrico Caruso had applied for a job as a chef, and, as a footnote, had written; 'I like to sing a bit of opera in the kitchen'.

As our own post-script to the Mona Lisa, another layer of fame was added in 1911, when the painting was stolen from the Louvre by a man named Peruggia. He was caught, two years later, at the Hotel Tripoli in Florence, with the painting hidden under his bed. The management immediately changed the name of the hotel to… yes, you've guessed it: Hotel La Giaconda. A master-stroke of marketing, and, even to this day, guests book-in specifically to see the particular room where the painting was found.

While in the Louvre, we also spent some time looking at examples of paintings which depict scenes from the Bible: The Supper at Emmaus by the Dutch 17th Century painter Rembrandt, and the monumental painting, by the 16th Century Italian Paulo Veronese, of The Marriage at Cana; where Jesus turned water into wine. "The perfect guest to have at a wedding reception," quipped George.

Flushed with Embarrassment

Fabulous paintings notwithstanding, our enduring memory of the Louvre is the toilets. Going to the loo in the Louvre was a unique experience. For some unfathomable reason, the toilet-flushing system was linked electronically to the cubicle door. To flush the toilet, you simply open the door. Ingenious. No need for ugly chains, or handles, or buttons on the floor. Except for one small problem; there were no instructions to explain this manoeuvre to the unsuspecting occupant. The bright spark who had introduced this innovative system hadn't quite thought it through. Queues of increasingly desperate people waited while occupants searched frantically for some clue as to how to flush. The last resort was to give it up as a bad job, so to speak, and open the door. The toilet would then flush and people would emerge with a look of great relief, in more ways than one.

For a time, Mona Lisa hung in Napoleon's bathroom. Perhaps *that* is the secret of her enigmatic smile, as she watched him try to work out the complexities of flushing French toilets! Now *that* is one theory I haven't read before.

You Know You Make Me Want to Shout

Mark Twain, 19th Century American author is quoted as saying; *"In Paris they simply stared at me when I spoke to them in French. I never did succeed in making those people understand their own language."* Perhaps, he should have tried the British technique: shout in English, and if the foreigners don't understand, then shout even louder. We didn't have any such problems being in George's company in Paris. Not only was he completely fluent in French, but the local Parisians at craft fairs or restaurants actually thought that he *was* French; the ultimate accolade for a teacher of foreign languages. Over lunch at a restaurant, our conversation turned to the subject of languages, and we raised the question to George of why the British public seem to be so very poor at grasping other languages. "*That* is the $64,000 question," answered George, with a slight air of resigned exasperation. He gave us some points to ponder: The British have an island mentality, English is the most widely-spoken language in the world, and English and American music, films and television are available practically everywhere on earth. Probably, the underlying fundamental reason is that English-speaking people feel as though they don't *have* to learn other languages. George, who is a natural bon viveur and raconteur, then began to tell us about some of the hilarious situations which have occurred during the GCSE French oral examinations at school.

I will let George take up the story from here…

I would sit in my classroom, with a tape recorder on the desk. Each candidate would have an allotted time to answer questions in French and, hopefully, we would be able to have a meaningful conversation.

There was a light, almost timid, knock on the door.

"Entrez!"

In walked Noel, hesitantly and trying to force a smile through nervous lips.

"Bonjour!" I said, encouragingly.

"Bonjour!"

"Ferme la porte, s'il te plaît!"

"Assieds-toi!"

Noel closed the door and sat down, as instructed.

"Ça va?" I asked.

"Très bien, merci," answered Noel, with an air of bemused bewilderment. I smiled, and gave him a nod of encouragement.

The theme for this particular assessment was concerned with food. I began by asking him, in French, what he had eaten for breakfast, and what was he going to have for lunch. The following conversation ensued:

"Qu'est-ce que tu as pris au petit-déjeuner ce matin?"

"Un bol de céréales."

"Qu'est-ce que tu vas manger à midi aujourd'hui?"

A blank stare was followed by confusion, then slowly, the dawn of recognition, as he realised I was asking him about his lunch. He leaned forward, almost conspiratorially, and patted his blazer pocket. With slow deliberation, in a comic, Inspector Clouseau French accent, he announced,

"I 'av a napple in my pockette."

The next candidate was required to role-play a shopping scenario. He was given an instruction card which asked him to buy some bread. He offered; "Eff yew a leurf?" It was pure 'Alo,'Alo.

One pupil was given the theme of booking into a hotel: "Avez-vous une chambre pour quatre poissons, s'il vous plaît?" Not surprisingly, the hotel did *not* have a room for four fish.

As we were laughing at George's stories, Shane came over to our table and held his hand out in front of me. I noticed some pink discolouration, so I asked him what had happened.

"It's okay now, but I nearly scalded myself in our bathroom last night," he informed me, indignantly. "Sir, will you complain to the manager?"

"To tell him that the water in your room is too hot?"

"No... to tell him that they've put a 'C' on the *hot* tap!"
George raised his eyebrows and smiled, ironically. After our entertaining coffee break it was time to explore Paris once more.

Show Me the Monet

The Orsay Museum, on the left bank of the Seine, has been described as 'The most beautiful museum in Europe'. The building was originally the Orsay Railway Station, which was abandoned in 1939. It re-opened as The Museé D'Orsay in 1986, to display modern works of art. It is a spacious, light area which retains the elaborate metal and stone work of the railway station. The station's huge ornate clock is still in its original position.

I was particularly enthralled with the paintings of the French Impressionists such as Monet, Renoir, and Pissarro. The wheel of fortune has turned full-circle, because, never in the history of art, has a group been so cruelly mocked. That includes today's era of un-made beds, cows sawn in half, and the often quoted pile of bricks.

In the 19th Century, the Salon, the French equivalent of England's Royal Academy, controlled public taste, and only paintings chosen by a selection committee were accepted. The Impressionists were the punks of the 1870s who rebelled against the establishment. They even painted outdoors, and had the audacity to exhibit these 'en plein air' canvases, rather than follow the traditional procedure of finishing a painting meticulously in the studio. When Claude Monet painted, 'Impression Sunrise, Le Havre', he explained that it couldn't really be described as a scene; more of an impression. The name stuck, and was regarded as a joke. As they had no chance of showing their work in the Salon, the Impressionists set up their own exhibitions between 1874 and 1886. They were ridiculed in the press as: 'the school of daubers'. The public would go to the exhibitions purely for amusement, and laugh out loud at the paintings. They were just taking the Pissarro.

"Sir, why did he keep painting the same thing, over and over?" asked one of the younger pupils, as we looked at Monet's series of 'Haystack' paintings. I explained that he was observing light and shade at different times of day, and during different seasons of the year.

Monet and his fellow Impressionists actually made significant discoveries about colour theory: when an object casts a shadow, the shaded area is tinged with the complementary colour of the object. For example, the shadow of a red post box would have a hint of green. Monet and Pissarro particularly enjoyed studying snowy landscapes, and the significant aspect is that the paintings are fresh and vibrant due to the tinge of blues, purples and lilacs in the shadows.

My attention was drawn to some muffled laughter, as Wayne, Shane and Kirky stood in front of a snowy landscape by Monet. The painting was called 'La Pie', a title which attracts Wiganers like moths to a flame.

For the benefit of those readers unaware of the cultural significance of pies in Wigan, let me explain: Wiganers are known affectionately as 'Pie Eaters', and have a self-effacing, self-deprecating humour; for example, pies on a skewer are called a Wigan kebab.

"Sir, who ate all the pies?" asked Wayne, while pointing at the title of Monet's painting.

"It means Magpie," explained George, scrutinising the scene, "Look, there it is, perched on the wooden gate. The thieving magpie must have pinched all the pies.

Pomp and Sewer Pipe

If the Museé D'Orsay is the 'most beautiful museum in Europe', then the Pompidou Centre must be her ugly sister. It is revolutionary in that all the structures normally situated *inside* a building, such as escalators and lifts, have been placed on the *outside.* The plumbing and various pipes are also on the outside, each painted a different colour corresponding to a different function: blue is the climatization plant, yellow the electrical installation, green the water circuits, and, presumably, brown for sewer pipes. Perhaps, French plumbers, electricians and heating engineers are required to have a further qualification in abseiling. It is fortunate that the architects, Renzo Piano and Richard Rogers, don't design aeroplanes. I wouldn't fancy using an outside toilet on a Jumbo Jet.

To Whom It May Concern

When I was planning the itinerary for our art tour to Paris, George advised me that the French embrace bureaucracy, almost as if they had invented the word. Presenting an official-looking document to a self-important French official tends to open doors, as if by magic, thereby avoiding long queues. So, I decided to put my calligraphy skills to good use, and I prepared a letter which included lots of official-sounding words such as; hereby, forthwith and whomsoever. It was typed in English and French on school-headed notepaper, and I also added the Wigan Borough Coat-of-Arms, (A Pie and Crossbones), lavishly embellished with copper plate lettering. The document needed several signatures, written with as many extravagant flourishes as possible. I required the school's two most important and authoritative persons to sign it. No, not the Chairman of Governors and Headmaster, I asked Christine and June, our formidable Caretakers.

The final piece-de-resistance, (even *I* was beginning to turn French), were lots of rubber stamps. The school office provided me with a box-full, together with an ink pad. All the usual stuff; library book issue and return, and permission to leave class to go to the toilet. I even made my own stamp from a lino cut, and I thought that the

French might be impressed by something in Latin. I decided to seize the moment. Something from Wigan, in Latin? I know, 'Car-Pie-Diem', which, I think, roughly translates as, 'No Pies Are Left in this Car Overnight'

Here Comes the Sun King

The Palace of Versailles, about ten miles outside Paris, was built for the Sun King; Louis XIV. The visual arts were recognised as a means of glorifying the King, a notion which can be traced back thousands of years to the Pharaohs. When we approached the awe-inspiring grandeur of the palace, it certainly evoked the intended effect. A sumptuously decorated, Baroque building, it is embellished with sculptures and columns. The term Baroque is derived from a Portuguese word for an irregular-shaped pearl. It is a reference to the over-extravagant forms used in the buildings and decoration of the 17th Century.

The Palace is surrounded by geometric, formal gardens, with terraces, sculptured fountains, hedges and statues. It was intended as an appropriate outdoor setting for the King's appearances in public, at the extravagant fetes. These festivities were the wonder of Europe, and every monarch wished to live the French style. In Russia, Peter the Great created St. Petersburg in the style of Versailles, and later Catherine the Great bought hundreds of works of art in Paris. Architects throughout Europe found their source of inspiration at

Versailles for the new palaces that their sovereigns had ordered them to build. The Palace of Versailles was the mother of all palaces.

Not surprisingly, the long queues stretched from the opulent, gold embellished main gate and snaked across the cobbled courtyard. This seemed an opportune moment to find out just how convincing my impressive-looking documentation really was.

"Okay, let's go and try it on," George said to me, not too confidently.

"Do you think it might work better if you wait here with the rest?" I suggested to him.

"But you don't speak French."

"Exactly."

George scratched his head and gave me a quizzical look, unable to follow my twisted logic.

"If you speak to them in fluent French, it makes it easier for them to ask you detailed questions about this," I suggested, holding up our letter of introduction.

So, I selected two of our youngest, innocent-looking pupils and told them to keep smiling. I decided not to take Wayne and Shane; there were too many cobbles to trip over. Several uniformed officials were on duty, collecting the entrance tickets at a box office. An intense-looking officer, who seemed to exude an air of seniority, stood watching.

“There’s our man,” I whispered to the kids, who were oblivious to my cunning plan. I approached the barrier and, with as much confidence as I could muster, beckoned to him.

“Je ne parle pas Français. Parlez-tu Anglais?” I asked, officiously.

What a relief when he replied, “No, Monsieur.”

I held a wad of entrance tickets in front of him, but he seemed unimpressed until I brandished the letter, pointing animatedly at the proliferation of stamps.

He took it to another official who was sitting at a desk in a small foyer. He carefully scrutinised my important-looking document, and beckoned me over. I took the initiative with a confident “Bonjour monsieur,” and our two pupils smiled at him, right on cue. He smiled back, gave us a couple of Gallic shrugs and opened his desk drawer. He took out a rubber stamp, which he banged down exaggeratedly on my letter, as if he was stamping, literally, his authority on the situation. He wrote his signature through the centre of the stamp, and handed it back to me, as if he was a celebrity giving his autograph to a star-struck fan. “Bienvenue a Versailles,” he said, with a welcoming smile. I looked at the letter and there it was; an authentic Palace of Versailles stamp; signed, sealed and delivered. It was well-placed between my lino-cut and the Caretakers’ signatures.

I waved the letter above my head, Neville Chamberlain-style, to signal to Janette to bring our party forward. We were all escorted through the barrier and welcomed as if we were V.I.P s. This proved to be the case throughout our stay in Paris; the Versailles stamp having authenticated the letter. By the time we got home it was festooned with stamps from various galleries and museums. I wish I had had the letter framed and entered it for the Turner Prize, with some outrageously pretentious title like; 'The Trompe l'Oeil of Bureaucracy'. But then again, I would probably have had more chance winning by entering one of the hotel's un-made beds. What a ridiculous idea that would have been.

Despite the stupendous, monumental exterior of the Palace of Versailles, Louis XIV was more interested in lavish interiors, with the intention that they should provide appropriate settings for himself and his court. The famous Hall of Mirrors (Galerie des Glaces) has been the setting for many important events, the most famous being the signing of the Treaty of Versailles, following the end of the First World War.

Our group, pupils and adults alike, looked round in open-mouthed awe at the sumptuousness of the crystal chandeliers, marble, bevelled glass and classical statues. The vaulted ceiling is entirely covered with paintings by the French artist, Le Brun; the main artistic adviser to the King. The tour of the Palace was like walking through a fairy-tale: a succession of drawing rooms named; Venus, Mars, Mercury, Diana, Apollo, War and Peace. Each room was as sumptuous as the next, and everyone seemed to be of the opinion that they had never been inside such a splendid building. A perfect ending to our memorable tour of the beautiful city of Paris.

As we are leaving Paris on the coach, it is time for me to time-travel, in an instant, and materialize back-in-time on to the Magic Bus, which is also just leaving Paris. I have got this time-travelling lark off to such a fine art, that I resume my seat at the exact moment I left. No-one has missed me. We are heading due east to Germany, and the historic town of Heidelberg.

Drink, Drink, Drink...

This area is actually the cradle of European settlement; The jawbone of Heidelberg Man was found in 1907, and, to the north, bones were found in Feldhot Cave in the Neander Valley; Neanderthal Man. Which brings me nicely to our Australian driver, Mick.

"Fancy a few beers, mate? I know a great German Bier Keller in town," he suggested.

Heidelberg lies on the River Necker, and our campsite enjoyed a tranquil setting on the river bank. Twinned with Cambridge, Heidelberg is an academic city, synonymous with its 14th Century university. Unlike Cologne and other major German cities, Heidelberg wasn't bombed during World War II, as it was earmarked by the Americans as a base for after the war. Consequently, it has retained its Baroque charm with narrow streets and picturesque houses of the Alf Stadt (old town), overlooked by Heidelberg Castle on the wooded hills of Odenwald (Odin's Forest). The Alte Bruke (old bridge) and pepper pot towers at the entrance to the bridge completed the idyllic setting.

Heidelberg became world famous through two Hollywood movies: 'The Student Prince of Old Heidelberg' was a 1927 MGM silent movie. It starred Ramon Navarro, who, incidentally, was also the original Ben-Hur, pre-dating the more famous Charlton Heston by some thirty years. The 1952 re-make of the 'Student Prince' was to star Mario Lanza but he was dismissed for several reasons and replaced by Edmund Purdom, who mimed to Lanza's already recorded singing. The most famous song was 'drink, drink, drink...', so we did. Our final stopover in Germany will be the city of Munich.

Ein Prosit

Munich means 'by the Monks', a reference to a Benedictine Monastery which became the old town in the 12th Century. Amongst a multitude of sights and attractions of a great city, the Franenkirche, (the 15th Century Cathedral of Our Lady) was impressive, and the Alte Pinakothek is one of the great art galleries of the world.

A few of us spent a couple of enjoyable hours viewing the old masters, but most of our new Aussie friends had other priorities. They wanted to re-visit some drinking establishments they had discovered during the Oktoberfest; a compulsory part of their European education. The Hofbrauhaus am Platz was the most famous. The steins, lederhosen and oompah band took me right by to my student days at the Leeds Hofbrauhaus. (Well, perhaps not the lederhosen).

I managed to find an art shop in town, and bought a sketch pad, coloured pencils, pastels and water colours. My intention was to record landscapes, people, and places of interest en route. This led to a few adventures in the Middle East; more of which later.

A Little Night Music

While relaxing at the campsite in Salzburg I started to draw portraits of our new friends. One of Nick was to come in very handy a few months hence, in Afghanistan. Clarry, our resident classical guitarist, started to teach me some guitar techniques, which I appreciated very much.

"It seems somehow appropriate to play music in the land of Mozart," I mused, as I looked around at the picturesque backdrop, straight off a packet of Alpen.

"Yes, but your rendition is more Ein Klein Knackered Music!"

"Thanks for that Clarry. I think you should be orchestrated."

There are certain places throughout the world in which famous celebrities have become part of the fabric; Gaudi in Barcelona, Shakespeare in Stratford-upon-Avon, and the Beatles in Liverpool, to name but a few. None more so than Mozart in Salzburg, Austria. He was born there in 1756, and today he is everywhere; portraits, plaques, name plates, and souvenirs. An over-used word is genius, but, in Mozart's case, I think we are on safe ground describing him as such. The composer Joseph Haydn wrote; 'Posterity will not see such talent again in one hundred years'. Mozart played multiple instruments, in particular the piano and violin. He was composing music at the age of five, performing at six, and was a court musician in Salzburg at the age of seventeen. He was such a precocious talent, that it had even been seriously suggested that he was actually a midget, masquerading as a child!

His father would take him on European tours, performing at the Courts of Paris, London, The Hague and Zurich. Mozart influenced the work of Handel and Haydn, and he gave lessons to Beethoven in Vienna. I can't help but wonder what kind of report Mozart must have written about his pupil. Possibly something like; 'He is a talented student, but he just *will not* listen.'

High on a Hill

Salzburg was the setting for the movie 'The Sound of Music', and, of course, we couldn't resist walking up into the hills to film our own version. We received a few sardonic glances from passing locals as we danced around like Druids at Stonehenge. Even the cows in the meadows seemed to give us a world-weary look, as if to say, 'Not another bunch of tourists pretending to be the Von Trapp Family!' Still, it gave us a laugh when we had a film night later in the year in Australia.

The beautiful city is world-renowned for its sumptuous Baroque architecture, accentuated by its situation on the Salzbach River, with a stupendous Alpine backdrop. The Hohensalzburg Fortress, one of the largest Medieval Castles in Europe, stands on Festungberg Hill, overlooking the city. It was well worth the walk up to see the breathtaking view of Salzburg, and its nearest Alpine peak; the Untersbergat. We loved Salzburg, and it remains one of our favourite cities.

The 100 mile, drive, southeast through the Alps from Salzburg to Graz, was so picturesque that it was like stepping into a thousand jigsaw puzzles, with a couple of chocolate boxes thrown in for good measure. We swept through endless Alpine villages with chalet-style houses decked out with brightly coloured hanging baskets and window boxes.

Memory Lane

Graz, which means small castle, is a student city, on the River Mur. We took a funicular railway, the Schlossberg, to the Stallbastei Fortress, which overlooks the city. Due to its position the architecture of Graz has been influenced by Italy and the Balkans, and the old town has examples of historic architecture from Gothic onwards. The mix of buildings from different periods provides a magical combination. The Schloss Eggenberg is a beautiful Baroque Palace, with an astonishing interior dedicated to astronomy and mythology. The Cathedral, the Domkirche, is Gothic while the Landhams has a fabulous Italian Renaissance courtyard.

All of these places brought back happy memories for Norma and me. We had hitchhiked through here several years earlier, as students. As we reminisced, we looked back with some amusement as we relived a particular incident. I feel a flux capacitor coming on; let's go back in time…

One evening, we were in a little bar in Graz, when a party of about a dozen locals came in. They were celebrating a birthday, and, as the drinks flowed, the laughter and animated conversation got louder. Some of the birthday party turned to us and offered an apologetic gesture for disturbing us. They spoke to us in German, and when we replied, in English, that we didn't mind at all, they spoke to us in English.

They invited us to join them, which we accepted. There was a guitar hanging up behind the bar, so I played a few songs, starting with, 'Happy Birthday to You'. Beatles' songs are always a safe bet, anywhere, and they sang the German version of, 'I Wanna Hold Your Hand': 'Komm, Gib Mir Deine Hand', and 'She Loves You': 'Sie Liebt Dich'. I also played the simple chords of Elvis's 'Wooden Heart', and everyone joined in with the German chorus. A great time was had by all, but I suffered with a dreadful hangover the following morning.

We managed to hitch a lift with a lorry driver and, somehow, I survived a queasy journey for a few hours. When he dropped us off, he pointed us in the direction of our next camp site. My aching head was pounding, with a steady throb which sent pain from the top of my head, down my neck to my shoulders, and then back again like an electric current along a cable. I felt as though a miniature symphony orchestra had crept into my cranium. It was playing Ravel's 'Bolero', with the percussionist sadistically using my brain as a set of drums, maintaining an incessant beat. All day, I had regretted my over-indulgence the previous night, as we trudged along a dimly-lit road. I was carrying our tent, which was strapped across the top of my backpack at neck height. This banged against the back of my head in time with the rhythm of my walking. The rattling of the tent-poles added to the sound going on in my head to create an out-of-body, stereophonic experience.

Norma was setting a frightening pace, as she marched on ahead of me. She was totally unsympathetic to my constant groaning and whinging, because, it was all my own fault. I felt as though I was undergoing a gruelling Special Forces survival course, as I prayed that we would soon arrive at our campsite. It didn't help when I kept asking, "Are we there yet?", as if I was six years old. Finally, as the 'Bolero' steadily built to a crescendo, I decided; enough was enough. I stopped dead in my tracks, and announced forcefully, "That's it! I cannot go one step further. I am exhausted."

"But the campsite must be very near, and it's almost dark," pleaded Norma.

"You've been saying that for the past half-hour," I said, wearily, as I took off my rucksack and sat down on a low, stone wall. I looked out over the field behind me and thought that if I really *had* been on a military training course, I would have climbed over the wall, there and then, and gone AWOL.

“Smell that beautiful Alpine woodland air,” I suggested, trying to prolong my break for as long as possible.

“And don’t forget the strong whiff of the farmer’s fields,” Norma observed, dryly.

“I’ve just had a brainwave.”

“I thought you’d been having them all day, take another Paracetemol.”

“Why don’t we just put the tent up in this field, and spend the night here?

Dubiously, Norma looked across the field, which was gently illuminated by the street lights and the moon, which was starting to rise in the clear September sky.

“What could be nicer than a night under the twinkling stars of a beautiful Austrian forest clearing?”

“We can’t just pitch-up in the middle of a field.”

“Why not? There’s no-one around, only a couple of small out-buildings, and we’ll be up and gone first thing in the morning.”

“Okay, let’s find a spot,” she finally announced, after giving it some thought.

We climbed over the wall, and walked about fifty yards across the field, which was hardly lush with grass. I spread out the groundsheet and took out our small, A-shaped tent and started to pitch camp. I used a rock to knock in the tent spraggs, which was surprisingly difficult on the hard, mostly bare dirt surface. Each pound of the rock against the metal peg vibrated up my arm and reverberated around my head. I could not wait to get into my sleeping bag. We threw our rucksacks into the tent, and I could barely get undressed. Norma gave me a Paracetemol and water from a plastic bottle, and I must have drifted into unconsciousness immediately.

A Rude Awakening

I was awakened by the morning sunlight flickering through the trees, as shadows danced and played on the white canvas of the tent. I opened my eyes very slowly and apprehensively, hoping that my head had resumed normal service. I looked over to Norma, who was on her side facing away from me, still in the land of nod. I exercised my neck and shoulder muscles and rolled my head. What a relief. Not a trace of a headache. The orchestra had finally packed up and gone home, and I vowed that I would not be booking them for a repeat performance. As I lay there for a few seconds, wondering whether to get up quietly without disturbing Norma, I listened to the sound of the leaves gently rustling in the breeze, and I could hear an occasional vehicle go by. I heard a light snoring sound from Norma, and I knew that if I just gave her a little nudge it altered her breathing pattern and cured the snoring. I pushed her very gently on the shoulder. She took a deep breath and muttered incoherently, and sure enough the snoring stopped. But only for a brief second as it started again, only this time louder. I gave her a slightly firmer push, but this caused her to make grunting sounds which I hadn't heard before. I sat up, alarmed, and leaned over to look at her, but she continued sleeping peacefully. The grunting got louder and I realized that the sounds were not emanating from Norma at all. I unzipped my sleeping bag, and stealthily rolled it down my legs. I crept tentatively towards the opening flap of the tent, and opened a little peephole to look outside. Momentarily, I couldn't quite identify the sight that confronted me. My full range of vision was filled with the incredible expanse of a huge, pink, hairy arse. The little curly tail was the giveaway. A monstrous pig was happily grunting away, and, as I popped my head out of the tent, I realized that he was not alone. Our tent was surrounded by an entire family of pigs; mum, dad, a couple of porkers and a brood of piglets. I gasped in shock, and looked back towards Norma, who was still asleep, blissfully unaware of our visitors. I undid the tent flap and climbed out to shoo them away, wearing just my underpants and vest (*Me* that is, *not* the pigs). The pigs looked at me inquisitively, but took the hint as I flailed my arms around and they trotted away. They turned, and, from a safe distance, just looked at me. Then, I began to sense that they were not the only sets of eyes watching me. As I stood there, arms still waving about like a windmill, I turned my head to my left. At the place where we had climbed over the wall the previous night, there was a bus stop with a queue of about a dozen people who were watching me; puzzled, bemused, and incredulous. My mouth dropped open and my waving arms slowly morphed into morning exercises as I pretended to stretch. As if camping and doing morning exercises in y-fronts in the middle of a pig field was commonplace. I yawned theatrically, stretched my arms in the air, scratched and nonchalantly retreated back into the tent.

"Norma, wake up," I whispered, frantically.

"W… w… what's the matter?" she groaned, startled, semi-conscious and confused by this rude awakening.

"Shhh… we are in the middle of a pig field."

She sat up in her sleeping bag and rubbed her eyes, wondering if she was still dreaming. By then, the nosey pigs had come back and were surrounding the tent, bumping into the ropes and casting exaggerated shadows, as the low morning sun made them seem even bigger.

"Don't worry, they are harmless. It's the people at the bus stop I'm more worried about."

Norma just shook her head in disbelief, as we both peeped out under the side of the tent. Sure enough, everyone was still there, mesmerized by this solitary tent, surrounded by pigs, standing on the hard, smelly ground. They probably wondered if they were on Candid Camera, or, perhaps, they thought that we were Installation Artists putting on a surreal performance.

Mercifully, the bus arrived within a couple of minutes, and we watched everyone climb on board, still looking in our direction as they took their seats. As the bus pulled away, we packed up our smelly tent quickly, before the next bus queue started to build up. We made our escape faster than from a drugs raid at a pop festival. We climbed over the wall and resumed our hike.

We laughed as we walked along, with our rucksacks on our backs, and, after only fifty yards, we came to a bend in the road at the top of a hill. We stopped dead in our tracks and didn't know whether to laugh or cry at the view ahead. Stretched out below us, a mere hundred yards away, was our intended campsite. Norma just looked at me with a wistful shake of her head, and said,

"I'm looking forward to breakfast at the campsite."

"Good idea. Somehow, I fancy a bacon butty."

Following that brief detour back in time to our student days, let us board our time-machine and re-join our bus, which is just leaving Graz.

Spectre

Another 100 miles took us through modern-day Slovenia to Zagreb, the capital of Croatia, although in the 1970s the whole area was known as Yugoslavia. It is situated on the Sava River on the slopes of Mount Medvednica, and is steeped in history going back to Roman times. But never mind all that history, the most important thing for me about Zagreb is that it was at the railway station, called Glavni Kolodvor, that 'Spectre' agent Red Grant, played by Robert Shaw, boarded the Orient Express in the James Bond movie 'From Russia with Love'. His vicious fight on the train with Sean Connery is regarded as one the most memorable in cinema history.

In front of the station is a beautiful garden modelled on Munich's Englischer Garten, which we had recently visited, which goes up to the Ban Jelacic Square, bustling with coloured trams. The old town is beautiful, like Salzburg, with houses that have red roofs and swirling decorations on yellow ochre walls. It rises above the city like the Castle District of Krakow or Montmartre in Paris. We spent just an afternoon and one-night stopover, and enjoyed sight-seeing amongst the churches, museums and art galleries. Particularly impressive was the 12th Century Cathedral and the Lotrscak Tower, which was built to protect the city gates. It provided us with a panoramic view over the city.

200 miles southeast of Zagreb, Belgrade, which translates to White City, is strategically situated at the confluence of the Danube and Sava Rivers. Its desirable position has led to many settlements, invasions and battles going back as far as 600 BC; It has been occupied many times: The Romans, Hungarians and Ottomans, amongst others. Belgrade has been destroyed more times than any capital city in Europe; 45 times in 115 battles in 3000 years. It is morbidly ironic that the bridge across the Sava is called the Bridge of Friendship.

We enjoyed a couple of nights in this bustling city, and I was particularly impressed with the Zemum district with its numerous spires, 18th Century facades of the Habsburg era, and the Art Nouveau, swirling tracery of the 1890s. The next leg of our journey was a 200-mile drive south to Skopje, nowadays the capital city of Macedonia.

The West Wing

There has been a settlement here on the Vardar River since 3,500 BC. It has been ruled by the Romans, the Byzantines and the Turks. The Ottomans introduced Islam and built mosques, baths (hamams) and caravanserai, which were stopovers and service areas for travellers. The Old Bazaar brings a touch of the East into Europe, a scene which will become very familiar to us from Turkey onwards. Much of the city was destroyed by a massive earthquake in 1963 when over one thousand people were killed. The Old Bazaar, ancient churches and mosques of the old town survived.

One afternoon we went for a meal at a most unusual restaurant. It was an aeroplane which had crash-landed in woodlands near to the city, and had subsequently been converted. Our tables were in the west wing.

After a couple of weeks of communal meals and nights in bars and Bier Kellers, our group was beginning to gel, as banter and repartee flowed naturally. The following conversation became typical...

A large wooden bowl of salad was placed in the middle of our table. It was presented with a flamboyant flourish, as if a work of art was being unveiled. Indeed, the arrangement of colours, shapes and patterns worked together to create a harmonious abstract composition. Huge tomatoes rested on a bed of salad, which enhanced the complementary colours of green and red. Slices of yellow peppers were juxtaposed with its complementary purplish colours of lettuce. It looked too good to eat, and no-one wished to ruin the aesthetic moment by being the first to take a helping.

"I love salads when I'm in a hot country. They're so much better than at home," announced Margaret, as she finally delved into the bowl with a matching pair of carved wooden serving spoons.

"Yeah," agreed Colin, "I think it must be the intense colour and natural dressings, and look at the bright red of these tomatoes. We never see such an *intense* red in England. It must be the climate."

"Not necessarily," interjected Bethan, joining in the conversation, "I believe in the theory that plants and vegetables are *living* things that respond to encouragement and touch. Even Prince Charles has admitted that he talks to his plants."

"Are you a 'tree hugger' who talks to the flowers?" asked Barry, slightly dubiously.

"No, but let me tell you about my grandad's experience. He rents an allotment from the local council, and he grows a wide range of vegetables. He has even won a few rosettes at agricultural shows. The adjacent allotment was tended by a friendly, middle-aged lady, and she often chatted to grandad over the fence. One day, she asked, in a tone of admiration, "How do you manage to grow your tomatoes so red?"

"Well, that is a trade-secret, but, since we are friends, I will share it with you. When there is no-one around, I take off my clothes and wander around the allotment, to feel at one with nature. I talk to them to heighten their awareness, and to stimulate growth. I think the tomatoes must be hypersensitive, because they turn *very* red, almost as if they are blushing."

"How very interesting. I must try that myself."

The following week, they chatted, as usual, over the fence.

"So, did you try my technique?" Grandad asked her.

"Yes, I did. I stripped naked and walked around."

"Has it worked?"

"Well, it didn't make any difference to the tomatoes, but my cucumbers are *massive*!"

We all laughed uproariously and enjoyed a convivial meal, which was, without doubt, the best I have ever had on any aircraft.

Fork Handles

125 miles south of Skopje, with great excitement, we glimpsed the turquoise blue waters of the Gulf of Salonika, an inlet of the Aegean Sea. Thessaloniki (also known as Salonika), in northern Greece, was founded in 315 BC and named after the sister of Alexander the Great, whose footsteps we will be following through the Middle East. It was a thriving port under the Romans and an early centre of Christianity, St. Paul having preached there.

It was an idyllic scene with brightly coloured boats in the harbour and fishermen repairing their nets along the dockside. There were lots of small churches and tavernas, and we were attracted to a restaurant that was preparing a barbecue.

The symbol of the city is the Lefkos Pyros, a 15th Century fort known as the White Tower. Under the Ottoman Empire the tower was used as a prison and a place of execution. When Thessaloniki was liberated from the Ottoman rule, the tower was whitewashed as a ritualistic act of purification and cleansing. It is no longer white, but it remains a symbol of freedom.

In the tent that night, our camping light had started to go on the blink, literally. I had bought some new batteries in Belgrade, but there wasn't much of an improvement. The lantern was beginning to show its age, but it still worked when we left home.

"Didn't you check it before we left?" asked Norma, rhetorically.

"It was fine last time I used it."

"And when was that?"

"1964."

Our top priority was to buy a decent replacement. The campsite shop was quite well-stocked with groceries and household utilities, but it did not seem to have much in terms of camping lights. They must have assumed that seasoned campers, unlike us, would already have such things. So it was right back to basics; candles as a temporary stop-gap. There was a vast array on display: Twirly, multi-coloured birthday candles, huge pastel-coloured candles, long ones, short ones, some in the shape of numbers. However, there were none of the straightforward, clear-wax packs of six.

We had far too much choice, and none of the signs were a great deal of help; it was all Greek to me. Just as we were about to ask for assistance, a lady barged in front of us and scooped up an armful of candles. They were wide, flat and set in circular tin-foil trays, like large cupcakes. We decided to follow her example and bought some of the same. Later that night, when we settled down in our sleeping bags to read, I lit two candles which immediately gave off a long orange flame. This seemed perfectly adequate for our purposes. It was a little smoky to begin with, but it soon settled down to a bluish flame, which I extinguished before settling down to go to sleep.

The following morning, I opened my eyes to see Norma lying on her side facing me, still fast asleep. I had to close my eyes again, gather my thoughts, shake my head slightly and slowly open them again to confirm what I was seeing. Her face was totally black, as if she had just finished a shift at a colliery. I gasped out loud, which caused her to open her eyes. She looked at me, and her eyes opened wide in total amazement, and her mouth dropped open. We burst out laughing. It was as if I had just woken up next to Al Jolson.

We sat up in our sleeping bags, which were the same colour as us, and I ran my hand over the roof of the tent to leave a line of white finger marks in the coating of black soot. Norma took out a small mirror from her bag, and held it up to my face, and then looked at herself. We concluded that it could only have come from the candles. Obviously a faulty batch, which I would return with a strong complaint. We climbed out of the tent, hoping that there was no-one close by, especially pigs. However, Colin, Barry and Margaret were having a cup of coffee as we stumbled out. At first they didn't recognise us; it was only our laughter that was a giveaway. Barry could usually be relied upon for a witty one-liner, but, in this instance, his mouth just dropped open and he spilled his coffee. We made a bee-line to the washrooms.

We went over to the camp shop and I asked the assistant about the candles.

"What does this say?" I inquired, pointing at the Greek lettering.

"It says sir; mosquito and insect repellent. It gives off a smoke to keep them away. Very useful for barbeques."

'And can they be used as bedside reading lights?' I almost asked.

Turkish Delight

Our final journey in Europe was the longest, so far, 300 miles along the northern coast of the Aegean towards Turkey, and the gateway to the East; Istanbul. Modern-day Turkey lies on the Anatolian Tectonic plate, and a geological fault line has had a profound effect on the history of the country. Over millions of years, the natural forces of the earth have created one of the world's most strategic areas in terms of travel, trade, cultural exchanges, and, sadly but inevitably, warfare. The Bosphorous is a crack in the narrow isthmus linking the Black Sea and the Sea of Marmara, which in turn squeezes through the narrow Dardanelles Straits. These two narrow channels are the only gateway by sea to the Aegean and

Mediterranean and hence the outside world. Consequently, this stretch of waterway has been of vital importance to all the civilisations that have ever bordered the Black Sea.

Up to arriving in Istanbul, our trip had seemed almost like an extended holiday through Europe before returning to homes and jobs. Reality was beginning to kick in. There was no home and there were no jobs for us to go back to. At least we had our tent.

Istanbul, as a bridge between Europe and Asia, was our first introduction to a different culture. Istanbul is a member of an exclusive club… one of the world's oldest continuously-inhabited cities, and we will be visiting several others along the way. For thousands of years, it was the terminus to the fabled Silk Road, stretching all the way to Xian in China. We will be following sections of this legendary trade route on our overland trek, following in the footsteps of Marco Polo, Alexander the Great, Genghis Khan, and of course James Bond.

Since Istanbul would be our introduction to the Islamic world, we felt that a guided tour would be beneficial. It would enable us to learn more about the architecture, art, culture and religion before embarking on our journey through the Middle East. A group of us hired a local guide and, after much good-natured bartering, we agreed a price and toured the sites in a battered mini bus. Our guide was called Bartu, who was in his mid- forties. He was short, thickset with strong hairy forearms and huge hands with sausages for fingers. He looked as though he was a retired Turkish wrestler. He displayed an excellent knowledge and had a good sense of humour.

Bartu explained that Islamic architecture, comprises two types of buildings; mosques and palaces. Mosques are intended to be multi-functional, acting as a church, town hall, school, and community centre, and there are three types of mosque; domed, open-plan and four-ivan (vaulted halls). Also mosques are of great artistic importance as they attracted the finest calligraphers, tilers and decorators to embellish all surfaces, in particular the mihab (niche) which points the way to Mecca.

Over the centuries the city has been the capital of the Roman, Byzantine and Ottoman Empires and has been called Byzantium, Constantinople and Istanbul. The numerous domes and minarets of the Hagia Sofia, Blue Mosque and Topkapi Palace rise above the Bosphorous to create a stunning backdrop; an instantly recognizable skyline. The Hagia Sofia was completed in the 6th Century by Byzantine Emperor Justinian as a Christian church. It was converted into an Islamic Mosque by the Ottoman Sultan Mehemet II, in the 15th Century. It is steeped in history, but I was thrilled most of all to be walking in the footsteps of Sean Connery in the James Bond movie 'From Russia with Love'.

Rhapsody in Blue

Adjacent to the Hagia Sofia is the Sultan Ahmet Mosque, known as the Blue Mosque due to the 20,000 blue tiles which adorn the elaborate interior. These tiles were manufactured not far away in Iznik, and were influenced by Chinese porcelain imported along the Silk Road. The predominantly cobalt blue and white reminded me very much of Delft pottery in Holland. Usually, Islamic Mosques have one, two or four minarets, but the Blue Mosque is unique in that it has six. This is thought to have been the result of a misunderstanding: when the Sultan instructed the architect that he required altin (gold) minarets, he thought he said alti, meaning six. Either way, the Sultan ended up with an impressive building; today one of the most photographed in the world. Five times a day a muezzin climbs to a balcony near the top of a minaret to call the faithful to prayer. This call is known as the adhan and it became the soundtrack which underscored our trek through the Middle East.

Cloak and Dagger

One of Istanbul's most historic buildings is the Topkapi Palace, which is situated on a promontory overlooking the Golden Horn and Sea of Mamara providing wonderful views of the Bosphorous. The Palace complex comprises many courtyards, gardens and fountains, and was the residence of the Ottoman Sultans for four hundred years from the mid-14th Century. It is a place of holy relics of the Muslim world, in particular the Prophet Muhammad's cloak and sword. It's attraction as a tourist destination was further enhanced by the 1964 Hollywood movie 'Topkapi', about a plot to steal the Topkapi emerald dagger, which is displayed in the treasury.

Bartu stopped at a doorway which was beautifully decorated with a gold border and blue and white tiles. Above was an Arabic sign of gold calligraphy on a black background, which was a work of art in itself.

"This room dates from the 16th Century," Bartu informed us, as we gathered round.

"What does the sign say?" I asked.

"Sunnet Odasi… the Circumcision Room."

Two skinhead guards in ceremonial uniform stood to attention on either side of the door.

"There should be four of them," quipped Clarry.

"*Don't* tell me they use the Topkapi dagger in there!" joked Nick.

"No sir… shall we go in?"

"May as well, what have we got to lose," Barry chuckled. "But if they've got a Eunuchs' Room, I think I will give that one a miss."

Mehmed II built Istanbul's Grand Bazaar (the Kapali Carsi) in the 15th Century as a means of providing finance for the Hagia Sofia. Initially, it specialised in cloth trading and then gold and precious stones. Today, it is one of the oldest and largest covered markets in the world with over three thousand shops. It is a giant labyrinth of endless tunnels, but the bustling, friendly atmosphere, with all the associated sights, smells and sounds, helped us to overcome any feeling of claustrophobia as we browsed the endless shops. Bartu gave us a lesson in the art of bartering, an essential skill which proved invaluable for the rest of our tour. The silk market and auctions are situated in the ancient centre, and Bartu told us that no two silk carpets are identical. The grids of streets are named after the craftsmen who once plied their trade there: slipper-makers, fez-makers, quilt-makers and jewellers. Along the shoemakers' street hung a sign which said, 'By Royal appointment to the Sultan, and Cobblers to the People'. (Okay, I admit I made that last one up).

The following morning, we went on a cruise along the Bosphorous. We boarded a ferry at the Eminonu Port area near to Galata Bridge, where the Golden Horn joins the Bosphorous. The long rods of numerous fishermen on the bridge seemed to form a guard-of-honour waving us off as the ferry dodged its way between oil tankers, freighters and other ferries. The flow of river traffic was as chaotic and shambolic as the city traffic and indeed, the pedestrians of Istanbul. As we sailed towards the mouth of the Black Sea, of added interest were the 'yali'. These are waterfront villas built as grand summer residences in the 18th and 19th Centuries. They had boathouses and jetties for mooring, and some of the mansions looked like miniature 16th Century Baroque Palaces, built in the style of the Palace of Versailles. The grandest was the Dolmabahce Palace, built as a symbol of Ottoman grandeur. At the narrowest point on the Bosphorous stands the Fortress of Europe built by Mehemet II in 1452, prior to his conquest.

A Turkish Pummelling

Being in the beauty therapy business, Norma felt that she couldn't leave Istanbul without experiencing an authentic Turkish Massage at a Turkish bath, known as hamams. She persuaded me to join her. We went to the historic Cemberlitas Hamam, which was built in the Ottoman era. On Yerebaton Street, close to the Grand Bazaar, it is a beautiful building with a domed ceiling; internal marble fountains, and circular arches. We were directed towards the appropriate male and female sections, and we gave each other apprehensive nods of encouragement as we parted company. I was greeted by a huge, intense-looking Turkish masseur who gestured for me to strip naked. He handed me a pestemal (loin cloth) to wrap around me and instructed me to lie on a large marble, circular plinth (gobek tasi), which was used as the communal massage area. The masseur measured over six feet, in all directions, with hands as big as plastic scoops that gardeners use to collect up autumn leaves. His forearms were of the same proportions, about the size of my thighs. He sweated profusely through every pore on the expansive dome of his totally bald head. Conversely, his back was the hairiest I have ever seen, on a human being that is. If he could have had it transplanted onto his head, he would have had more hair than Jimi Hendrix. Without any warning, he poured a bucket of cold water over me and started to soap me up with a sheepskin glove. Or it could possibly have been a full sheep. I was flipped over, lifted up and dropped back down again with the ease of a cat tormenting a half-dead mouse. I just tried to go with the flow and anticipate his next throw in an attempt to minimise any pain. I was covered in more foam than teenagers at a rave as he sat me up and washed my hair. His left hand held the back of my head rigid in a vice-like grip as he massaged my scalp with his fingers and knuckles. It was more like Chinese burns than a Turkish massage. The worrying thing was that all of this was merely the prologue prior to the main event. He then proceeded to systematically work me over with a succession of techniques as though he was a chef tenderising beef. Once I had recovered from the initial shock, pain and numbness I actually began to relax. Or was I just slipping into a coma? He finished off by turning me over as if he was flipping a beef burger at a barbeque, so that I was lying face down. The really disturbing thing was that he then climbed onto the slab behind me and grabbed my legs. 'Oh no,', I thought, with an air of resigned inevitability, 'he's got my helpless naked body in the wheelbarrow position... Brace yourself'.

He then twisted my legs into some sort of knot, which seemed more like a wrestling move than a massage technique, and leaned forward to grab my hands so that he could pull on my arms. My torso was lifted up gradually from the marble slab, as each vertebrae from my neck down to my lower back cracked in turn. A medieval rack must have sounded very similar each time it was ratcheted-up a cog. When he eventually released me and I was able to stand up I felt six inches taller. That was because I *was* six inches taller. I didn't need a shower. He threw another bucket of cold water over me and gestured that the massage was over. What a relief. Actually, I felt great, and after getting dressed gave him a well-earned tip. I sat in a sunlit courtyard and waited for Norma, who eventually emerged from the dark interior glowing as though she was radioactive. We exchanged experiences as we walked along the cobbled street, ready for a well-deserved coffee. Norma told me that her masseur was a huge woman who wore only a pair of enormous, slightly ripped, black knickers. They were big enough to rig out a sailing boat on the Bosphorous. She had pendulous breasts which looked like a dead-heat in a zeppelin race, and her tree-trunk thighs and ample buttocks had more dimples than a golf ball.

"Instead of Cemberlitas, perhaps they should re-name this place Cellulites Hamam," quipped Norma. She continued her story by telling me that once she had stripped naked, the Turkish lady, without warning, threw a bucket of ice-cold water at her with the force of a tsunami. This sent her sliding backwards across the tiled floor. All Norma could do was laugh, which set off the masseur, and they both continued to giggle all though the pummelling ordeal, which seemed to follow exactly the same procedure as my massage.

We had arranged to meet Barry, Colin and Nick for Turkish coffee at the 'Pudding Shop', in the Sultanahmet area of Istanbul. This was a popular meeting place for travellers on the hippie trail in the 1960s. It was first opened in 1957 by the Colpan brothers as a patisserie called 'Lale Pastanesi'. It became popular with overlanders as a place to exchange travel advice and leave messages on the notice board. It was featured in the Alan Parker movie 'Midnight Express' a couple of years after we were there.

Our few days in Istanbul certainly opened our eyes to the delights awaiting us over the next couple of months, but our next destination was to a place close to the hearts of all Australians and New Zealanders… The Gallipoli National Historic Park.

We headed west towards the Gallipoli peninsula, following the coast of the Sea of Marmara. The ANZAC (Australia and New Zealand Army Corps) War Cemetery is in a peaceful setting overlooking the Dardanelles Straits. It must have been like hell in 1915, as the Anzacs were bombarded by the Turkish troops from inaccessible high ground. Many of our Antipodean friends were able to look for names of relatives lost in battle, and they took photographs to take back home to family and friends.

Chapter Two

Eastern Promise

During the next leg of our journey, we will encounter a couple of Wonders of the World, gods, gladiators, saints, wars, invasions, 'the face that launched a thousand ships', and even Santa Claus.

Beware of Greeks Bearing Gifts

We took a ferry across the Dardanelles to our next destination of Canakkale. The strategic importance of the entrance to the Dardanelles Straits was highlighted by the Gallipoli campaign of the First World War. This was a relatively recent event when compared to the history of conflict in the area. The Trojan Wars against the Greeks took place as long ago as the 12th Century BC, and it is difficult to separate historical evidence from myth. Everyone is familiar with the story of the wooden horse, when the Greeks came up with a cunning plan to break the deadlock of a ten-year siege of Troy. They pretended to withdraw and left a wooden horse as a leaving present. The Trojans dragged it inside the city walls, unaware of the soldiers hiding inside. The rest, as they say, is history… or mythology. Guess what greeted us as we arrived at Troy? That's right, a giant wooden horse. Of course we just had to go inside it and wave for a photograph. The main source of the story is from the 'Aeneid', an epic poem by the 1st

Century BC Roman poet Virgil, who modelled it on the 'Illiad' and 'The Odyssey' by the 8th Century BC Greek poet Homer. In a nutshell, a war was fought over Helen of Troy (who was a Princess of Sparta), the most beautiful woman in the world; hence the phrase: 'The face that launched a thousand ships'. She was abducted, but rescued by her twin brothers, Castor and Pollux, (now come on, what kind of parents would give a child the name Pollux). Helen survived to live happily ever after, marrying King Menelaus of Sparta.

The ruins of Troy were first excavated by German archaeologist Heinrich Schliemann, in 1873, and he discovered that there are many different cities, each built on top of the ruins of a previous city. They are known by numbers and it is difficult, if not impossible, to match up particular stories of Troy with a particular layer of the ruins. Still, the wooden horse seems to have survived. Must be all that creosote.

We camped overnight at Bergama on the Aegean coast, and spent some time exploring the great acropolis of Pergamum. In addition to the usual temples and theatre, Pergamum was known particularly as a great centre of learning, and the ruins of a large library can still be seen. We always try local dishes, and we had musakka, and kofte, which were meatballs made with parsley, egg and breadcrumbs. We enjoyed local wine while looking across the beach to see the setting sun reflecting off the Aegean.

Bird Island

Next stop was at a beach campsite at Kusadasi, which means Bird Island, overlooking the beautiful turquoise blue Aegean Sea. We were ready for some sand, surf and sex-on-the-beach cocktails. This was our base for excursions to Ephesus, one of Turkey's most famous ancient sites and one-time capital of the Roman province of Asia Minor. Like Pompeii in Italy, Ephesus evokes a feeling of community life and as we strolled along the marbled main street, Curetes Way, it didn't take a great leap of imagination to be able to visualise a bustling town of people going about their business. We could almost hear the sound of chariots rattling along the wheel-worn grooves of the streets.

Before the Romans arrived, Ephesus had been a major Greek settlement for centuries, built around the Temple of Artemis, one of the seven wonders of the ancient world. She was the daughter of Zeus, King of the Gods, and she was a multi-functional Goddess of many things. It was believed that she would bring fertility to worshippers, and it is wonderfully appropriate that the only part of the temple to survive is a single erection; a lone column standing proud in memory of Artemis. Greek gods must have a sense of humour.

As we walked through the Magnesium Gate, it was with cruel irony that one or two of us were starting to suffer from the dreaded Delhi Belly. See what I mean about Gods having a sense of humour. The theatre, known as the Odeon (Meeting Hall), was carved into the side of Mount Pion by the Greeks. The porch of the Temple of Hadrian still stands, but the most impressive building at Ephesus is the Library of Celsus. The Arcadian Way is a grand parade flanked by porticos and columns, and which was lit at night by street lamps.

Ephesus was a very important religious centre of early Christianity, and St Paul preached there, as mentioned in 'Acts', in the Gospels. St. John the Evangelist also preached there, and it is believed that he took the Virgin Mary with him, in AD 37, so that she could spend her later years in Ephesus. Her stone house and shrine, a few miles away in Meryemana, are revered by both Christians and Muslims.

To symbolize fertility, the statue of Artemis is adorned all over with bull's testicles. Somehow, I can't see this catching on at the Milan fashion week. Due to its strategic coastal position, Ephesus became a very rich port at the mouth of the River Cayster. This attracted the attention and invasion by King Croesus of Lydia, from the area of modern-day Western Turkey. The Lydians panned gold from River Pactolus and had gold and silver mines. They were renowned silversmiths, but the main contribution of Lydia to human history was the introduction of coinage. The King was the richest man in the world and his name, even today, is synonymous with enormous wealth; 'As rich as Croesus'.

While we are on the subject of money, allow me to digress and time-travel to relate an amusing classroom incident. While teaching at Cowley School in St. Helens, I was covering an English class for an absent colleague. The pupils were making notes from a set-book, when one boy put up his hand.

"Sir, who was Ava Rice?"

"I don't know," I confessed. "Do you mean Archie Rice? He was a character in John Osborne's 'The Entertainer'."

"No, Sir, it definitely says Ava."

"In what context is she mentioned? Read out the sentence to me."

"He was rich, beyond the dreams of Ava Rice."

Another Fine Mess

At Ephesus, archaeological excavations have discovered a gladiators' graveyard. Forensic research and analysis of skeletons, such as cut-marks and bone-density, has led to some interesting and surprising discoveries. Contrary to popular belief… Gladiators were *fat*. They were fed a high carbohydrate diet that developed fatty layers to protect muscles from superficial wounds. Think of the following Hollywood movies: Russell Crowe as the Roman General Maximus Decimus Meridius in 'Gladiator'. Victor Mature in 'Demetrius and the Gladiators'. Kirk Douglas as real-life 'Spartacus'. Hold that thought for a moment. Now, consider this; replace the actors with; Oliver Hardy, W.C. Fields and Fatty Arbuckle, (or should that be Fattius Arbucklius). Not exactly an Oscar-winning casting. Cecil B De Mille or D.W. Griffith would turn in their graves at the thought. I can just imagine a contest in the blood and sand of a Roman arena: Flabius Jellybum versus Gluteus Maximus Enormus. The Romans advertised these gladiatorial combats on tablets. What a fantastically advanced civilisation it must have been to have tablets in the 1st

Century AD. I didn't get a tablet until Christmas 2015, and even then I thought I could get it on prescription.

Nights in White Satin

A 20th Century Bulgarian installation-artist called Christo had a unique specialism, some would say gimmick. He would wrap things up. Natural forms, public buildings and even bridges. He has covered the Reichstag in Berlin and the Pont-Neuf Bridge in Paris in white fabric to create stunning sculptural forms which have attracted huge crowds. Was he the world's first wrap artist!? I don't know if Christo ever visited the travertine pools at Pamukkale; they are nature's modern-art installation. They look as though they have been wrapped in cotton sheets. Indeed, the name Pamukkale means 'cotton castle' in Turkish, and the terraces are not so much a natural form, but more a work of art created by calcium deposits of thermal spring waters. In the glistening sunlight, it looked more like the Antarctic than Anatolia. To create 'Wrapped Coast' in 1969, Christo covered cliffs near Sydney, Australia with white fabric tied with ropes. Check out the photographs. In my opinion they look uncannily like the natural formations at Pamukkale where the pools have been used for bathing for thousands of years. The underground volcanic activity which creates the hot springs has also forced carbon dioxide into a cave, which is called the 'Plutonium', meaning 'Place of God'. Today the name plutonium has a slightly different connotation. Remember the television commercial for 'Ready Brek'? On a cold winter's morning, kids went off to school glowing in the dark. I think a bath in plutonium would have a similar after-effect.

Bodrum was the ancient Greek city of Halicarnassus, another Wonder of the World. The tomb of King Mausolus, who died in the 14th Century BC, became known as the Mausoleum, and this is the origin of the name used today. The crusading Knights of St. John used many of the stones from the Mausoleum to construct the Castle of St. Peter, which stands today as Bodrum's most distinctive landmark on a promontory between the harbour and Kumbahce Bay.

From Bodrum our final destination in Turkey was Antalya. The Roman city walls have survived, and border the picturesque harbour. Hadrian's Gate is a huge triple-arched gateway, built to honour a visit by the Emperor. Compared to this, I wonder how impressed he was with our wall in Britain? Hadrian's Wall was built to keep out the invading hordes from the north. It was intended to be impregnable, and the Emperor is quoted as saying, 'The Picts can try to breach the wall until they are blue in the face.'

The next stage of our journey will bring us into contact with someone even more famous than Hadrian: Father Christmas.

Little Saint Nick

In a museum in Antalya, is a shrine which contains holy relics of St. Nicholas. He was Bishop of nearby Myra in the 3rd Century AD, and was known for his kind deeds. He gave a bag of gold coins to three sisters following the death of their parents. He left them anonymously at night, and this has led to the legend of Santa Claus. St. Nicholas has gradually evolved into the Santa Claus we are all familiar with today; 'A big fat man with a long white beard', as Bing Crosby sang in the 1934 song 'Santa Claus is coming to town'. This image was created by Clement Clarke Moore's 1881 poem, 'A Visit from St Nicholas', which was illustrated by the caricaturist, Thomas Nast. He was probably influenced by earlier myths and legends: King Frost of Saxon Britain, and the Viking God Odin, who wore a long white beard and gave gifts to the needy. Also, there is the Germanic Winterman, who dressed in furs for the festival of Yule. The Dutch shortened Sint Nikolaas to Sinter Klaas and took it with them to New Amsterdam, which eventually changed its name to that most Christmassy of modern-day cities… New York.

Travelling through Turkey was a richly rewarding and educational experience, which gave us a sense of history and whetted our appetite for our next country, Syria.

We realized that Turkey was very much a link, or stepping stone, to the east as we crossed into Syria. We had been gradually inducted into different cultures as we made our way along the southern coast of Turkey, and as we travelled towards the northern Syrian city of Aleppo, I felt as though I had made the transition from tourist to traveller.

Northern Syria is flat, dry and arid and is strewn with ruined ancient settlements. It is known as the region of 'Dead Cities', some of which are just rubble while others are recognisable villages. The decline of the Roman Empire resulted in a decline in trade. The people moved to more fertile land to grow crops, leaving ghost towns behind them. Syria's central position has made the area a target for other expanding empires; Egyptian, Assyrian, Persian and others have destroyed and rebuilt over thousands of years. The troubles continue right up to the time of writing.

Milk Makes a Prophet

Aleppo is another of the oldest continuously-inhabited cities in the world. In Arabic, Aleppo is known as Halab, which is derived from the word halib, meaning milk. This is because the Old Testament prophet Abraham passed through on his way from Ur to the Holy Land, and milked his cow on the hill where the Citadel now stands. He gave this milk to the poor as an act of charity and kindness. Blessed are the cheese makers.

The 12th Century Aleppo citadel is one of the most distinctive medieval fortresses in the Middle East. It is the biggest sandcastle I have ever seen. It looked as though it could have been made by using giant square moulded buckets, the type that children use on a beach. The old city encircles the citadel and if we thought that the bazaar in Istanbul was huge, this one was the largest covered market in the Middle East. Walking through the souk, our nostrils were assaulted by the combined smells of spices, fruits, meats, perfumes, horse and donkey manure, rubbish and sewers. We were surrounded by the technicolour of carpets, silks, vegetables, jewellery and metalwork.

Amongst the jostling crowds, we shared the humour of street vendors, hustlers and entertainers, and felt sadness seeing disabled beggars. Huge brass lanterns hang on heavy chains and shafts of daylight find a way through to reflect off glassware and brass. It is the longest roofed market in the world; a labyrinth, a warren, a maze to get lost in. Donkeys pull rattling carts across cobbled floors and the smell of manure competes with the smell of coffee and tea from mobile chai sellers. Old men sit in groups playing chess or backgammon while smoking the Aleppo-made narghile (hubble-bubble pipes).

The railway station, with its 'Garnier of Paris' clock, was where Agatha Christie's Hercule Poirot boarded the Orient Express. If he thought that was murder, he should have tried travelling by bus. After the First World War, the League of Nations awarded France control of Syria, and French influence still lingers in Aleppo. The boulevards and balconied apartments are reminiscent of Paris, and the park, statues of poets, and fountains are modelled on the Luxembourg Gardens in Paris.

The Great Mosque is the most important religious site, founded in the 8th Century after the Muslim conquest. Aleppo is a seething cauldron of humanity, with a backdrop of fabulous Islamic architecture, but my one over-riding memory is of bananas and custard.

When we pitched up at the campsite, to our usual soundtrack of Clarry playing 'Romanza', it was our turn to make the evening meal. Mick gave us the allocated funding from the kitty and off we went to the local markets. Going over budget was not an option, after all we still had a long way to go to Kathmandu. We bought the now customary melons, and Norma came up with a flash of inspiration; bananas and custard for afters. Obviously, bananas were plentiful and cheap, but I hadn't spotted any tins of Bird's Custard.

"I will make my own custard," she said confidently, "with milk, eggs and vanilla from the spice market."

We bought eggs from a stall run by a local dairy farmer, and he gave us some milk in an old, scratched, stained and battered plastic container. I didn't like to ask which animal the milk came from, and I certainly didn't want to know about the dark floating flecks. It looked as though Abraham himself could have milked it. For main course we bought vegetables and rice and could just about stretch to pieces of chicken. As we got back to the campsite, fate took a hand. We were enticed by a beautiful smell of cooking emanating from a nearby group of tents, and we found ourselves stopping and gazing, like a couple of waifs and strays. As in the Bill Halley and the Comets song, 'Shake, Rattle and Roll', I was 'like a one-eyed cat peeping in the seafood store'.

A group of Danes, from Copenhagen, welcomed us and we chatted congenially, as English is widely spoken throughout Scandinavia. They had travelled overland on a route very similar to ours, and were going as far as Jerusalem. The chef was cooking chicken and kebabs, and he explained to us that he had just received a late message informing him that some of their party had been delayed on an excursion, and would get something to eat in Aleppo. They invited us to join them, but we explained that we were with a large party, and we were cooks for the evening. Hence our bags of shopping.

"Please, why don't you take some of our food with you? It will only go to waste."

"Are you sure?" I asked nonchalantly, feeling like the 'one-eyed cat' that had been thrown a fish.

Later that evening, when we called our group to dinner, everyone's face was a joy to behold as they held out a plate to receive a ladle of chicken casserole and a kebab. Norma's vanilla custard was a triumph, and the whole meal was achieved miraculously under budget. We never did confess our secret assignation with the Danes.

We christened ourselves Johnny and Fanny Craddock. For the benefit of younger readers, they were the most famous TV chefs of the 1950s and early '60s. Fanny was unbelievably bossy, and Johnny, who wore a monocle, drank his way through the programme. His most famous parting line was when he looked into the camera and raised a glass to the viewers with the words, "Here's hoping your vol-au-vents turn out looking just like Fanny's."

Our journey south from Aleppo was a relatively short hop of about 100 miles to Homs for an overnight stopover on the way to the capital city of Damascus. Homs, another ancient city, was founded around 2300 BC, and today it is a commercial centre with an oil refinery. The highly reflective metal-domed mosque dominates the old town. It is dedicated to Khaled Bin Al-Walid, known as the 'Sword of Islam', who captured Homs in the 7th Century. We visited the Al-Zenar Church (Church of the Virgin's Belt), which holds the relic of Mary's belt, which is kept in a box in a small shrine inside the church. Also, we visited the obligatory bazaar, which sold a vast array of goods, in particular brightly coloured silks, printed cotton and woollen textiles. We stayed at a campsite overnight and after breakfast set off south for another 100 miles on the Biblical 'Road to Damascus'.

Bring Me the Head of John the Baptist

Damascus is thought to be *the* oldest, continuously inhabited city in the world; dating back to beyond 3000 BC. In view of its age, it is hardly surprising that Damascus has been conquered by a succession of armies and civilisations throughout the millennia, and evidence of each can still be traced; the usual suspects mentioned in Aleppo. There are countless Islamic mosques and the domes and minarets create a magical cityscape when silhouetted by the setting sun. The famous Umayyad Mosque is the grandest and most important, and it is considered to be the fourth most important in the Islamic world after Mecca, Medina and Jerusalem. We went on a guided tour of the mosque, and Norma was issued with a black, hooded full-length chador. At first, the guide thought that she was a local worshipper because her hair was very dark, her face tanned and she was wearing clothes that she had bought at bazaars en route: a block-printed skirt and scarves round her head and shoulders. He spoke to her in Arabic and did a double-take when she looked at him. Her blue eyes were the giveaway, and he seemed mesmerised. The photograph of her in the main courtyard with a square minaret as a backdrop looked like an advertisement for Scottish Widows' Insurance.

The site of the mosque had previously been occupied by Pagan and Roman Temples and also the Church of St. John The Baptist. As we know from the Bible, his head was cut off as a present for Salome. There is a green-domed shrine, which contains the head of John the Baptist, who is honoured as a prophet by Christians and Muslims alike. The inner courtyard is about the size of a couple of football pitches with a two-storied arcade on three sides. The fourth side has the giant prayer hall which is covered with gold and green mosaics. It is believed that the design of St. Mark's Square in Venice was based on this courtyard. Damascus prospered under the rule of the Saracens, their most famous leader being Saladin whose tomb is contained in the Umayyad Mosque. Saladin is a name inextricably linked with his greatest adversary the English King Richard the Lionheart, who spent years in the area with the Crusaders. So much so in fact, that during his reign, from 1189 to 1199, King Richard spent less than a year in England. He preferred France, couldn't speak a word of English, conspired with his brother John to overthrow his father, Henry II, and just popped home occasionally to collect taxes to finance his gallivanting. I don't think Robin Hood and his men would have been quite so merry if only he had known the truth.

After the Prophet Muhammad died, in the year 632, he was succeeded by leaders (or Caliphs) from his family and followers. His cousin Ali, who also became his son-in-law, was assassinated and the Caliphate passed into the hands of the Umayyads, who were relatives of Muhammad. They moved to Damascus and founded the mosque. As part of the tour, our guide went on to explain the fundamental differences between Shiite and Sunni Muslims. The former is an abbreviation of Shia-t-Ali, the party of Ali which believes that Muhammad's family and hereditary descendants should lead Islam. Sunni Muslims believe that there is no basis in Islam for hereditary privilege. It is a political rather than secular divide since all Muslims follow the 'Pillars of Islam'.

Walking through the bazaar was like stumbling onto the set of a Hollywood Biblical epic, but my modest super-8 film was more Cecil B De Meadows then Cecil B De Mille. The assortment of goods was mind-boggling, and since Damascus gave its name to the reversible woven designs of damask, there were garments and lengths of cloth available everywhere in silk, wool, linen and cotton. At the time of writing, in 2016, it is sad that the civil war in Syria is forcing hundreds of thousands to flee north to Europe. I hope the situation is resolved soon, because Syria was friendly, welcoming country which we enjoyed very much. As we will see as we travel through Iraq, Iran and Afghanistan, due to their strategic positions, they have a history of invasion and war stretching back thousands of years. The countries have always survived and re-built, and I hope this proves to the case again.

After the hustle and bustle of the capital city it was almost a relief to get back on the road and share experiences chatting with our travelling companions. We continued south to the Jordanian border and then on to another capital city.

Philadelphia, Amman for all Seasons

Our next stop is Philadelphia. No, we are not time-travelling to Pennsylvania; it was a previous name of Jordan's capital, Amman. The original Philadelphia pre-dates the American version by over 2000 years, and was named in honour of the Egyptian Pharaoh Ptolemy Philadelphus. We had arranged to stay in the garden of a city-centre YMCA hostel, where we pitched our tents and had use of an outside cold water tap. Luxury. We used Amman as a base, for day trips and overnight excursions.

The main street of Amman was only a short stroll down the hill and it was a bustle of traffic, shops and street hawkers. We had been recommended to try a speciality of Amman; thick milkshake of banana or mango which were for sale at many little stand-up booths. We queued along the street with the locals. When it was our turn to be served, Norma was aghast when the proprietor merely took a cracked and stained glass from one customer, filled it up from the dispenser and handed it to her. No such thing as a rinse under a tap. Health and safety or hygiene did not appear to be a top priority. She looked at her banana milkshake with revulsion and passed it onto the man behind her. I drank mine, but at least I lived to tell the tale.

The souks glistened with the gold and silver on display; bracelets, rings, earrings, chains and charms. Carved brass and copper goods were plentiful, and kaftans were popular, embellished with gold and silver threads.

Brief Encounter

We went from Amman to Israel for a few days. We crossed the border amidst the tight security of high fences topped with barbed wire, turnstile gates and the constant scrutiny of armed guards. The general atmosphere was not as intimidating as we had expected as families, shoppers, and dusty old cars moved in both directions. Faded Manchester United and Liverpool football shirts worn by teenagers jostled for position amongst the traditional or everyday clothes as streams of people moved through at a steady rate. In the customs hall, our group was divided into males on the left and females to the right as we placed our bags on a row of trestle tables. The officer who dealt with me pointed to my camera bag, and gestured for me to place it on the table.

"It is a cine camera," I volunteered, before being asked.

"Please open."

The camera was quite modern for its day, but, nowadays, it would be regarded as a period-piece found only in bric-a-brac shops, or specialist places that still sell projectors and convert treasured home movies or weddings on to DVD. The camera had a handle and a trigger and was operated by pointing it like a gun. The officer ordered me to point at the ceiling and pull the trigger. It made a whirring sound for about five seconds, and since the ceiling remained intact, he nodded and gestured for me to zip it back into its carrying case. Incidentally, it has been announced recently in Britain that electronic gadgets must be operated at airports to prove that they are indeed what they purport to be. Flat batteries mean confiscation of goods. Has it taken nearly forty years for British customs to latch on to that one?

"Have you packed your bag yourself, sir?"

"Yes."

"And does everything in the bag belong to you?"

"Yes."

"Has it been left unattended at any time?"

"No."

The officer then clicked open my small suitcase and lifted the lid. He looked inside and rummaged about, and then raised his eyebrows and looked at me over the top of the lid. He looked to his left and gestured to his colleague, who was dealing with Nick next to me, to look at something in my case. I felt my throat become dry, and my knees go weak as Nick gave me a concerned look. My mind started to race. What has he found? Has someone slipped a stash of drugs into my bag? The officers remained expressionless as my eyes darted frantically in an attempt to glean some kind of clue from their faces.

Maintaining his dead-pan poker face, the officer picked up something and lifted the irrefutable evidence out of the case. My mouth dropped open as he held aloft two items above his head.

"So *these* belong to you?" he stated, loudly and accusingly.

I couldn't speak; I just shook my head slowly as I felt everyone in the room looking at me. From his left hand, he dangled triumphantly a lacy black bra, and in his right hand the matching knickers. It was only when I detected just the slightest hint of a smile and mischievousness in the officers' eyes that I realised that they were having a bit of fun.

"Oh, only at weekends," I responded, with a casual shrug.

To my great relief, the two Israeli customs officials burst into uproarious laughter, which had a ripple effect along his line of colleagues. I looked behind me to the ladies' section and gave Norma a woeful look, but she was joining in the laughter. She marched over to our side and retrieved her underwear from the officer. The light-hearted exchange eased our transition through the formalities. The Middle East was relatively peaceful at the time, and the only country that was unsafe to visit was Lebanon. Again, at the time of writing the only place which is safe to travel to *is* Lebanon. When will the cycle ever end?

Jerusalem, the capital city of modern Israel, has a history dating back five thousand years. It is the holiest city in Christianity and the third holiest in Islam (after Mecca and Medina in Saudi Arabia), and it has been fought over and ruled by the Egyptians, Assyrians,

Babylonians, Persians, Greeks, Romans, Byzantines, Arabs, Crusaders, Mamaluks, Ottoman and British. The panoramic skyline is dominated by the golden Dome of the Rock, which glistens in the reflected sunlight of the day and appears to glow at dusk, which accentuates the 'light of the world' ephemeral, religious quality. It is situated on the Temple Mount and is sacred to Christians as the place where Abraham prepared to sacrifice his son Isaac, and also to the Muslims as the site where Muhammad ascended to heaven. It is an Islamic shrine built by the Umayyads of Syria. It dominates Temple Mount, along with a mosque built for Friday prayers.

"John, what is the name of the mosque?"

"Al-Asque."

"Oh, I thought you would have known, having studied architecture."

"I do. I have just told you."

"I thought you said you were going to ask."

"No. It is called the Al-Asque Mosque. It means the Farthest Mosque."

The walled old city is at the centre of Jerusalem between the Jewish west and Arab east, and it is divided into four quarters: Armenian, Christian, Jewish and Muslim. The winding alleyways of souks and markets were alive with the hustle and bustle of shopkeepers, traders and street vendors; a sight which could hardly have changed in over two thousand years. We made our way to the Church of the Holy Sepulchre, the site of the Crucifixion, and then followed the Way of the Cross, the route along which Jesus was forced to carry his cross. However, I managed to cover the distance a lot quicker than Jesus did.

Run for Your Wife

"RUN, RUN!" screamed a local stallholder, pointing along an alleyway. I had been filming the street scenes for my forthcoming Biblical epic when a local woman had wandered past and into my shot. Even though she was carrying a basket of fruit on her head, her peripheral vision made her aware of my intrusive lens. Without breaking stride, she turned towards me, eyes blazing, and dropped into a low crouch as I watched her through my viewfinder, transfixed. She was like a tiger silently and stealthily moving in on a kill. The next thing I felt was the sweep of her hand across the top of my head as I managed to avoid a left hook which Henry Cooper would have been proud of. It caused me to fall over, but I didn't need a second invitation to run as I sprinted off along the cobblestones, cine-camera still filming. My heart was pounding due to the sudden shock as I realised that I must have inadvertently transgressed a religious law and greatly offended the lady. I negotiated the crowded alleyways with a series of rugby sidesteps and the occasional hand-off. I didn't dare look back over my shoulder as I had visions of the irate woman gaining on me, inexorably, like an Egyptian mummy in a black and white B-movie. To the astonishment of a market trader, I vaulted over his table and took refuge behind a pile of watermelons. I blended in well because, by then, my face was probably a similar shade of green. All I could do was to look at the small crowd now looking down on me and put my index finger over my lips in a pleading, pathetic manner. I gave it a couple of minutes to be on the safe side before hesitantly popping my head over my safe haven of melons. I couldn't have had more trepidation if I had been a First World War soldier in the trenches. To my great relief, I saw Norma standing not far away looking anxiously in all directions. When our eyes finally met across a crowded street, she just burst out laughing as she spotted my head amongst the melons.

"It's safe to come out," she laughed, as I sheepishly apologised to everyone around me. As I walked over to her I noticed that she was accompanied by the man who had originally warned me to run. He had left his shop to find out what had happened and he grinned broadly. I was glad I'd brightened up his day.

Uncle Moustache's

We had arranged to meet some of our friends at a well-known restaurant known as Uncle Moustache's, just inside Herod's Gate. After my stressful ordeal, I was desperate for a cup of tea. It was late afternoon and Barry, Colin, Nick, Ruth and Bethan were already seated at a table waiting for us.

"We have ordered a traditional Israeli dish of chicken, rice and soup," said Barry, greeting us cheerfully, "it's called 'falafel'."

"Very appropriate," joked Norma, "cause this fella just fell."

That seemed to be my cue to relate the tale of my frantic great escape. We began our meal to the sound of laughter filling the restaurant. We noticed that the walls were covered with numerous drawings, many of them cartoons, of figures which we presumed were members of staff. Notable amongst them were images of a gregarious character proudly sporting an outrageous moustache, obviously the eponymous Uncle Moustache himself. Without asking me, Colin went over to a waiter and asked for a piece of paper and pen. The waiter immediately adopted a pose, as if it was part of his job. I accepted the challenge and after a few minutes a small crowd of diners from the other tables came over to watch. Just as I finished the drawing, to a slight ripple of applause, a large jovial gentleman, dressed in an all-white chef's uniform together with a cartoon-like hat, came over. The moustache was a giveaway. It was large, black and luxuriant combed in a handlebar style which would have been the envy of any World War II R.A.F. Pilot. It curled up slightly at the ends and, together with his dark, twinkling eyes, gave the impression that Uncle Moustache wore a permanent smile. He cleared a space on our white table cloth by moving our dishes to one side with a sweep of his arm. He handed me a large black felt-tipped pen and then stood back proudly with his chest out, legs apart and hands on hips; the kind of stance Henry VIII favoured when posing for Hans Holbein. He grinned warmly and gestured with both hands towards his face and then pointed at the white table cloth. I regarded it as a great compliment that the owner of the restaurant should request a complete stranger to draw on his table cloth. The crowd of onlookers remained in place and were joined by some of the waiters as I sat looking apprehensively at the daunting virgin canvas in front of me.

"Make it a good one," whispered Norma, encouragingly. No pressure there. Fortunately, my drawing started to turn out well, and, after about five minutes, drinks for our party were delivered to our table. Being on a tight budget, we protested that we hadn't ordered further drinks only to be reassured that they were on the house.

"Stretch it out as long as you can," whispered Colin mischievously, as he took a sip of beer.

Uncle Moustache appeared delighted with the finished portrait and he insisted that I sign it. He then cut out the centre of the table cloth and pinned it up on his wall. More plates of food were served. Again, on the house.

"From now until Kathmandu," announced Barry, raising his glass, "I am going with you to every restaurant. I'Il save a fortune!"

The following morning, we continued sightseeing. The Western Wall is one of the holiest sites in Jerusalem, and is thought to be the only remains of Solomon's Temple. It is often referred to as The Wailing Wall, a term coined by the British following reports from travellers that Jews pray out-loud in front of the wall, while gently rocking back and forth. Worshippers push kvitelach, which are prayers written on paper, in the spaces between the stones to be received by God. The wall is also sacred to Muslims who call it the Al-Buraq Wall. It is named after the winged stead (with a human face) which the Prophet Muhammad rode on his night flight. It is thought that he tied Al-Buraq to the wall before he ascended to heaven.

Mud, Mud, Glorious Mud...

We were all looking forward to our visit to the Dead Sea, mainly to find out if it was true that you can, literally, sit in the water and read a newspaper while floating. A photo-opportunity not to be missed. The Dead Sea is the lowest point on Earth at 417 metres below sea-level and, due to evaporation, approximately a third of its volume is a concentration of salts and minerals including calcium, potassium and bromine. This has created an environment totally unsuitable for any marine life, hence its name. Contrary to widely held belief, the Dead Sea is not the saltiest body of water on Earth as there are places in Antarctica and Africa with even greater concentrations. However, it is the most famous, and since ancient times Dead Sea mud has been valued for its healing and cosmetic properties. To this day, it is still used to treat many ailments including acne, psoriasis, cellulite and muscle aches. The ancient Egyptians used it in mummification, and legend has it that the Queen of Sheba believed in its healing properties. Cleopatra used it in her make-up and it is thought that she opened cosmetic factories near the Dead Sea. She wrote a book on cosmetics, and I wonder if she ever opened a beauty salon, thinking up the obligatory pun like 'Look Dead Good' or, after mummification, 'Look Good Dead'. We had great fun caking ourselves in mud and couldn't resist writing slogans on our bodies ready for a group photograph. We entered the water steadily, carefully avoiding any contact with the eyes for obvious reasons, and I slowly sat back into the water. It is an amazing feeling to be floating so effortlessly, and the sensation was like sitting on an inflatable plastic armchair. It is impossible to swim because you lie practically on the surface, like pond insects that walk on water without breaking the surface tension.

I was wearing just a pair of denim jeans, cut-off at knee length as shorts, and I decided to let them dry off naturally as I sat in the sun. Before long, white marks started to appear like dried sweat-stains, and the denim started to feel as though it had been washed with too much starch. I started to feel as though I was sitting in wet concrete, which was beginning to set, like the victim of a Mafia hit man. Gradually everything around my nether regions started to stiffen and harden. Well, almost everything. I blamed the bromine.

The surrounding landscape was made up of a palette of lilacs, pinks, ochres and crimsons. The scene reminded me of a 19th Century painting in the Lady Lever Gallery in Ellesmere Port called 'The Scapegoat', by the English Pre-Raphaelite painter William Holman-Hunt. It depicts the scapegoat, as described in the Bible, in the Book of Leviticus; on the Day of Atonement a goat would have its horns wrapped in red cloth, representing the sins of the world or Christ's Crown of Thorns (depending on which account you read). Holman-Hunt travelled to the Holy Land and bought a goat which he tethered on the salt shoreline in front of the Dead Sea, with the mountains as a dramatic backdrop. He then proceeded to paint it, but unfortunately the poor animal died of exposure and neglect. A scapegoat indeed. I thought it was the artist who was supposed to suffer for his art, not the model.

Back at the hotel in Jerusalem, we were in desperate need of a hot shower, or even a desalination plant. Overnight, I left my semi-stiff shorts on the tiled floor of the bathroom, and the following morning found them standing there petrified (as in turned-to-stone, not frightened). I picked up my shorts, now completely dry, and put them on the floor of our room as Norma sat up in bed. I tapped on the side of them with a spoon to demonstrate how solid they had become.

"There's a hollow sound echoing down my pants leg."

"No comment," she replied, sardonically.

I should have kept my shorts as a freestanding piece of modern sculpture and given it a baffling name; something like 'The Dead Sea Scrolls Through the Genes'. A certainty for the Turner Prize.

Scroll Down

Which brings me to our next excursion; the Israel Museum to see the Dead Sea Scrolls. It is uncanny how many inventions and discoveries have actually been made by accident. The Terracotta Army in China, Richard III under a car park in Leicester, Velcro and Viagra. The Dead Sea Scrolls were found in 1947 near the ancient ruins of Qumran. A Bedouin shepherd, called Muhammad Edh-Dhib, fell into a cave and came out with the scrolls. Sounds painful.

They are the original Old Testament manuscripts, some of which can be found in the Bible and others which were not included such as psalms attributed to King David and Joshua. They are mainly written in Hebrew, with some in Aramaic, which is the language Jesus would have spoken. A small number were written in Nabatean, an interesting Bedouin tribe who we will learn about as we travel through Jordan.

Seeing Stars

Bethlehem is only five miles from Jerusalem and Norma, Nick and I took the local bus primarily to visit the Church of the Nativity. It is the oldest Christian church in the world which is still in use, and was built in the year 326 by the Emperor Constantine. It was partially destroyed two hundred years later by the Samaritans, (they must have been the *bad* Samaritans). During the Persian invasion of 614 almost every Christian church in the Holy Land was destroyed, but the Church of the Nativity was spared. Apparently, a huge mosaic depicting the Wise Men in flowing robes helped persuade the invaders to let the church stand, because they were similar in image to Persian priests (the Magi). During the first Crusade of 1099, the church was restored and improved further.

We entered the Church of the Nativity from Manger Square through a small door which led to a nave of two double rows of Corinthian columns of red limestone. The floor is made of marble slabs from the Crusader times, and steps lead down to the grotto where Jesus was born. The grotto was not much bigger than a squash court, but it seemed much smaller as it was crowded with visitors. The three of us became separated as we tried to pick our way through the heaving throng. Norma and Nick were ahead of me, and they signalled that they would wait for me on the steps. I eventually threaded my way to the niche, in which a silver star is set in white marble to mark the actual spot of the nativity. I leaned forward to put my head inside the niche and it was a moment which, literally, brought tears to my eyes. It wasn't a religious experience or an overwhelming feeling of Christian love emanating from such a sacred place. Without any warning, countdown or signal, the entire congregation in the grotto sang in unison, at full volume; "Hallelujah, Hallelujah." I jumped out of my skin and banged the back of my head on the top of the niche. I must have seen a hundred stars… of Bethlehem, naturally. I thought I was going to pass out there and then, right over Jesus's birthplace. I literally would have been away in a manger. I managed to struggle to my feet practically nose to nose with a group of Italians, who continued to sing inches from my ears. My head was pounding but I was trapped with no chance of escape. I had to stand there grimacing with pain as tears rolled down my cheeks. They must have thought I was overcome by the emotion of the occasion. As I looked over a sea of heads towards the exit staircase, I saw Nick and Norma standing half-way up the steps. They had witnessed my plight, but they were more concerned with stifling their laughter as respectfully as possible. Eventually, I found my way outside, more or less carried along by the crowd like leaving a football match. The strong sunlight intensified my throbbing headache, but I was wasting my time looking towards Norma and Nick for sympathy. Their bottled-up laughter was finally flowing out over Manger Square as they held their sides and started to complain of having a stitch. Ever since, when I receive a Christmas card depicting the adoration of the Magi, I get a slight migraine.

It was time to return to Amman, and this time I made sure I wasn't used as a courier for ladies' underwear.

In the Groove

A memorable day trip from Amman was to see the Roman ruins at Jerash. It is quite easy to become complacent or blasé when visiting so many historic ruins. You can become over-faced and lose sight of the fact that the standing columns or remnants of buildings were once the centre of vibrant, thriving communities, no different to modern towns and cities today. The most famous example of a ruin which still *lives*, is Pompeii, because it was buried as a time-capsule by the eruption of Vesuvius in 79 AD. In a similar way, the ruins of the Graeco-Roman city of Jerash give out similar vibes because it was buried under sand for centuries in a valley in the Gilead Mountains, until its re-discovery in the 1920s. The Temple of Artemis dominates from a raised platform looking out over the Triumphal Arch of Hadrian, a forum, baths, theatres and hippodrome. Running water and fountains were common because Jerash was built on a natural spring. Water sports were popular and water battles were re-enacted for the entertainment of the public. It was a major centre on the east-west caravan route and became rich by trading spices, silks, herbs, gems and ivory. As we walked around the town the feature which really brought the place to life were the pronounced grooves along the road created by chariots and traders' carts. We could almost hear the ghostly clatter of horses' hooves and wheels on stone.

Siq, and Ye Shall Find

In 1845, Petra was described as a 'rose-red city half as old as time' in a prizewinning poem by John Burgon. Not bad for someone who hadn't even been there. Petra was unknown to the western world until 1812, when it was re-discovered by Swiss explorer Johann Burckhardt.

Today, it is Jordan's most popular tourist attraction, and a regular excursion from cruise ships in the southern port of Aqaba. When we arrived there in the 1970s, very few of us had heard of it. We were simply told by Mick that there are some ruins at the end of a canyon and we would be sleeping down there overnight. Millions of years ago an earthquake created an extensive valley which stretches from the Dead Sea to Aqaba, and, today, Petra is located in this valley. We set off with a local guide, named Sanad, on a three kilometre hike along a dark, narrow gorge in the sandstone rock. It was only a few metres wide, and is known as a siq (meaning a shaft or narrow pass).

The rock-face was carved by water and wind erosion into smooth-flowing shapes and the layers of grey, blue and copper-reds created one of nature's natural works of art. It reminded me very much of Arizona. I enjoyed taking photographs and cine film, and often I would walk ahead of our main party to capture everyone making their way along the siq. At one stage, I walked backwards for a few steps as I filmed Norma coming towards me. Then she stopped, open-mouthed with an amazed expression and shouted excitedly,

"John, look behind you."

"Oh no," I joked, pretending to freeze in terror, "don't tell me it's that woman from Jerusalem still after me."

I slowly turned around to view one of the few sights in my life to have literally taken my breath away. The side walls of the siq framed a sunlit magical image, giving us a tantalising glimpse of a section of a cathedral-like building, right there in the middle of the desert. If we had seen photographs, or had any inkling as to what to expect, the impact would not have been as surprising, emotional or dramatic. It had the same effect on me as when I looked across the Grand Canyon for the first time. We emerged from the siq into an area, about the size of a football pitch, to view the full splendour of Al Khazneh, which is popularly known as the Treasury. It has a classical façade of a Greek or Roman temple, with full-size columns, friezes and pediments and, it is worth repeating, all carved from solid rock. The colours of the natural sandstone were the same as we had seen in close-up during our walk along the siq, and they changed in tone and intensity depending on the angle of the sun. A magical place.

We stopped for refreshments, and our guide took the opportunity to give us some background information and history. The word Petra means rock in Greek, and it is from this name that many modern-day terms derive; such as petrology (the study of rocks), petroleum, and petroglyphs (ancient rock carvings such as those found in North America and Australia). The city was established in the 4th Century by Arabs of Bedouin stock, called the Nabateans. They carved houses, three and four-bedroom apartments, tombs, temples, theatres, palaces, stables and warehouses out of sheer rock walls. Compared to these achievements, Michelangelo's sculpture of David from a single slab of Carrara marble seems unambitious. Sanad asked us to look up at the vast urns which form the upper sections of the Treasury, and he pointed out bullet holes. These were caused by Bedouin horsemen shooting their rifles under the mistaken impression that treasure was held inside. They were hoping that they would eventually hit the jackpot and coins would cascade out like some ancient slot machine. At that moment, as if rehearsed, a group of local horsemen rode out of the siq and off into the valley, disappearing in a cloud of billowing dust.

The Nabateans earned a living by operating their own caravan routes, and traded far and wide. Apparently, they also ran a lucrative little side line as a protection racket. Petra was perfectly situated in a strategic position on trade routes from north to south, and even more so from east to west as goods were transported from Persia, India and as far away as Cathay (modern China) bound for Jerash, Jerusalem and Hebron. For a fee, the Nabateans guaranteed safe passage and Petra provided secure stopover accommodation for traders and travellers.

"Is it true," asked Ruth, an RE teacher in Australia, "that the three wise men in the Nativity story will have passed this way?"

"That is a very interesting question, which I am glad you have asked." answered Sanad.

He went on to tell us that it is almost certainly true that they will have been granted safe passage, by the Nabateans, to travel through their territory, and that the Magi will have stayed overnight at Petra. We were impressed by our guide's knowledge of Christianity, even though he himself was a follower of the Islamic faith. He went on to tell us that, in the Bible, the Magi are mentioned only in the Gospel of Matthew, and there is no reference to their names or how many, only 'some' wise men. Magi were well-known figures in the ancient world and the word is derived from the Persian word 'magush' – wise man. Persian Magi, Zoroastrian priests, were considered the genuine keepers of true and ancient wisdom, while Babylonian Magi were largely sorcerers, magicians and astrologers and widely regarded as tricksters and charlatans; the origin of the modern-day word: magic.

The Magi story gathered pace over the centuries in art, history and literature. By the 8th Century, the three Kings had acquired names and kingdoms: Melchior, King of Persia; Caspar, King of India and Balthazar; King of Arabia. Matthew was making a specific point with the gifts: in Jewish ritual, only three kinds of people were anointed; Kings, priests and prophets. Gold is a gift for a King, Frankincense for a priest and myrrh (which was used in embalming) for a prophet. These three gifts meant that Jesus was *triply* anointed; 'the anointed one', which is a translation both of the Greek 'Christos', and the Hebrew 'Mashiach'. Matthew was writing to demonstrate that Jesus of Nazareth was the Christ, the Jewish Messiah.

Several of us complimented Sanad on his knowledge of the bible, and he replied that such knowledge is necessary for his job as a guide. He pointed out that the two religions of Christianity and Islam are closely linked. Many Old Testament prophets are revered in Islam, and Jesus is mentioned more times in the Koran than the Prophet Muhammad himself. It's surprising what you can learn on a visit to somewhere I had previously never heard of. There is a quote by Benjamin Disraeli, which is worth mentioning in this context: 'Travel teaches toleration'. I don't think any further comment is necessary.

Everyone was ready to move on, but Norma, Nick and I realised that we were the only ones who hadn't actually been inside the Treasury. Sanad assured us that we could just catch up with them further along the road. Nick and I finished our sandwiches and Norma strolled over to the Treasury entrance and went inside. A couple of minutes later we walked over and looked inside and, to our great surprise, discovered that the hollowed-out room was only about the size of a tennis court. Incidentally, a few years later we couldn't help but laugh when Norma and I went to the cinema to see the movie 'Indiana Jones and the Last Crusade', which was filmed on location in Petra. When Harrison Ford entered the Treasury he looked down upon a cavernous expanse of fire and tribal rituals. The power of the film editor. When Nick and I went into the treasury, we were alarmed to find that Norma was nowhere to be seen. We called out her name, which echoed eerily off the smooth walls. We began to worry as we wondered if there were any hidden doors, trap doors or chambers which she had stumbled upon by inadvertently touching some secret handle. In front of us was a stone structure which resembled some kind of ancient sarcophagus. We stepped onto a couple of ledges and climbed high enough to see over it. As we peered simultaneously over the ledge, an un-earthly, deathly groan echoed around the chamber as a body slowly raised up into a sitting position. We were so startled that Nick and I screamed and stumbled backwards, only saving ourselves from falling onto the stone floor by our fingertips. Panic over. We had found Norma, whose ghostly wailing had now turned into hysterical laughter as we scrambled down.

"Where have you been? I've been lying up there for ages."

"But what if it *hadn't* been us, and you had frightened some poor stranger to death?" I replied.

Norma was still laughing as she scrambled down to the floor. We picked up our sleeping bags and rucksacks, and the three of us set off along the path. As the surrounding rock became redder in the late afternoon sun, we must have looked like the scarecrow, tin man and lion from 'The Wizard of Oz' as we followed the red-brick road.

After about ten minutes, we became aware of a commotion about fifty metres ahead of us. A few loud bangs and cracks resonated around the valley, and my first reaction was that there was a firework display taking place. However, Nick pulled Norma and me back by the arms, and forced us into a crouch with the solemn warning, "Stay down, that sounds like gunfire."

We knew that Nick had lived in America for quite a few years, so we followed his advice without hesitation, realising that his assessment of the situation was likely to be more accurate than my innocent English-orientated viewpoint. And he was right. We took refuge behind a rather inadequate rock, as we witnessed a gun fight right in front of us. Local tribesmen were firing rifles at each other across the pathway, separated by only about forty metres.

"Perhaps they are making a movie," I spluttered half-heartedly, still unable to comprehend what I was witnessing.

"Maybe," replied Nick, not taking his eyes off the action, "but I doubt it."

"There is no way to get through or round them," said Norma, in a worried tone of voice, while forlornly looking at the steep rock faces surrounding us. After a few moments, one of the armed tribesmen spotted us and he started to walk along the path in our direction. We kept our heads down, silently praying that we hadn't been seen, but to no avail as we heard a voice shout, in broken English, from about twenty metres away.

"Please come out from behind the rock."

Instinctively, we put our hands in the air. After all, that's what they always do in the movies. As we stepped out tentatively onto the path, the gunman laughed out loud.

'Is that the crazed laugh of an unhinged gunman?' I thought, as we hesitantly lowered our hands. I trawled further into my useless reservoir of cinema clichés and thought 'Don't make no sudden moves.' The gunman came right up to us, and, with a wide, friendly grin wrinkling his leathery face, he assured us that we were in no danger.

"It is a small dispute about wages," he told us, matter-of-factly. He then shouted, in his own language, for a ceasefire, which happened immediately. He then gestured for us to walk along the path with him. We hesitated, but agreed to accompany him in view of the fact that his gesture was made with his rifle. As we approached and passed through the centre of the conflict, the tribesmen on each side waved to us, some with their hands and some with their rifles. We waved back enthusiastically, but decided not to stop for a chat. We were led to a safe place, and our escort shook our hands and apologised for the inconvenience, or botheration, as he called it.

"Oh, don't mention it," we replied, with an undisguised exhalation of relief, from most orifices. We continued at a much faster rate to catch up with our travelling companions and we soon heard the wages negotiations resume. What kind of a job negotiates pay deals with a gunfight? Had they never heard of the conciliation service ACAS? We never did find out.

Our experience reminded me of a scene from the movie 'The Man Who Would Be King', starring Sean Connery as a character called Danny, and Michael Caine as Peachy, based on the book by Rudyard Kipling. A full-scale battle was taking place in some unspecified Himalayan Kingdom, when suddenly everyone put down their weapons and lay face-down silently on the ground. Peachy and Danny stood and watched, mystified, as a group of Holy men walked through the middle of the battle. This resumed in earnest once they had departed.

When we caught up with the rest of our group we apologised for the delay.

"Sorry, we were held up in a gunfight."

"I have heard some excuses in my time," replied Colin, "I'll remember that one next time I am late for work."

Sanad was now ready to give us some more information. He told us that the Romans had invaded Petra, and that they had built all their usual trademark buildings: hot baths, paved roads, a theatre and of course triumphal gates, in this case the Arch of Trajan. Sanad also pointed out Jabal Harom, (Aaron's mountain), where the tomb of Aaron the brother of Moses, is said to be located. Petra faded into obscurity from the 4th Century due to changing trade routes as the camels were replaced by seagoing vessels for transporting goods.

Moreover, the Romans started to withdraw from the area due to the gradual decline of the Empire. A few Bedouins continued to live in the valley throughout the subsequent centuries, and were re-discovered in 1812.

As we proceeded further into the valley, greenery appeared in the form of oleander bushes on either side of a stream bed, which is dry for most of the year. Sanad took us to our accommodation for the night, just as the sun was beginning to set. The late afternoon light displayed a glowing palette of rich, warm colours across the sky. We were led into a couple of the two-thousand-year-old Nabatean caves, which was where we would be sleeping. We were to be overnight troglodytes. They were good-size rooms with perfectly straight, flat walls and ceilings carved out of rock. The strata of different coloured sandstone created a timeless effect, almost as if they were covered in modern-day wallpaper. We set-up our sleeping bags and started a fire to cook an evening meal, just outside the apartments. To call them *caves* would be almost insulting to the high level of craftsmanship of those Nabatean builders, two millennia ago. As the stars started to twinkle in a totally cloudless sky, we became aware of the clarity, free of any light pollution, and the silence, which was total and absolute. This was broken only by the chatter, banter and laughter of our group, as we covered a wide range of topics; alien abduction (we thought that we would be perfect targets that night), anecdotes and the inevitable campfire ghost stories.

"Is our room full-board with room service and a drinks fridge?" I asked Sanad.

"No," interjected Barry, quick-as-a-flash, "we are all on Bedouin and breakfast."

After a very quiet, peaceful night's sleep, we retraced our steps out of Petra. Fortunately, the gunfight at the OK Corral was over and we boarded the bus to travel south.

Travelling by bus through the desert landscape of southern Jordan reminded me very much of my greyhound bus travels through Arizona; the complementary colours of blue sky and the orange of the land, each intensifying the other. It has the same desert rock formations, carved by wind erosion, sandblasted over millions of years, to form beautiful smooth curves like giant sculptures by Henry Moore. We stopped at Wadi Rum, the largest wadi (valley) in Jordan, also known as the Valley of the Moon, carved in the granite and sandstone rock. It is home to the Zalabia Bedouin, and the area became famous for its connections with the British army officer T. E. Lawrence, who passed through several times during the 1917-18 Arab Revolt against the Turks. The epic David Lean movie, 'Lawrence of Arabia', starring Peter O'Toole, was filmed on location there.

The following morning, we set off early for the journey north back to Amman for one night, before embarking east through the Jordanian desert towards Iraq.

Desert Storm

We were up at dawn to make an early start for the long-haul east towards Baghdad. We boarded the bus with slight trepidation, as we would be encountering the vast open desert for the first time. On the straight road from Amman on our way to Baghdad the calm and serenity of the endless desert landscape was suddenly interrupted as strong winds started to whip up a desert storm. Dave had to reduce his speed to a crawl, as slow as if we were travelling on a British motorway. It was like a thick fog; a London pea-souper. In the middle of a sand storm in the Jordanian desert, it was more like a tomato-souper. It was as if a veil of orange fog had enveloped the bus, like a scene from a James Herbert novel. It was eerie, and unlike anything I had seen before. Nick and Colin volunteered to walk in front of the bus to guide the way with flashlights, as they covered their heads and faces with a keffiyeh (Arab head scarf) to protect themselves from being sand blasted. We kept going as we felt that it would be more dangerous to stop and risk being hit from behind. When it had cleared, Nick and Colin received a round of applause when they re-boarded the bus.

The Iraq border crossing gradually came into view, and a few small huts emerged through a sandy haze, as rising desert heat refracted the light to create a shimmering mirage effect.

Calmer Chameleon

In 1726, the writer Daniel Defoe coined the famous phrase; 'Nothing is certain, except death and taxes.' I would like to add one other, which is an absolute certainty for travellers through Asia; Delhi belly, or the Turkey trots, or the Shiraz shi… Well, you get the idea. Everyone was affected to some degree. Norma and I got off quite lightly, but one or two others had been laid low for a couple of days. One Australian woman, Kay, was permanently afflicted, and, for about two weeks, she was never without a toilet roll; always tucked under her arm.

A strong desert wind began to pick up as we drove along the straight road towards Baghdad. Kay's husband, Peter, suddenly screamed for Mick to stop the bus. He immediately responded by slamming on the brakes, wondering what had happened. With no time to explain, Peter jumped off the bus and sprinted across the desert sand quicker than a camel on heat. He found a few small rocks to protect his modesty, which, by that stage, was of minor concern to him. He whipped off his trousers in double-quick time, and squatted behind the rock. At least he had the presence of mind to aim down-wind, as the alternative doesn't bear thinking about. Peter was oblivious to the fact that his ablutions had become a spectator sport. The wind built up, in more ways than one, and he held on grimly to his trousers, which he held aloft above his head, well out of harm's way. They billowed wildly like a windsock at an airport. As he squatted behind his very small screen of desert rocks, I felt particularly sorry for a chameleon which happened to be out for a morning stroll, innocently minding his own business. Unfortunately, it walked straight into the line of fire, like a spray-tan salon. The poor thing was left totally confused because brown wasn't a hue in its range of colour-changes. Peter even managed to smile (or perhaps it was a grimace), but he lost concentration, and, more importantly, he also lost his trousers. The swirling wind lifted them airborne, like a helicopter, and swept them away. It was like Wagner's 'Ride of the Valkyries'.

"I know that this is the land of magic carpets, but I didn't realize there are also flying trousers. They will get to Baghdad before us!" quipped Nick.

We all erupted with howls of laughter. I gripped my aching sides, and one or two people started to look concerned, as they clutched their stomachs. It's the most fun I have ever had watching someone go to the toilet. Mercifully, Peter's trousers snagged on a rock about twenty yards down-wind, and Mick chivalrously ran to retrieve them, neatly sidestepping the newly-discovered species of Iraqi brown chameleon. As Peter boarded the bus, he could not resist a deep, flamboyant bow. Or was he just doubling-up in pain?

Genie with the Light Brown Lamp

Baghdad is situated on the River Tigris, in the area originally called Mesopotamia, ('land between the rivers'). It is the cradle of human civilisation, pre-dating the Egyptians, Minoans of Crete, the Greeks, Persians and Romans. The bazaars were filled with goods from the Silk Road, and it became the richest city in the world by trading in incense and pearls from Arabia, gold and slaves from East

Africa and spices and dyes from India. On the east side of the river is the historical al-Risafa district, with monuments, bazaars and mosques, the most prominent being Jami al-Khulafa and Mirjan.

We visited the Iraq Museum, and I was impressed with the sculptures and carvings of the Sumerian and Assyrian civilisations from this area. The human race owes a lot to the early inhabitants: we saw a clay tablet which is the world's first calendar, the Sumerians invented the wheel, started schools, established laws, writing and developed agriculture. All this, 1500 years before the pyramids, and when Britain was still in the Stone Age.

The smells from restaurants reminded us that it was lunch time, and we were spoiled for choice; hummus, olives, grilled lamb or chicken and rice everywhere we looked. A local speciality was mazgouf (fish), freshly caught in the Tigris, and kept live in tanks. Walking around the old town and bazaar, we were attracted by an enticing aromatic smell, which lured us into a small restaurant. We popped our heads inside, more out of curiosity, but the owner was on to us immediately, and welcomed us as if we were regular diners. He shooed away a couple of locals drinking tea at the best table in the window alcove, and sat us down. Our minds had been made up for us. He told us proudly that he was making a traditional Iraqi beef stew, with okra and tomatoes. He insisted that we go over to the kitchen to see it cooking. The cooks were so startled, that one of them even took his cigarette out of his mouth. The floor-to-ceiling tiles were of indeterminate colour, but, beneath whatever was covering them, we could make out the odd glimpse of white and blue.

I had lost track of how many weeks, or months, we had been on the road, but, by then, our levels of hygienic expectations had lowered considerably. As the chef stirred the cauldron with his ladle, carefully avoiding flicking cigarette ash into the stew, the owner added an ingredient called baharat; a mix of nutmeg, black pepper, coriander seed, cloves, cinnamon and paprika chilli. It was delicious, and unbelievably cheap, so we left a well-deserved, generous tip. As we were leaving the café, the proprietor came out into the street and shook each of our hands as if to say goodbye to old friends. Fantastic hospitality! Next stop, a place which appears 252 times in the Bible… Babylon.

Rivers of Babylon

The Greek historian Herodotus, the first man to suggest the concept of Wonders of the World, described Babylon in 450 BC as, 'Surpassing in splendour any city in the known world'. It was three hundred years later, that an actual list was compiled by Antipater of Sidon, and it is that same list, which is still recognized today, especially in pub quizzes. Hands up anyone who can name them. The only one to survive to the present-day is the Great Pyramid of Giza in Egypt, and the only one which cannot be given a reasonably accurate location is The Hanging Gardens of Babylon.

There is debate over whether they actually existed, or were indeed in Babylon. How could they have been anywhere else? The name is perfect. I hope future archaeologists don't find evidence and re-locate it. Somehow, The Hanging Gardens of Basildon wouldn't have quite the same magic. So with a combination of blind faith and 'suspension of disbelief', we set off to see the site where it might have been. I am not quite sure what I was expecting to see. Something like the Southport Flower Show? What about the gardens of Versailles? Or perhaps Monet's garden of water lilies at Giverny? Compared to these examples, The Hanging Gardens of Babylon defy description. There was nothing to describe.

To be fair, a reproduction of the Ishtar City Gate, (dedicated to the Goddess Ishtar), was impressive. It illustrates the new Babylonian technique of building with individual bricks, decorated with rows of bas-relief sirrush (dragons), and aurochs (which sound like creatures from Tolkien's 'Lord of the Rings'). Each brick was glazed in blue and kiln-fired. Perhaps that is the reason why Nebuchadnezzar built his fiery furnace.

I remember a scene in the TV comedy series Fawlty Towers, when an irate, hard-of-hearing guest, called Mrs. Richards, complained that the view from her hotel window 'Was not good enough'. Basil Fawlty countered with, "It's Torquay madam, what were you expecting to see? The Hanging Gardens of Babylon?" Well, let me assure Basil Fawlty that if the view *had* been of the Hanging

Gardens, then Mrs. Richards would certainly have had grounds for complaint.

Of course, we had our photos taken in front of a battered old sign; we stood in front of what looked like the footings for the foundations for a new housing estate. We looked like proud owners who had just put down a deposit on a plot off-plan. Just to take that analogy a stage further, I think Herodotus would have made a fantastic estate agent. In his description of Babylon, he refers, in glowing terms, to fortresses, temples, massive gold statues and the famous Tower of Babel, built by King Nebuchadnezzar II. He gives specific measurements of lengths of walls and heights of buildings, but subsequent archaeological excavations have proved that they had more modest dimensions. The moral of this tale; always take a tape measure when viewing one of his show-houses.

According to legend, the King built the gardens for his Queen Amyitis, the daughter of the King of Medes, whose homeland to the east of Persia was green and mountainous. Apparently, she found the flat sun-baked terrain of Mesopotamia depressing, so the King built her a green, leafy artificial mountain with ascending terraces of over-hanging foliage. I can empathise with his way of thinking, because I once built a rockery in our back garden for Norma. The reason it was regarded as a miracle, or wonder of the world (The Hanging Gardens that is, not my rockery) was the incredible feat of engineering. There was an ingenious system to transfer water from the Euphrates River, and raise it up for irrigation of the gardens. I had the same idea for my rockery, and the only reason I didn't do it was because it was an exceptionally hot summer and there was a hosepipe ban.

Eden Project

After an interesting few days in Baghdad, we headed towards Basra. We decided to have a brief stopover in paradise. I had been to Paradise before, but that was a town in Michigan. This time, it was for real; the site of the earthly paradise of the Garden of Eden, as described in the Book of Genesis. As with the Hanging Gardens of Babylon, there is dispute as to the location. The most commonly recognized site is at the confluence of the great rivers Tigris and Euphrates, which combine to form the Shatt al-Arab river, which flows to the gulf.

There was indeed a small wall around a tree, plus a sign to remind us where we were. It wasn't the healthiest-looking tree I have ever seen, and it was definitely not an apple tree. The 'Tree of Life' looked in need of the kiss of life, and, would you Adam-and-Eve-it, we all posed for photographs holding an obligatory apple. These were sold to us by an enterprising group of children in charge of a bullock cart. We gave the kids some sweets and pens, and chatted to them. They were having great fun jumping in the river, and, as the temperature was about 30 degrees, I was tempted to join them. I decided against it because I didn't think it would be too wise to go swimming in a river called Shatt.

East of Eden

The area of Mesopotamia is, in effect, a huge basin into which flows countless rivers from the Zagros Mountains in the northeast, Saudi Arabia and Syria to the west and Kurdistan to the north. These fertile plains support endless palm trees, and it has been a major centre for date-growing for thousands of years. There are crops, vegetables and plants... particularly *industrial* plants. As we got nearer to Basra, the petroleum refineries seemed to be everywhere, with their distinctive flare stacks, lit like candles on a giant birthday cake. The flames are to burn off excess gasses from pressure-relief valves. We stayed overnight near Basra, sleeping out in the open next to a pipeline, and the following morning we were quickly out of our sleeping bags as the sun rose. In that part of the world, it seems to rise almost vertically, and very quickly, over the horizon, as the heat becomes searingly hot. Once we had burned off our excess gasses, we headed for the Iranian border.

Arabian Nights

From Basra, it was only about 30 miles to the Iranian border, and then we travelled east through the flat plains north of the Persian Gulf. The scenery became more spectacular as we made our way through the southern slopes of the Zagros Mountains, heading for Shiraz.

"Here is a quiz question for you," announced Mick, as we sat down for a cup of tea at a little roadside stall.

"What's the connection between the song 'Layla' by Eric Clapton, the theme from the film '2001 A Space Odyssey', and the 1888 classical piece 'Scheherazade' by the Russian composer Rimsky-Korsakov?"

Mick was reading from his dusty, sun-faded ring-file binder, which contained his travel notes, local information, hotel addresses and also titbits of information that he had picked up along the way. I love general knowledge trivia so I offered a vague answer.

"I think Scheherazade is something to do with the Arabian nights. Was it set in this country?"

"Very good," replied our question master, "but what about 'Layla'?"

"Was Eric Clapton born in Iran?"

"No."

"Was the riff in 'Layla' taken from a piece by Rimsky-Korsakov?"

"No."

We were all completely stumped by the '2001' connection.

"Do you give up?" asked Mick, smugly.

"Yes."

"The answer is Iran, or Persia as it used to be called. The three pieces of music have a connection with this country."

Mick then explained that the story of 'Layla and Majnun' was written in the 12th Century by a Persian author called Nezami. It is about a Bedouin poet, called Qays, who fell in love with Layla, but her father forbade marriage. He wandered the desert and became insane because of his love for someone unattainable. (Majnun means 'mad man' in Arabic). When Eric Clapton read this story seven hundred years later, he related to it because of his own similar situation with Patti Boyd, who at that time was the wife of Beatle George Harrison. The classic song 'Layla' was the result.

The Stanley Kubrick film, '2001 A Space Odyssey', opens with the music 'Also Sprach Zarathustra', (thus spoke Zarathustra), and was written by Richard Strauss in 1896. Zoroaster (Zarathustra in Persian) was a prophet in Persia around 1000 BC. He preached that God communicated through dreams. These were interpreted by Zoroastrian priests, known as Magi (from the Greek magoi, meaning wise men). They studied the night sky, in the belief that what was observed in the stars reflects events on earth. They developed the twelve signs of the zodiac that are still used today. Personally, I don't believe in Astrology and I am very sceptical about Horoscopes. But then again, that's probably just me; a typical Capricorn.

It has been suggested that Zoroastrian priests from Persia were the Magi in the Biblical story of the Nativity, as told to us in Petra by our guide Sanad. This also ties in with what we were told in Bethlehem; the Church of the Nativity was spared destruction because the paintings of the Wise men reminded the invaders of Zoroastrian priests.

Rimsky-Korsakov was inspired by Scheherazade, who was a Persian Queen, who told stories based on fairy tales, fables and legends over a period of one thousand and one Arabian nights. They included characters well-known to us today, especially during Pantomime season; Sinbad the Sailor, Ali Baba, and Aladdin. These stories were a life-saver for Scheherazade, quite literally. The Persian Sultan Shahryar was convinced that all women were unfaithful and vowed to put to death each of his wives on the wedding night. When he married Scheherazade, she managed to prolong her life by telling him a different story every night for a thousand and one nights, until he eventually repudiated his vow. By my calculation, that works out at over two and a half years. She must have dreaded getting writer's block, but I suppose there is nothing like an imminent death-sentence to focus the mind. She lived happily ever after as a Sultana. Brown and wrinkled; it must be the desert sun.

After we finished our refreshing cup of tea, we got back onto the bus and, before setting off, Mick rummaged around in his cassette box. We drove off to the sound of, you've guessed it, 'Layla'.

A Glass or Two in Shiraz

Shiraz is an ancient city in South West Iran. It was originally a centre for trade and the arts, and from the 9th Century became a place of Muslim pilgrimage. The city was the capital of Persia in the 18th Century, and many of the buildings still standing today date from that period. Vakil (Regent's) Mosque is one of the most impressive, with a beautiful ceiling in the prayer hall, and a myriad of colours fill the room as sunlight filters through the stained glass windows. It is a

University City, known as the city of poets, literature, wine and flowers, and it has many beautiful gardens and tree-lined avenues. A colourful, timeless scene was along the banks of the Dry River, (so called because it is seasonal) as crowds of women chatted and did their washing. There are numerous crafts to be admired amongst the bazaars, notably inlaid mosaic work and silverware, and particularly carpet weaving, and, of course, wine.

Traces of wine and grapes have been found in pottery jars, unearthed in archaeological sites of Neolithic villages in the Zagros Mountains; evidence that winemaking in the area has a history dating back to the 6th Century BC.

We visited a local vineyard for a pleasant afternoon learning about wine, and, of course, tasting. Apparently, there is some confusion over Shiraz wine. Legend has it that returning Crusaders brought shoots of the grape variety from Shiraz, but it is thought that there was something lost in translation somewhere along the line. The red Shiraz wine, particularly from Australia, has no historical connection with Shiraz in Persia. Just to cloud the issue, if not the wine, Shiraz wine (from Shiraz) is actually white. So there we have it, but I found that it all became much clearer with each glass. Cheers.

The Place of Forty Columns

Persepolis derives its name from the Greek, meaning Persian city, and is located 50 kilometres north of Shiraz, at the foot of Kouh-e Rahmat, (Mountain of Mercy), in the plain of Marv Dasht. It was an impressive Palace complex, founded by Darius the Great, around 518 BC, as his seat of government and centre for ceremonial festivities. Subsequently, it was improved and expanded by his successors, notably Xerxes. Persepolis lasted barely two centuries; it was looted and destroyed by Alexander the Great in 331 BC. After drunken celebrations of victory, Persepolis was burned, almost ceremonially, as a symbolic act to avenge the destruction of Palaces and Temples in Athens by the Persians, under Xerxes, some 150 years earlier. Even though the ruins of Persepolis were almost totally buried by the surrounding desert for centuries, it was still known to the locals as the, 'place of forty columns', which were exposed periodically due to shifting sands.

Since we were following in the footsteps of Alexander the Great, we decided that we should also follow his example and have a drunken night as well. It would be rude not to. Mick, whom I had befriended ever since I had happened to notice him loading a case of whisky on the bus in London, came over to join us and suggested a drink. We were to spend that night in our sleeping bags in the car park, under the endless sky of sparkling stars. Our mentor Alexander would have been proud of us. We had a great party.

The following morning, we were awakened by the light and heat of the sun as it climbed very quickly above the horizon. I sat up with a thumping hangover, and looked over towards the ruins of Persepolis.

‘If Alexander felt the way I do now,’ I thought, ‘I wonder if he remembered burning down the Palace the night before. I’ve been to a few house-warming parties, but nothing like that’.

Incidentally, two names crop up regularly during our travels: Alexander the Great and James Bond. Here is an interesting touch of trivia which links them: Alexander’s epitaph and James Bond’s family motto both happen to be... ‘The World is not Enough’.

The ruins of Persepolis today are dominated by the remaining standing columns, and, to me, it was a scene reminiscent of industrial chimneys, particularly when silhouetted against the setting sun. Somehow, it seems to almost foretell the numerous oil refineries which blight the desert landscapes throughout Iraq and Iran. The original buildings were organised in a grid on a raised platform, with the Hall of a Hundred Columns at the centre. The great staircase of the Apadana, (Audience Hall), is decorated with detailed relief carvings of conquered nations bringing offerings to the King. There are double-bull columns, and a mythological griffin (Homa); the guardian of travellers. This has been adopted as the company logo for Iran Air.

“Hey Clarry,” shouted a couple of the girls, laughing, “I think you must be a reincarnation of a Persian soldier. Come over here and look at this.”

We all went over to the staircase to see a relief sculpture of a row of Clarry-look-alikes. The figures were life-size, about 5ft 7 inches tall, all with identical beards, wearing hats, standing in a row, carved in profile. Clarry laughed in agreement, and joined the back of the line. A photo opportunity, not only for us, but also for a few other amused tourists.

Knickers in a Twist

We departed Persepolis and continued north on a good quality road through the mountains. Not far from the town of Qaderabad, Mick pulled over to the side of the road.

"Anybody fancy a shower?" he asked.

"Why, are you trying to tell us something?" Nick joked.

"Where are the facilities?" inquired Bethan, as we all looked around at the barren landscape.

"The stream in the valley has some small rapids and waterfalls, and is perfect for washing and filling-up water bottles. I have stopped here before."

"I could do with a shower," I announced, picking up my towel.

Everyone trudged down the hill, just a couple of hundred metres, and the sound of the stream got louder as we got closer. The threadbare grass on either side was evidence that it was a popular place for picnics, or washing clothes on the flat stones, even though the place was deserted. The stream flowed from the Zagros Mountains and joined the Zahandeh River to Shiraz. It was only about ten metres wide, and could be crossed by stepping stones, smoothed by a couple of thousand years' worth of footsteps. There was a small cascade of white water, created by a natural rockery, and Mick told us that by hanging on to the rocks we could enjoy a *horizontal* shower. I tested the temperature by tentatively dipping my foot in the water. It was freezing, as one would expect from a mountain stream, but after long hours sitting on a hot bus with no air-conditioning with just a warm breeze for ventilation, everyone was eager to take the plunge. You know how athletes often sit in a bath of iced water after training, or spend time in a cryogenic chamber to aid recovery from injury? Well, they are like the waters of the Caribbean compared to this stream.

We wrapped towels around our waists as we changed into swimming costumes or shorts. The stream was about waist-height, and was surprisingly fast-flowing just down from the cascades. We had to hold on to each other, or to a rock, to avoid being swept over by the sheer force of the water. Bethan had forgotten to bring her swimming costume from the bus, so she decided to strip to her bra and knickers. Travelling and living together does tend to strip away inhibitions. No one lingered for very long in the water, and we were soon back to the bank in the warm sun. Bethan was last to go in. She made for the cascades and announced, bravely, that she was going to have a horizontal shower. She sat on a rock and slowly eased herself into the freezing water, gasping as she felt her back being jet-washed, with the force of a hose used by riot police for crowd control. She managed to turn over as we encouraged her from the side. She clung on to a couple of crevasses in the rock, face down and breathing from the side as the white water thundered over her. It made a power-shower seem like a dripping tap. She easily had the strength to maintain her grip, but unfortunately the same could not be said for her knicker elastic. Slowly, gradually, inexorably her white knickers started to move south. The suntan line across her back emerged to highlight the tonal contrast to her white knickers, and even whiter bottom. They filled up with water, and ballooned like a spinnaker in a strong wind. Bethan could feel her knickers slipping down, and the laughter from the bank confirmed her suspicions. As gentlemen, we felt as though we should avert our gaze, but we were transfixed. Momentarily, Bethan tried to put one hand behind her back to pull them up, but she had to quickly resume her two-hand grip, due to the force of the water.

"Trust me, I'm a doctor," laughed Barry, as he stretched across to try to restore her modesty. I held on to Barry's other hand. He reached out and was tantalizingly close, when the water just pulled the knickers out of reach, as if an invisible pair of hands had started to play a game with him. Bethan's bottom, jet-blasted by now, appeared like the moon coming up over the sea. Barry adjusted his position and, with a final stretch, managed to get within touching distance. But too late! The knickers had started to pick up speed, and moved down her thighs. From then on, they were on the home straight in their bid for freedom. Over the knees, down the calves, snagged for a second on the ankles, and then they were away, down-river faster than a barracuda. We watched Bethan's knickers disappear with fascination, and the roar of our laughter matched the roar of the water. Then the girls took over, and absolutely insisted that we consider Bethan's embarrassment and look the other way. They helped her out of the water and wrapped her in towels. I doubt if Cleopatra would have had more attendants as she stepped out of a bath of ass's milk. Talking about asses, Bethan laughed as she assured us she had never had such a clean bottom. Too much information.

"I am really glad that didn't happen to me," commented Colin.

"Why?"

"Getting out of freezing water… naked. Now that really would be embarrassing!"

As we walked back to the bus, we all had a good laugh and speculated as to the fate of Bethan's knickers. My theory was that they would be carried all the way back to Shiraz, and get caught up in a woman's washing on the banks of the river. Probably a large, fierce-looking woman with blazing eyes, similar to the one who chased me through the streets of Jerusalem. She would inadvertently scoop up the knickers with the rest of her washing, put them in a basket and take them home. I would love to have been a fly-on-the-wall when her poor, unsuspecting husband was confronted with the damning evidence of the rogue pair of Marks and Spencer knickers, as his wife demanded an explanation.

I could just picture him sitting there like a scene from a film noir; thick set, thinning hair, hairy arms, unshaven, wearing a white vest which exposed his hairy shoulders. After a few moments of dumbfounded, thinking time, he would proclaim his innocence by spluttering;

“Isn’t it obvious? An English woman, travelling overland to Kathmandu, must have lost her knickers in a fast-flowing river. They have floated off and found their way into your washing basket, and here they are, in my house.”

Good luck with that one! Even Scheherazade would have rejected that story as being too far-fetched.

The Emerald City

As we approached Isfahan, turquoise, blue and emerald domes and minarets seemed to grow organically from the desert sands. It was like the Emerald City in the ‘Wizard of Oz’, except that this one was real.

There are certain cities around the world which conjure up a particular image or mood based on its architectural style. I am thinking of pastel-coloured Art-Deco Miami Beach, Regency Bath, or the iron balconies of Creole New Orleans. Add Isfahan to this list; a city which is the exemplification of Islamic architecture. Its name originally means ‘Place of the Army’, and grew as an oasis for the caravan trade in the Dasht-e Kavir Desert. It is situated on the Zahandeh River, which flows from the magnificent backdrop of the Zagros Mountains. Laid out in 1598, it is a beautifully proportioned city, with one of the largest squares in the world, as we drove over the Pol-e Shahrestan Bridge, the sight below us would have hardly changed in centuries, as the river became the local launderette. The women chatted in groups, some pummelled brightly-coloured washing on flat river-stones, while others just pummelled their husbands while holding aloft white knickers. Women were coming and going all the time, with reed baskets of washing balanced confidently on their heads. The river bank was as colourful as a carnival, with washing laid out to dry in the sun.

We enjoyed the atmosphere of the Qeisarieh Bazaar, and we were by now well accustomed to the familiar smells and colours, and yet, each bazaar seemed to have its own particular character. Besides the ubiquitous Persian carpets, there were countless fantastic crafts; engraved metal plates, vases, drinking goblets and trays, block-printed textiles and embroidered tablecloths.

We had lunch at a city-centre restaurant, tiled from floor to ceiling, of course, and ordered an Isfahan delicacy of Beryani; minced lamb, topped with seasoning and spices. This was followed by Gaz, which sounds like someone's nickname, a chewy nougat with pistachios and almonds.

In common with most of the Middle Eastern cities we had visited so far, we discovered that Isfahan has a rich heritage, with Islamic architecture from the 11th to the 19th Centuries. The golden period was during Safavid Dynasty, particularly during the reign of Shah Abbas in the 16th Century, when Isfahan became the capital of Persia. So many cultures and nationalities met, traded and worked there, that it became known as Nesf-e-Jahan, or Half of the World.

The Masjid-i Jami, or Great Mosque, of Isfahan was built in the late 11th Century, and to give it some historical context, it was constructed at about the same time that William the Conqueror was building the Tower of London. The mosque is one of the finest examples of the four-ivan type in which ivans, or vaulted halls, lead off from each side of the inner courtyard. It was a beautiful, serene, peaceful environment, as the bright sun glistened on the acres of intricately decorated glazed tiles. The light shimmered on the many shades of blue and turquoise as if flickering across a tropical ocean. Unique to Isfahan are The Shaking Minarets (Menar Jonban), when one is shaken, (not stirred), it can be felt throughout the building.

We thought we had seen perfection at the Great Mosque, until we visited the Royal Mosque (Masjid-i Shah), which dates from the 17th Century. The semi-dome of the portal looks almost like a natural form, like stalactites in a cave, with every surface decorated with unimaginable detail. As we saw in Paris, the French Impressionist painter Claude Monet made a famous series of paintings of the portal of Rouen Cathedral, at different times of day to catch the changing light. One can only imagine what he would have created if he had been able to visit Isfahan in the 1870s. (The names of some of the mosques and squares in Isfahan have been changed since the Iranian Revolution).

The next leg of our journey was approximately 200 miles north to the capital city of Tehran, situated on the southern edge of the Alborz Mountains.

When compared to many of the ancient cities we had visited throughout the Middle East, Tehran is a new town a mere two centuries old. Although it is the capital city of Iran, it does not have the same aesthetic appeal as Shiraz and Isfahan. It is a huge, crowded and choking in traffic jams and exhaust fumes, and yet it was its natural setting which attracted the Safivad Kings in the mid-16th Century. In the 18th Century, Agha Muhammad Khan made it his capital, and himself the Shah of Persia.

What Tehran lacks in architectural balance and harmony, it more than makes up for with its many museums. The National Museum is particularly impressive and houses a marvellous collection of carvings, stone figures and ceramics, some dating back 7000 years. As one would expect, relics excavated from Persepolis feature prominently, and we found that we could relate to them having visited the ruins a few weeks earlier. Persian carpets are world famous, so we decided to visit the Carpet Museum. The carpet industry has a history going back 2500 years, and the designs reached their zenith during the Safavid Dynasty. This was at approximately the same time as the High Renaissance of Leonardo, Michelangelo and Raphael, and it could be argued that the Persian carpets of the period were works of art in themselves. The designs were based on the geometric layout and symmetry of Islamic gardens (char bagh), the prayer niche, and hunting scenes. Trade with Europe prospered along the Silk Road, and the carpets flew off the shelves, so to speak.

My greatest memory of Tehran is that of Ali. I don't mean the son-in-law of the Prophet, but Muhammad Ali the boxer, the Greatest. His fight in the USA with Ken Norton was due to be broadcast live on Iranian television in the early hours, and I inquired at the hotel if it would be possible to watch. A few of the waiters, chefs and kitchen staff were boxing fans, and especially fans of Ali, and I asked if I could join them. They were very hospitable, even though I was given the job to knock them up the following morning. They gave me a list of their rooms, which were in the basement and adjacent to boilers, fuse boxes, meters and air-conditioning units, along dark corridors festooned with ducts, tubes and a web of cables, looped precariously from walls and ceilings. I gave each door a firm *rent-man's knock*, waited for a groaning, mumbling answer and carried on with my rounds. In the kitchen a huge kettle was already boiling, and a smiling chef handed me a mug of hot tea.

It was four o'clock, but I was wide-awake because I was quite used to some very early starts on our trek. Gradually, everyone gathered in the kitchens from the dark corridors, invariably yawning and scratching. They all seemed to have been cloned from the same seed. Unkempt hair the colour of coal, swarthy complexions, dark bluish stubble, very hairy arms and legs, and all wearing vests of varying degrees of white. They soon woke up when the fight started, as we gathered around a small black and white television. Everyone cheered for Ali, who won a very close fight on points over fifteen rounds. I enjoyed the camaraderie amongst us, and they very kindly treated me to breakfast of scrambled eggs on toast during the fight.

From Tehran we travelled north through the mountains on the main road towards the Caspian Sea. We reached the flatter land of its southern edge at Amol, where the road turned east via Babol towards Gorgan.

Nessum Dorma

We stopped for the night on the shores of the Caspian Sea, about 20 miles from our next major destination of Gorgan. We set up camp near sand dunes at the beach, and as we looked out to sea in a northerly direction the sun started to set over our left shoulders. The beach was quite deserted, apart from a few families packing-up to go home. I commented to Norma that it reminded me of Ainsdale Beach near Southport, and this was re-enforced by a lone horseman galloping along at the edge of the water, since I had once seen the famous Grand National Winner Red Rum on a training run. Ominously, heavy cumulonimbus clouds began to gather, painted with the reds and oranges of the setting sun, to fill the sky with a Turneresque palette of mauves, purples and magentas.

We enjoyed a beach barbeque and settled down for the night, but not for long. After about two hours our tent was lit up by lightning, followed almost immediately by a clap of thunder which rattled the tent poles. Norma and I settled down in our sleeping bags. There must be something in the human psyche which makes us feel safe and content listening to the sound of raindrops on canvas. Like watching the hypnotic flames in a fireplace, or listening to the shipping forecast on the radio on a Sunday evening. Just as I was about to drop off, the most dreadful scream cut through the sound of rolling thunder, followed by another, and cries of terror. Our tent started to move to the sound of scurrying all around, as we knelt together in the middle of the tent.

"Not pigs again?" I said, with a touch of bravado trying to mask my own rising terror. This time, the sound of squeaks and squeals were certainly not piglets. I jumped out of the tent. Our camp was being overrun by a plague of rats. It has been said that the rats in the mud of the First World War trenches were as big as cats. Well, in the pouring rain, with a thunderous soundtrack and sheet lightening intermittently floodlighting the sand dunes, these rats seemed to be monsters. Instinctively, everyone ran towards the bus about a hundred yards away and clambered aboard, screaming.

"Don't panic," spluttered Mick, "they are probably more frightened of us than we are of them."

Our woeful expressions spoke volumes. It was two o'clock in the morning, and we were all soaked to the skin as we took our seats. Steam began to rise. The windows quickly steamed-up and the whole bus began to smell like a wet shaggy dog.

"John, is this the trip of a lifetime that you have been promising me for years?" whispered Norma, morosely.

I slept fitfully through a restless Arabian night; probably the same as Scherehezade had done. I drifted in and out of consciousness dreaming that I had just won the Grand National at Aintree on Red Rum. Barry was a close second on Shaggy Dog, pursued by Mick on Drowned Rat, closely followed by Prince Caspian and Aladdin Sane.

We were awakened by the morning light, as the heat of the sun re-activated the steam. Getting off the bus was like emerging from a Turkish bath in Istanbul. Mercifully, there was no sign of the rats, even though I had visions of them lying in wait to ambush us, like in James Herbert's terrifying novel; 'The Rats'.

The Biblical torrent had flushed the rats out of a sewer pipe, and they had run for their lives in terror. Then they saw us and became *even more* terrified. Poor things. According to our driver that is. The hot sun quickly dried off our tents, sleeping bags and clothes as we had breakfast… Ratatouille (sorry, couldn't resist that one.) We loaded the bus and moved on to a campsite near the town.

Gorgan is another of the many places we had passed through which owes its existence to a strategic trading position, in particular the legendary Silk Road. The bazaars had the usual collection of textiles, spices, and carpets, and, bizarrely, it had an incredible number of taxidermists' shops. Even when we stopped at a little coffee shop in an intricately-tiled courtyard near Shohada Avenue, we felt uneasy at being stared at by stuffed birds and small animals. An uninterrupted gaze of beady eyes.

"This must be how Rod Taylor and Tippi Hedren felt as 'The Birds' congregated in Bodega Bay," I whispered to Norma, as if they could hear me.

Our final destination in Iran was the holy city of Mashhad, a place of pilgrimage for over a thousand years. In the 9th Century, a Muslim cleric, Imam Reza, a descendant of Muhammad, was murdered at a small watering-hole settlement, called Sanabad, along the caravan route to Turkmenistan. The small town became known as the 'Place of Martyrdom'; Mashhad, and it grew into an important Shia Muslim religious site, and place of pilgrimage, or Ziyarah. The turquoise dome of the shrine of Imam Reza is prominent on the skyline, contrasting beautifully with the golden dome of the Gowhrzhad Mosque.

We found it to be a very pleasant city, with lots of beautiful parks. Mashhad has one of the oldest libraries in the Middle East, and contains the oldest manuscript of the Qur'an (Koran). Some of the best Persian carpets are from Mashhad, easily recognizable we were told, by their complex curvilinear floral designs, in dark blues and reds.

It was with great sadness that we said goodbye to Iran, the magical land of Scheherazade and the Arabian Nights, the splendour of Isfahan and the historic ruins of Persepolis, but everyone was excited and looking forward to our next country; Afghanistan.

Chapter Three

A Passage to India

The desert border-crossing from Iran to Afghanistan was interesting to say the least. As we walked through passport control, our route took us through an exhibition which must be the ultimate deterrent to the smuggling of drugs. It was a display which exhibited various methods by which travellers had attempted to smuggle drugs. Hollowed-out heels of shoes, metal tubing of rucksacks, tent poles or secret compartments in suitcases. The most chilling aspect was the background information, which was printed in several languages, and stated calmly and coldly the nationalities of the culprits, and the sentences they had received. For example: ‘Swiss couple, age 19 and 21. Sentence: 15 years in prison in Kabul’. ‘German male, age 32. Sentence: Death’. ‘British female, age 25. Sentence: 20 years in prison in Mashhad’. (Which has a prison built specifically for foreigners). Truly frightening.

There was a great feeling of exhilaration and anticipation as we entered Afghanistan. The dusty road to Herat gave us our first sight of the famous Afghani trucks, affectionately known as jingle trucks, due to the sound of chains hanging from bumpers, with beads and pendants everywhere. Each truck was brightly painted in patterns or landscape scenes, and they reminded me of customized cars and vans usually shown at motor shows or steam-rally fairs.

Jingle all the Way

Herat dates from the time of our old friend, Alexander the Great. Mainly due to its strategic position on the fabled Silk Road, it has been invaded many times: The Mongol invaders Khengis Khan and Tamerline, the Uzbeks and the Safavids of Persia have all destroyed and re-built a city that has seen it all, right up to modern times of the British, Russians and Americans. Its long history of resilience suggests Herat will probably still be there in another two thousand years, when London could look like the Forum in Rome, or New York like the final scene from the film 'Planet of the Apes', with the only recognisable landmark being the top of the Statue of Liberty trying to resist a final burial. Who knows? All civilisations throughout human history rise and fall in cycles.

The Masjid-i-Jamei (Friday Mosque), is the most famous in Afghanistan. It is decorated in stunning mosaic of blue, turquoise, green and gold, and the great prayer hall is flanked by two massive minarets, each of which is topped-off with small turquoise domes.

Chahr Suq is the central square, which has a lively atmosphere accompanied by the clatter of brightly coloured tasselled gharries (horse-drawn taxis). The bazaars sell silk, carpets, kuchi jewellery, while traditional Herati glassblowers demonstrate their skills. Herat is famed for the quality of lapis lazuli, a natural precious stone mined only in Afghanistan, and several shops specialised in this beautiful blue jewellery. It has been exported for 7,500 years, and has been found in ancient Egyptian jewellery, Tutankhamen's funeral mask and the Romans ground it as an aphrodisiac. Incidentally, lapis lazuli provided the blue pigment for Renaissance painters, and, due to its rarity and expense, patrons in the west would specify exactly how much could be used when commissioning work from artists such as Raphael or Titian. This is why the Virgin Mary would be the only person in a painting who could be dressed in blue. We strolled around the metal bazaar, in which the Afghani craftsmen worked at the front of their shops, beating and engraving brass and copper pitchers, trays, cups and vases.

The bazaars of Herat will have changed very little over two thousand years; a maze of compact streets, with impromptu sun shades strung haphazardly from one side to the other. The dusty atmosphere accentuated the shafts of sunlight, which danced in time with the billowing sheets. The smells wafting through the air was a combination of spices such as saffron, coriander, cardamom and black pepper, mixed with fruits and vegetables and freshly baked bread.

In the mid-1970s, there was a fashion revival of Afghan coats, following a surge in popularity in the late 1960s. Remember the Beatles of the 'Sgt. Pepper' era: long hair, luxuriant moustaches and wearing embroidered Afghan coats. They attended a course of transcendental meditation with the Maharishi Yogi at an exotic destination… Kathmandu? Kashmir? Or perhaps Goa?... Well, actually they were on their way to Bangor in North Wales.

"We can't travel all the way through Afghanistan without buying an authentic Afghan coat," suggested Norma, as we strolled through the bustling streets of Herat, browsing in various shops, all of which had the same distinctive smell. Firstly, there were mints and herbal tea. Every shopkeeper offered us a cup of tea, accompanied by a mint-flavoured boiled sweet. Even though we made it clear that we were not intending to buy anything, it made no difference as everyone was happy just to offer warm hospitality. The other predominant smell was of yak; the animal which provided the skins for the coats. Let me see if I can offer some kind of description of this smell. Imagine a wet dog that has been sprayed with WD40. The Afghan coats had a certain fragrance of the natural oil on the fur. Add to this the pervading surrounding smells: dusty rugs mixed with the aroma of fruits, vegetables and spices wafting in from the streets. Each shop had row-upon-row of the coats, plus sleeveless jackets, all hand-embroidered in a bewildering range of colours and designs. However, we were shocked by the prices, which were far in excess of our budget, even taking into account the obligatory bartering ritual. In the 1960s and '70s, there was a lucrative passing trade of travellers, hence the high prices. Not only those on the hippy trail to India, but busloads of overlanders, mainly Australians and New Zealanders.

I noticed that many of the shops in Herat proudly displayed family photographs and occasional drawings or cartoons. This gave me an idea. I suggested to Norma that we should take some of my drawings to a few shops, to see if we could negotiate a deal; a portrait of the owner in exchange for an Afghan coat. It was worth a try. When I asked Nick if I could borrow his portrait, he offered to come with us as proof of a good likeness. We went to a shop where Norma had seen a couple of coats she quite liked. It was on the main street, Shari-i-Nan, and sold postinchas (sheepskin coats and sleeveless jackets), and sheepskin slippers, all beautifully embroidered by hand. The shopkeeper had a face which demanded to be drawn; a shock of thick, black, shiny hair, and heavy dark eyebrows. He had a shoe-brush of a moustache, Stalin-esque in its magnificence, which he stroked and preened with the flamboyance of a pantomime villain of the silent movies. It was obviously his pride and joy. He had warm, friendly dark brown eyes, and his swarthy complexion was etched with lines; a map of his life. It was a face you could almost read. He couldn't speak any English, but fortunately his 12-year-old son could, with a slight Antipodean accent, which was no doubt picked up in the bazaars rather than in school. He was a very friendly, helpful boy who seemed to relish the opportunity to practise his English, and, while his father put the kettle on, he told us that his name was Jafaar. We introduced ourselves and I took the drawing out of its cardboard tube. Nick held it up, while pointing at his own face; a gesture which I was hoping would be unnecessary. Both father and son seemed impressed, smiling broadly and nodding approvingly. This seemed an opportune moment for me to put forward my proposal.

"Would your father like to have his portrait drawn by me?" I asked the young boy, who then translated the question. His father raised his substantial eyebrows in surprise, and then asked, through his young interpreter, "How much?"

"Oh, I don't want any money from you," I replied, nonchalantly, as if I was a market trader, "Just a coat for my wife."

"Are you a famous artist?" asked Jafaar.

"Of course," lied Norma and Nick, in unison, before I had time to answer. He had a brief conversation with his father, and then Jafaar turned to me and said, "My father must 'ave a beeg moostash."

"Pleased to meet you Mustafa," I said, offering my outstretched hand.

"*No*, my father's name is Gulyar, and he must have a big moustache on his portrait," repeated Jafaar, and this time emphasising the point by placing his index finger across his top lip. Norma and Nick tried their best to stifle giggles over my faux pas. Norma casually strolled over to the coat rail, which was a 10-foot-long pole sagging in the middle under the weight of Afghan coats, and she started to flick through as a way of demonstrating our suggestion. However, this was met with a vigorous shaking of the head as the shop owner simply replied, "No."

We realized that Norma had started at the expensive end of the range, but, with a twinkle in his eye, Gulyar retaliated by walking to the other end of the rail, and putting his hand on the cheapest coat in the shop. Norma and Gulyar faced each other. Who would blink first? Without a word, she took one step forward and placed her left hand on a coat. Gulyar did the same with his right hand. It was like a scene from 'High Noon', as they stared each other down. Who would be first to draw? Well, actually I was hoping it would be me. Silent negotiations continued. Eventually, step by step, they met in the middle of the rail and shook hands, much to the amusement of Nick, Jafaar and me.

I asked Gulyar to sit near to the window at the front of his shop, and I started to draw his portrait. I always start with the eyes, then general layout and relative proportions and angles. The first half hour is probably the hardest, since it requires intense concentration and decision making. To add to the pressure, a few people gathered in the doorway behind me to watch the portrait develop. It seemed that most of them were Gulyar's relatives. After about thirty minutes I was able to relax because I had managed to capture a good likeness as the eyes in the portrait started to look back at me. Favourable noises of approval from my audience gave me confidence.

It was time for a cup of tea. Generally, I prefer sitters not to look at a portrait until it is well under way, but, in this instance, I didn't have a great deal of choice; his relatives picked up my sketch pad and took it to Gulyar. I watched anxiously for his reaction, which seemed to be favourable. He then whispered something to his son, who came over to me and said,

"My father says please make sure you give him a big moustache."

"Of course," I replied, with a nod and a thumbs up to Gulyar.

He gave me a big smile and stroked his moustache as if it was his pet. After a tea break, I did another hour and reached a suitable stage of the drawing to break for the day. We arranged for a final sitting for the following day. As we waved goodbye, Gulyar couldn't resist a final farewell mime, pointing at the sketch pad, and then caressing his moustache.

As we walked back to the hotel, Nick observed dryly, "Gulyar seems to think that the more he strokes it, the bigger it gets."

"Pardon!" exclaimed Norma, in mock horror.

"His moustache, I mean."

"I can't wait to tell everyone about you," laughed Norma, pushing me playfully.

"About getting a commission to draw a portrait?"

"Er, no… 'Pleased to meet you, Mustafa!"

The three of us had the giggles as we strolled back to the hotel.

Norma and I returned the following day, and I continued with the drawing. This time, I had an even bigger audience. After about an hour, we were very pleasantly surprised as a group of ladies, presumably family members, came into the shop, laden with bowls, pots and plates. They proceeded to lay out a table for lunch. Gulyar introduced his wife, Makai. I made a feeble joke about her name sounding Scottish. They smiled politely, with a bemused expression.

Jafaar told us that the meal had been prepared especially in our honour, and we were really touched by the genuine warmth of their hospitality. They explained each dish as they served us. Qabli pulao, (steamed rice with lamb), qorma (meat with fried onions and spices), and steamed dumplings, called mantu. We followed everyone's lead as they ate with their right hands, using nan bread as scoops. The atmosphere during lunch was convivial, and we were introduced to Gulyar's other relatives. One or two of them could speak some English, having been brought up working in the bazaars. Everyone was keen to hear about our travels, and they seemed particularly pleased and proud when we told them how much we loved Afghanistan, and the friendliness we had been shown by its people. When we happened to mention the name of our hotel, there was a buzz of excitement from everyone, and Jafaar told us that his sister, Ghezal, would be having her wedding reception at the same hotel the following evening. She happened to be sitting next to Norma during the meal, and, after speaking to her father, Ghezal took us completely by surprise by inviting Norma to her wedding. We were both delighted, naturally assuming that the wedding invitation included both of us, until Jafaar said,

"No, Mr. John, you are *not* invited."

"My drawing isn't *that* bad, is it?" I joked, while wondering what was going on. He explained that the men and women would be at separate celebrations, until they all get together at midnight.

Over lunch, Jafaar told me that his father had reiterated, again, his obsession for a large moustache. I rolled my eyes to Norma, and whispered that I can only draw it like it is.

"Perhaps you could exaggerate it just a little," she suggested, "just to keep him happy."

After lunch, we had one more sitting to finish the portrait. I was reasonably happy with it, and showed it to Gulyar for his approval. He smiled broadly, and I received a spontaneous round of applause from everyone in the shop, especially Makai. I signed the drawing and presented it to Gulyar with a handshake, and we took some photographs of the occasion. He then stood on a stool and from the wall, he lifted off a slightly dusty, gold gilt frame, which contained long-faded, barely visible photographs, and indicated that his portrait would be mounted in that particular picture frame.

Gulyar then gestured for Norma to choose a coat, and she went to the point in the middle of the rail where they had met and shaken hands. However, to our surprise, he shook his head and said loudly, "No."

Norma looked quite shocked, and I assumed that he was about to renege on our deal. He went over to her with a stern look on his face, and lifted her arm off the rail. Just as I was about to protest, and wishing that Nick had come with us, Gulyar led Norma along the coat rail… to the *expensive* end. He let out a booming laugh, and invited Norma to choose an Afghan coat. When we returned to the hotel, Norma proudly modelled her new coat for all our friends.

The following day, the function room at the hotel was beautifully decorated with colourful streamers and wall hangings. Norma was looking forward to the wedding reception, and she was particularly pleased because the invitation gave her the opportunity to wear a turquoise silk dress, which she had bought in Damascus. When she returned to our hotel room, in the early hours of the morning, the first thing she did was to proudly show off her henna painted hands and ankles, almost paisley-like in design. These were symbols of a good life and good luck. She told me that the whole experience was unforgettable. Following the wedding ceremony, Ghezal had entered the reception room, wearing a beautiful white wedding dress, trimmed in gold. She was then mobbed by everyone in a chaotic scene, as all the guests rushed towards her and pinned money, the Afghani, to her dress. A guest followed with hot coals on a shovel, which was presumably a tradition possibly similar to a chimney sweep at home. Amongst the ensuing scrum, the coal carrier stumbled, scattering red-hot coals across the floor. Some fell onto the train of Ghezal's dress, and left unsightly scorch marks. Norma was horrified, but no-one else, including Ghezal, seemed the slightest bit concerned. Norma told me that everyone made her feel very welcome, but she became a little uncomfortable when she was surrounded by all the ladies and children who pointed to her face, seemingly fascinated. A few of the guests spoke English, and one lady told Norma that everyone was intrigued by her bright blue eyes, even though she had very dark hair, and a dark, suntanned face. Once the music started, everyone danced enthusiastically to an eclectic mix, including; Afghani, Middle Eastern, and Indian music, and, surprisingly, English and American records. Norma said that she followed everyone's lead and tried to join in with the traditional dances, but was in her element when Chubby Checker started singing 'Let's twist again'. The whole room joined in, and there was no holding them back once Bill Haley started singing 'Rock Around the Clock'.

We had informed Gulyar that we would be leaving Herat in a couple of days, on our way to Kandahar, and he told us that the bus route out of Herat went passed his shop. They promised to wave us off. As the bus negotiated the narrow streets, sure enough, the family was standing outside the shop waiting for us. As soon as they spotted Nick, Norma and me, they started to wave enthusiastically, and Gulyar pointed proudly towards his shop window, where his newly-framed portrait was on display.

"Oh my God," screamed Norma, as she put her hands to her face in horror "Look what he has done to your drawing." Everyone on the coach burst out laughing. My mouth just dropped open as I slowly shook my head. Gulyar must have thought that his moustache *still* wasn't quite macho enough, so he had decided to enlarge it *himself*... with a large black felt-tip pen!

I had spent about three hours, over two days, taking a great pride to not only achieve a good likeness, but also to make it a good quality drawing, with subtle nuances of light, shade, texture and colour. I should have realised that all that was needed was a magic- marker moustache. Overnight, he had changed from Stalin to Marx. No, *not* Karl… Groucho.

"I never forget a face, but in his case I *will* make an exception!"

It didn't take me too long to overcome the disappointment of having my drawing vandalised. After all, it didn't quite rank alongside Marcel Duchamp's painting of a moustache on the Mona Lisa (on a reproduction I hasten to add). As we departed from Herat, on the straight road to Kandahar, the beautiful Afghanistan countryside opened up before us. The main road through the country skirts the Hindu Kush mountain range to the north, and follows a broad u-shape through Kandahar in the south, and on to Kabul in the northeast. The endless colour-changes of the mountains provided continuous fascination as the sunshine from the south highlighted cool shades of lilacs, purples, turquoises and blues, to warmer oranges and pinks.

Desert Silver Service

After a couple of hours, we pulled off the road on to the forecourt of a modern-looking glass and marble hotel, which seemed incongruous in such a desert setting. As we got off the bus, we noticed a tiled swimming pool, but, on closer inspection, we realised that it did not contain any water, just green algae, mosses and weeds. There was a patio area of white plastic tables and chairs, which looked reasonably new, but hardly ever used. A few tumbleweeds blew across, just to add to the slightly surreal atmosphere; a landscape made for Salvador Dali. The place seemed totally deserted, and just as we were about to return to the bus, a waiter came out of the building. He was immaculately dressed in a crisp white shirt, bow-tie, waistcoat, and striped, formal trousers. He carried a silver tray at shoulder height, as if he was serving on a cruise ship. In such a situation, he reminded me of Kenneth More as the butler on a desert island in the movie 'The Admirable Crichton'. We ordered tea, which he served with the aplomb and panache of a silver-service waiter. As we sipped our drinks from best quality china cups and saucers, little fingers cocked, naturally, the waiter explained that the hotel had never actually opened after completion. It was Russian-built, but unfortunately an unforeseen major problem occurred concerning mains supplies... There weren't any. Consequently, they were only able to open to serve light refreshments. It must be the poshest and most expensive tea stall in the world. Today, the team of architects and builders are still working on a different project. I believe the building site is somewhere in Siberia

Candlelit Kandahar

We stayed at a small, friendly, family-run hotel, which was adequate for a brief stopover. Let's just say it had seen better days. We decided to use our sleeping bags, since the top sheet on the bed looked more like the Turin Shroud. The narrow, windowless corridors were painted in a shade of mint green, and the dining room in an unappetising purple. To make matters worse, we were warned that power cuts were likely during the couple of nights of our stay; different sections of the city were being cut-off in turn. We enjoyed a few enforced candle-lit dinners, which actually enhanced the ambience of the hotel dining room. The meals served were surprisingly tasty. We tried palaws, (rice, meat and vegetables), Afghan kebab and ashak (ravioli stuffed with leeks and topped with yoghurt).

It is said that the sense of smell evokes memories more than any of the other senses. The dim lighting and the smell of candles reminded me of the miners' strike and the winter of discontent back home in the early 70s; when the spirit of the Blitz was re-awakened by candlelight. It was as if St. Helens was celebrating Diwali, the Hindu Festival of Light. When, as a student, I used to arrive home from Leeds University, for the occasional weekend, if there was no-one at home, I knew exactly where mum and dad would be; the Parr and Hardshaw Labour Club. To certain sections of the community, bingo was almost a religion; their place of worship on Fridays being Mecca… the bingo hall, that is. Showing indomitable spirit, everyone played bingo by candlelight. I remember one night when the bingo caller announced from the stage, "Ladies and gentlemen, the power-cut will soon be over. A bus has just gone past with all its lights on."

I'm not sure to this day if he was serious or joking. I like to think it was a great example of Northern humour. The Army and Navy Store in St Helens must have employed a marketing genius. There was a sign in the window which read, 'Now Is the Winter of Our Discount Tents'. Brilliant.

Kandahar province is a large, fruit-producing area, and has long been a favourite overnight stop for travellers due to its strategic position; linking India and the Middle East. Kandahar, like Herat, was founded by Alexander the Great. It was a major trading centre for wool, textiles, grapes, pomegranates and opium.

In Kandahar, we had, by now, become used to the chaos and vibrancy of Middle Eastern bazaars, and we visited the Shahidam Chawk (Martyr's Square) in the centre of town. Nearby, four Bazaars, namely the; Kabul, Herat, Shah and Shikarpur, run along four streets and meet at Char Suq. So far, during our travels in the Middle East, we had started to recognise that each area has its own local specialities. Kandahar seemed to specialise in silks, mirror work, and, in particular, numerous ornamental bird cages. The famous embroidered shirts of Kandahar, popular with hippies, but not quite my style, were impressive, but not worth negotiating a drawing for. As we had seen in Herat, there were jewellers' shops specialising in lapis lazuli. I haggled for a good price for a bracelet for Norma.

After a pleasant stay in Kandahar, enjoying the customary Afghani friendliness and hospitality, we were now looking forward to continuing our journey. Next stop; the capital city of Kabul.

The surrounding landscape was unchanging, but never monotonous or boring, and we punctuated the drive with occasional stops at traditional roadside tea houses, (called Chaikhanas). These were popular with the local Jingle truckers, who drove the ubiquitous world-famous, extravagantly decorated Afghan lorries. We took turns having photographs taken in front of them, paying the drivers a couple of Afghanis for the privilege.

Ten Camels for My Wife

The city of Kabul is situated high on an Afghan plain, and it is one of the highest capitals in the world, at an altitude of 5,900 feet, providing incredible views of the ever-changing colours of the mountains. Kabul is dominated by two hills, the Asmai and the Sherdarwaza, and Nick and I climbed to the top of one of these to view a stunning panorama. We were surprised to find that cannons from the 19th Century Anglo-Afghan wars are still in place. The hills are separated by the Kabul River, which doubles as a local launderette. Similar to other cities we had travelled through, it was a colourful spectacle as groups of local women gathered and chatted at the river bank to do the family washing.

In the 16th Century Babur, the founder of the Mughal Empire, established Kabul as his capital, and he loved the area so much that he decreed that his tomb should be built there. Today, it can be visited in Babur's Garden.

The Afghanis have a tradition as bird-fanciers, and near to the river is the Ka-Farushi (bird market), along a narrow, dusty lane, selling fighting birds, canaries, song birds and pigeons. Hence the number of shops throughout Afghanistan selling decorative bird cages.

The main bazaar is the Char Chatta (Four Arcades) near to the Pul-i-Khishti Mosque, which was pretty much the same as those in Herat and Kandahar. The main hub of activity was Chicken Street, which had a friendly atmosphere and was popular with overland travellers enjoying the many tea shops and restaurants. We were amazed at the number of local people who quietly asked us if we wanted hashish. A firm but polite 'No thank you' was our unhesitating reply, especially in view of the stark and chilling exhibition we had seen at the border on entering Afghanistan.

An absolute must-see experience for us was the famous Kabul Camel Market. After a very early breakfast, we drove the short distance to the market, and we had been advised to take some pens and sweets to give to the local children. It was a fascinating experience wandering around the market, feeling almost like the Pied Piper of Hamelin as we were followed by hordes of happy lively children. The historic camel market is as old as the city itself. Traders and buyers, all dressed in traditional Afghani robes and turbans, haggled and argued for the best deals. Many conducted business sitting cross-legged in small groups on the dusty floor, while drinking tea. They seemed quite used to having inquisitive visitors watching the proceedings, and were very obliging when we asked for photographs. I took pictures of lots of friendly, wrinkled, suntanned, smiling faces. Every one of them had yellowing teeth, with just as many gaps as teeth. In fact, most of the camels had healthier-looking teeth. We chatted to one of the camel traders, a very friendly man who could have been aged anything from fifty to eighty. His face was covered in more lines than the cross-hatching on a Rembrandt etching. He took a fancy to Norma and put his arm around her. He offered me eight camels in exchange for her.

"No," I replied forcefully, "are you *seriously* suggesting that I would sell my wife for eight camels? You must be joking… I couldn't possibly let her go for less than ten."

As we were leaving the market, one or two of our ladies were quite indignant that they were only valued at four camels; they really got the hump when others bragged that they were worth twelve. We travelled back to the hotel for lunch, but I found my accommodation had become slightly more crowded. The rooms were obviously not designed to sleep ten camels.

That afternoon, we were taken to a sporting event, the like of which I had never seen before, nor since. It was called Buzkashi, which apparently is the national sport of Afghanistan, and involved teams of horsemen attempting to dump a headless calf into the opposition goal. I can't understand why it has never achieved Olympic status. The crowds of spectators just gathered around the perimeter, no such thing as a grandstand, and so much dust billowed that it was like watching a foggy football match in an English midwinter. Another traditional sport of Afghanistan provided a sideshow, as two wrestlers entertained a small crowd. The contestants were fully clothed, and the spectators formed a circle around them. It was reminiscent of a fight in a school play-ground, or perhaps it was a real fight over tickets. Anyway, everyone seemed to have great fun.

Carry On Up the Khyber

Sadly, it was time for us to leave Kabul, and Afghanistan, as we continued our journey (with Norma, that is… I had the camels on sale or return). It was a truly wonderful experience, and we both agree, looking back many years later, that it was one of our favourite countries. It is a country which has witnessed many wars and invasions over the centuries, and hopefully it will emerge from the current conflicts to a brighter future. Until the next war, that is.

The Kabul River passes through the Kabul Gorge, known locally as Tang-i-Gharoo, and we followed the Torkham highway through this imposing sheer-canyon. The Mahipur Falls are a roaring cascade, which enveloped our bus in a dramatic mist as we passed close by, heading for the fabled Khyber Pass. It is situated in the Sulaiman Hills, which form the western barrier of Pakistan, and the pass varies in width from parts as narrow as fifty feet to other sections opening up wider than a mile. The strategic importance of the Khyber Pass is enshrined in the history of many countries and great armies, notably (again) Alexander the Great in 327BC, have passed through. We continued to follow in his footsteps as we looked forward to another country; Pakistan and the border town of Peshawar.

It began its existence as a frontier-town, strategically situated near to the mouth of the Khyber Pass, as a gateway to the Indian sub-continent. From its hilltop position, the Mughal Bal Hisar Fort looks down over the old city, as the ubiquitous black and yellow Morris-Minor taxis competed with Qingqi rickshaws for passengers. Leather-craft was a common trade and a particular product of the area was the leather Peshawar chappals (sandals). An interesting architectural feature of the town was the Sethi houses, which were built with wooden frames, with un-baked bricks to guard against earthquakes. The houses were several stories high, with carved heavy wooden doors and intricately decorated balconies. Turbaned tribesmen sat in samovar houses, smoking and drinking tea in the Chowk Yadgar (Square of Remembrance).

We strolled through the renowned Qissa Khawanni Bazaar, which translates to the Market of Storytellers. This is a place where travellers and visitors in the past were entertained by professional storytellers in the evenings.

Yogi Town

No, I don't mean in Jellystone Park, it is our next destination; Rawalpindi. The town's name is derived from the Rawals, a tribe of yogis who founded the original village. It is better known historically as a major British military outpost from 1849, after the occupation of the Punjab. Today, it is an industrial town, with an oil refinery, gasworks and an iron foundry. There is also a brewery, sawmills and factories, producing textiles, pottery and leather. It is also a major railway junction, and, as we watched the trains go by, we were amazed to see that there were as many people huddled together on the roof, and hanging on the sides, as there were passengers actually inside the carriages. It reminded me of faded black and white photographs that my dad had taken during his National Service in the Navy, in India and Ceylon. Yellow taxis and auto rickshaws were everywhere, the latter being a precarious ride, to say the least. We enjoyed touring the two main bazaars; Raja in the old town, and the Saddar bazaar which, despite its name, had a happy, lively, friendly atmosphere.

One evening, Barry, Colin, Peter and Kay, (with her toilet-roll tucked under her arm, as usual), were sitting with Norma and me in a little café in Rawalpindi. We were enjoying convivial conversation, while most of the local customers were glued to the cricket on television; Pakistan versus New Zealand in a test match. The renowned batsman, Javed Miandad, (who Norma thought was a father and son), was at the crease and the commentator was waxing lyrical over his cricketing prowess.

"His stroke has such a smooth follow-through," the Pakistani television commentator observed, oozing National pride.

"*That* is just what I have been trying to avoid for the past fortnight," commented Peter, morosely, while tapping his stomach.

"What?" we replied.

"A smooth follow-through!"

A beautiful shaft of wit.

All that Glisters

We were really looking forward to arriving in Lahore; we had booked into the International Hotel. After sleeping under canvas, or under the sparkling stars of desert skies, or even in caves, we couldn't wait for a little luxury; hot showers, soft beds and lazing by the pool.

The main buzz around town when we arrived in Lahore was the impending State visit of King Abdullah of Saudi Arabia. The city was being prepared for his presence, including temporary gold decorative pavements in places he would be walking. The disabled beggars, ragged street vendors and hollow-eyed, bedraggled children were cleared away out of sight by officials who had a sense of occasion and importance, but hardly a sense of priorities. We managed a brief glimpse of the King as his cavalcade passed by. He is probably like our Queen, thinking that the indigenous smell of the world is of wet paint.

Lahore boasts some fine examples of Mughal architecture, notably the Lahore Fort (Shahi Qila), which commands a hilltop position overlooking the city. The fort dates from the reign of Mughal Emperor Akbar the Great in the 17th Century. It is a complex of fortifications, built in distinctive red brick, and mosques and palaces of marble.

We visited the famous 17th Century Shalimar Gardens, built for Shah Jahan, (of Taj Mahal fame). The garden is an oasis of calm, surrounded by high walls, incorporating distinctive, brick fretwork. There are over 400 fountains in marble pools, all fed by a marvellous feat of engineering; a canal which brings water from over 150 kilometres away. The tranquil sounds of running water provided an idyllic ambiance as we strolled among almond, apple, apricot and mango trees. The garden is designed in the form of three terraces, which, in ascending order, have the Urdu names: Life, Goodness and Pleasure. It was the kind of scene that we had expected to see at the Hanging Gardens of Babylon.

We enjoyed a beautiful afternoon of serenity, before returning to the old city of Lahore; bazaars, rickshaws, donkey carts and street hawkers, the now-familiar colour sensations of textiles, spices and fruits, and the full range of smells; from fragrant to pungent.

Jewel in the Crown.

Quote: *'India, the one land that all men desire to see, and having seen once, by even a glimpse, would not give that glimpse for all the shows of all the rest of the globe combined.'* Mark Twain.

Since leaving England, we had travelled through well over a dozen countries, and, invariably, on the eve of departure from any country Colin would rub his hands in anticipation. 'A new country tomorrow', became his catchphrase, but I must confess that I was particularly excited at the prospect of going to India. The thought of it gave me a warm glow of anticipation, or perhaps it was another touch of Delhi belly.

To visit India had been an ambition of mine for as long as I could remember, mainly due to dad's stories. My sister Linda and I grew up listening to his stories about India, and life aboard the aircraft carriers 'The Formidable' and 'The Indomitable' (or the 'Formid' and the 'Indom' as they were popularly known). As kids, we only had to make the slightest comment about heat, be it the weather, the kitchen or the coal fire, and we were met with his stock reply; "It's hot in India." Even to this day, Linda and I still jokingly use the same phrase.

Drink of the Gods

Our first destination in India was the North West city of Amritsar. The Golden Temple of Amritsar, in the Punjab, is a cultural and spiritual centre; the holiest shrine in Sikhism. Amritsar was the name of an ancient lake and means the 'pool of ambrosial nectar', and Amrit means 'drink of the gods'. Buddha, who is also an important figure in the Sikh religion, visited the lake to meditate during his search for enlightenment. It is believed that an underground spring from this ancient lake feeds the present Amritsar pool, and it is where, two thousand years after the Buddha's visit, another philosopher, Saint Guru Nanak, founded the Sikh religion in the 16th Century. Sikh means student, and the word guru refers to a teacher, spiritual leader, or mentor. Over subsequent centuries, Sikhism was spread by ten further Gurus. Similar to Hinduism, they believe in the constant reincarnation until enlightenment is achieved; called Waheguru in Sikhism.

The temple is covered in pure gold and decorative marble, and the impressive dome is an inverted lotus-shape. The golden reflection in the sacred water enhances the magical scene dramatically. It stands in the middle of the square lake, reached by a marble causeway, and the courtyard surrounding the lake is of decorative inlaid marble. All around, people are praying, chanting, playing drums and flutes, and preparing food. The dazzling gold of the temple was framed by a multi-coloured kaleidoscope of the brightly coloured silk of people who thronged the causeway around the lake. Visitors of all religions are welcome to join in the experience, and, as an appreciation for visiting, are given free food.

Not one to pass up the chance of free food, I eagerly led the way. As we entered the Golden Temple, we were greeted warmly, and a 'teeka' was placed on our foreheads. This is the dot which represents the mind's eye in the Sikh religion, enabling us to see beyond physical reality into the spiritual world. In other words, it is a third front eye, similar, I suppose, to Mr Spock's 'final front ear'; a different religion altogether. We were given dahl, which was a traditional Indian vegetarian dish of beans, rice, vegetables and chapattis. The intention is that everyone sits on the floor, while eating, to show that everyone is of equal importance and will eat side-by-side, even if you are a Pope, a King, a Jedi Knight or even a Captain Kirk.

The next leg of our journey took us north to Kashmir via Jammu.

'If there be a paradise on earth, it is this.' Shah Jahan

The drive to Srinagar in Kashmir was hair-raising, to say the least. Our fear of the sheer drop to the valley below us was intensified by the sight of the occasional wrecks of buses lying in the valley; rusting, skeletal and reclaimed by nature. It was a heart-in-the mouth ride, more terrifying than any fairground roller coaster, and the worst seats were at the back of the bus which swept over the edge of the precipice at every hairpin bend. We could see some lorries and local buses ahead of us, and Mick was anxious to maintain a decent speed so as not to hold up traffic behind us.

"They wouldn't overtake us on this road… Would they?"

"You'd be surprised," replied Mick, ominously, not taking his eyes off the road for a second. To make matters worse, we had to negotiate the occasional landslide, with the wheels of our bus struggling to keep a grip as they skidded on the loose terrain. We were on the edge, both physically and mentally. I had visions of us balancing precariously over the edge, like at the end of the Michael Caine film 'The Italian Job', with our driver saying to us 'I've got an idea', as we sing 'The Self-presentation society'.

Robert Louis Stevenson wrote; 'It is better to travel hopefully than to arrive'. Obviously, he had never travelled on this road to Srinagar. We all breathed a 'good-to-be-alive' sigh of relief as we arrived, but I have to admit that our anxious few hours on the road were worth the effort.

Mona Lisa Reunion

Kashmir is a spectacularly beautiful place, comparable to anywhere I have seen in the world. The lakes in the lush valley are surrounded by dramatic snow-capped peaks, but it is the pleasant climate which has made Kashmir a popular summer retreat for centuries. Srinagar lies on the banks of the Jhelum River, a tributary of the mighty Indus, and, over the centuries, Mughal Emperors have built beautiful mosques and gardens; such as Chasma Shahi (Royal Fountains), and Pari Mahal (Palace of Fairies). There are wooden shrines with distinctive pagoda style roofs, narrow lanes of wooden houses with intricately carved balconies, a bustling market and ancient bridges spanning the river. Today, Srinagar is probably most famous for the houseboats on Dal Lake, and these originate from the days of the Raj. The houseboats were a British idea to circumvent a law which stated that outsiders were not permitted to buy land. They exploited a loophole, since there were no rules against owning floating homes. The houseboats are made of deodar wood, a local Himalayan cedar, which is a species of pine with a distinctive aromatic smell which permeates the interior. Incense and some aromatic medicines are made from the wood. The boats are oblong shaped, highly decorated and the wood is exquisitely carved. They have a balcony, lounge, dining room and bedrooms with en-suite bathrooms. Each houseboat has its own water-taxi, called a shikara, a canopied, gondola-style boat with a resident boatman. Norma and I were allocated a houseboat called 'The Mona Lisa'; it was like seeing an old friend again after visiting the Louvre. She smiled at us (enigmatically, of course) from the lounge wall. We enjoyed a few lovely tranquil days on board, mainly sitting on the roof terrace while observing everyday life on the lake.

Dal Lake covers approximately eight by four kilometres, and is a maze of intricate waterways. Inevitably, it has been dubbed the 'Venice of the East'. Vegetables are grown in floating gardens, which are artificial floating islands of reed rafts. A thriving community lives and works on the lake, and as we toured in our shikara, we were surrounded by a rainbow of colours from shops and boats selling silk saris, embroidered shawls, Kashmir Pashminas, fruits, spices, copperware, and hand-woven woollen carpets. Flower sellers were everywhere as they sailed around in small boats, which were full of the most colourful, exotic flowers imaginable. Walnut carving was a popular craft, and a speciality seemed to be knife and fork carving-sets. Perhaps the most common product on Dal Lake were objects made of papier maché, an art form which originated in Persia and was highly favoured by the Mughal Emperors of the 15th and 16th Centuries. From small boxes to huge vases and plaques, they are brightly coloured and highly lacquered to give the impression of glazed pottery.

A few of us arranged an excursion on horseback up to the Sonomarg glacier. Norma and a few of the others declined the offer, deciding that the last thing they needed after a bone-shaking bus ride was to sit in a saddle for a day. Mercifully, the saddles were well-upholstered as a thick sheepskin provided welcome suspension on our pony-trek. The scenery was out-of-this-world, with jaw-dropping beauty, and to be out in the open on horseback under a blue sky simply intensified the aesthetic experience. We stopped at a little hut, imaginatively called: The Hindu Tea Stall. We didn't have a choice, our horses knew exactly where to go and stand. The sun glistened on the snow-capped peaks, and the glacier was so reflective that we needed our sunglasses. From the serene tranquillity and clear mountain air of Kashmir, we would soon be heading towards a completely opposite environment, the capital city.

City of Mughals

Delhi is actually two separate and distinctive cities; Old Delhi, romantically dubbed the City of Mughals, and New Delhi, based on a grand design by British architect Edwin Lutyens in the 1920s. The main shopping district, Connaught Place, is modelled on the Royal Crescent in Bath. The main street, Chadni Chowk, was alive with traffic, people, cycle rickshaws, and bullock carts transporting everything imaginable. Locals would stroll along casually with a decoratively painted elephant lumbering alongside, as if walking a dog. Cows wandered about aimlessly. They may be sacred animals in

India, but that didn't prevent street vendors giving them a sharp slap with a stick if they helped themselves to their produce. The haphazard bazaars were the usual riot of vibrant colours of textiles and spices, with the associated smells of incense, food stalls, all underpinned by the all-pervading stench of sewage. Rudyard Kipling, a name synonymous with India, wrote 'The first condition of understanding a foreign country is to smell it'.

We were surrounded by street hawkers, snake charmers, card tricksters and find-the-pea conmen. I was persuaded to have a haircut, just sitting in a battered old wicker chair by the roadside. The barber told me it was his ambition to own his own shop. I asked him if he had heard of the English tradition of naming hairdressing salons with a terrible pun. He didn't have a clue what I was talking about. I suggested the name 'Urdu'. He just rolled his head in that uniquely Indian way.

The shops sold high quality crafts similar to other cities we had visited, a speciality being fabulous jewellery which could be made to order. I bought a large batik of the trinity of Hindu Gods; Brahma (the Creator), Vishnu (the Preserver) and Shiva (the Destroyer) as a resource for future jobs teaching art. I also purchased a selection of Mughal paintings, which are a combination of Indian, Persian and Islamic styles. They began with Persian artists in India who became influenced by local styles and developed into Mughal paintings. The main themes are battles, court scenes, legendary stories, wildlife and hunting scenes, and they evolved between the 16th and 19th Centuries.

My collection of artefacts from around the world did become a valuable teaching resource. Let us briefly go on a time-travel detour, and materialise in about twenty years into the future in my art room at the Deancry High School in Wigan... I was beginning a project about India. On display were some of the above, including a painting of Lord Ganesh, the Elephant-headed Hindu God of Success. I always began a lesson by explaining some of the culture and the history of a particular topic. In my class were a couple of Indian children who of course knew the names of the Hindu Deities. To give some of the other children a chance to answer, I pointed at the painting of Ganesh, and asked if anyone knew who it was. I was amazed when about half a dozen pupils put their hands up immediately.

"Yes," I said, choosing a pupil to answer the question.

"It's Ganesh."

"Correct. Did you *all* know that?"

The ones who had had their hands up all nodded.

"Have you done a project on this in Geography or History?" I inquired.

"No Sir. He was in 'The Simpsons' last night!"

I shook my head and smiled. I wonder if that episode was called Homer's Oddity? After that slightly surreal detour, let us beam ourselves back to India.

Shah Jahan moved the capital of India from Agra to Delhi in the 17th Century, and built the Red Fort as his main residence. We entered by the Delhi Gate, and as we walked up the road we had a panoramic view of the city. There are marble palaces, mosques, gardens with marble fountains, and grand audience halls. The Diwan-i-Klas (the Hall of Private Audiences) used to have as its centre piece the Peacock Throne, which was taken to Iran in 1739 and became the famous throne of the Shahs of Persia.

A Sweeping Statement

At our hotel late one afternoon, after showering and changing ready for dinner, we were enjoying a quiet few minutes reading in our room trying to stay cool beneath the large, noisy, wooden fan on the ceiling. I was sitting in a bamboo chair which squeaked and creaked every time I shifted position, while Norma lay on the bed. Without warning, our tranquillity was interrupted as the door burst open, allowing shafts of late-afternoon sunlight to flood into the room. No-one appeared in the doorway, and momentarily I assumed that a breeze had blown it open. Norma suddenly sat bolt upright on the bed and pointed towards the floor. I immediately sprang to my feet ready to fend off whatever had come in, provided it wasn't a crocodile of course. But then again, it had to be something big enough to push open the door. I could hear swishing and shuffling sounds along the floor. Could it be our worst nightmare? A huge snake? Then I saw something moving; shiny, black and hairy just above the level of the bed. 'At least it isn't a snake,' I thought, breathing a sigh of relief, before my imagination raced off again; 'are there black panthers in India'? Then, I realised that Norma, who had a much better view of our uninvited guest, seemed unconcerned, or was she simply frozen with fear? Tentatively, I peered over the bed to see the cause of my heart palpitations. It was indeed shiny black hair, but it was on the head of an Indian man whom I could now see just above the level of the bed… No, he wasn't that short. He was in a crouching-sitting-squatting position with his head practically between his knees. He shuffled along on the soles of his bare feet as he swept the floor with a switch, made of a bundle of twigs and tied at one end with string. It was a sawn-off witch's broom. He held a plastic dust-pan in his other hand and circled the bed, sweeping underneath as he passed. It was safe to assume that this was our cleaner. He approached me and I automatically lifted my legs to a horizontal position, as you do at home when the vacuum cleaner approaches. He went into the bathroom and Norma and I exchanged bemused smiles as he emerged and made his way to the door, which he closed behind him. Not once had he looked up from the floor. There was neither acknowledgment, eye contact nor a word spoken. Not even a toothy grin. We laughed, and our minds worked simultaneously as we both looked in the mirror and asked,

"Have we become invisible?"

We were laughing as we went into the dining room, only to find that everyone else had had the same experience.

"We could have been doing anything as he burst in without warning," I announced in mock horror.

"What, in this heat... I don't think so," replied Norma, sardonically. There followed silent nods of agreement from all the ladies.

Someday my Prints Will Come

Later that evening, I announced with more than a touch of frustration and exasperation, "I think I'm having trouble with my sprockets."

"Sounds painful," joked Colin.

"I will give you some tablets," added the droll Doctor Barry, "it should clear-up the problem."

"How many photos are on this roll of film?" I asked Norma, holding up my camera.

"About 24 shots I think, why?"

"Because I have taken about 40 already, and the dial still clicks round."

Colin, a keen photographer, gave my camera a cursory inspection and confirmed my worst suspicions. The sprocket holes on the roll of film had failed to link up with the flywheels and, consequently, the film was still inside the canister. (For the benefit of any younger readers of the digital generation; just ask your Grandad). I had lost a couple of days' worth of photographs. I would sooner have lost my clothes. Fortunately, everyone assured me that I could have copies of their photographs. Panic over.

After breakfast the following morning, we were back in our hotel room getting ready for an excursion and I decided to try to fix my camera. Even with the curtains drawn, the room was not quite dark enough for me to open up the back of the camera, so I stepped inside the freestanding ramshackle wooden wardrobe as a makeshift darkroom. There were one or two fine shafts of light piercing through a couple of cracks in the doors. Just enough to enable me to see what I was doing without risking exposure to the film. When I was satisfied that I had rectified the problem, I pushed open the wardrobe door and leapt out with a triumphant 'Ta, dah!' It was at that moment that I finally saw the whites of our cleaner's eyes. Unknown to me, he had come into our room to sweep the floor and he just happened to be crouched straight in front of the wardrobe at that precise moment. He couldn't have looked more startled and terrified if I had been a snarling Bengal tiger leaping out at him. He let out a piercing scream and fell over from his squat position and completed a backward roll by landing on his feet. I lunged forward to help him to fully stand up, but this only made matters worse. He sprang away from me in terror, dropping his brush and pan. He obviously thought that I had been lying in wait to ambush him. As he made his escape, he looked back and gave me a haunting look, as if he had just escaped from the clutches of a deranged, predatory killer. As the door slammed behind him, I stood there, camera still in hand, almost as shocked as he was. I looked at Norma, who had witnessed this drama from the wicker chair. She had been trying to control her laughter, but to no avail as the dam burst.

I thought that I should find the cleaner to explain and apologise, and also to return his pan and broom. He spoke little English and it was difficult for me to work out if he understood me, because Indian people tend to shake their heads in a rolling manner when they mean yes *and* no. Very confusing. What's wrong with a firm nod in the affirmative and a shake in the negative? Talking of negatives, I don't think he quite grasped the gist of my explanation about my roll of film. Our conversation must have looked more like Basil Fawlty talking to Manuel, because, despite my best intentions, the story got out that the crazy man in room number 6 had; "Come out of the closet because he was frightened of being exposed."

Are the Stars Out Tonight?

Quote: *'We owe a lot to the Indians, who taught us how to count, without which no worthwhile scientific discovery would have been made'.* Albert Einstein.

A fascinating excursion was to nearby Jantar Mantar, an outdoor astronomical observatory, which is one of a series of five in India, built in the 18th Century. The name was derived from two Hindi words, Janta, which means instrument, and Mantar, meaning formula or calculation. Accurately calibrated to monitor the movement of the stars and planets, its curving geometric buildings looked like a cross between an enormous abstract sculpture and a skateboard park. It wouldn't look out of place in the Yorkshire Sculpture Park, amongst the Henry Moore's and Barbara Hepworth's. I was reminded of the time, when, as a student, I was sketching a sundial in a park in St. Helens. A flat-capped, old codger engaged me in conversation.

"That sundial has been there since I were a lad," he said, in a broad Lancashire drawl, "and it *still* keeps good time."

Our Indian guide could have made the same claim about Jantar Mantar, as he displayed his substantial, or perhaps I should say astronomical, knowledge.

As human beings, we have difficulty understanding the vast distances and periods of time, which are beyond our comprehension. Distances are measured in light-years (the distance travelled in one year, at the speed of light). A familiar analogy often used to illustrate the age of the earth, is to condense something like four and a half billion years down to one year, something we can visualize mentally. Into this artificial timescale we find it easier to relate to significant developments such as separation of continents or the extinction of dinosaurs. The human race first appeared at approximately one minute to midnight on New Year's Eve.

Similarly, with the stars in the Universe; our guide explained to us that a figure such as a trillion, trillion stars means absolutely nothing to us. But when he suggested that there were the same number of stars in the universe as grains of sand in all the deserts and on every beach on Earth, then we had something to grasp hold of. But then again, how could anyone possibly know that? After all, we have only been on this planet for one minute! … Happy New Year!

Someone Left a Cake Out in the Rain.

Quote by Kipling: *'The hilltop palaces of Rajasthan are like a tiered wedding cake standing on a plinth. The intricate marble latticework and inlaid precious stones are as delicate as sugar-sprayed lace with piped borders. The glistening reflection of the sun is the icing on the cake. The palaces seem to have been designed by confectioners rather than architects'.*

In case you are wondering where Kipling wrote this descriptive passage, let me explain that I don't mean Rudyard… I am talking about *Mister* Kipling (he of the 'exceedingly good cakes'). Alright, I will own up… I made the quote up, but I stand by the analogy. The Indian palaces *really do* look good enough to eat, and, after all, the last Viceroy of India was a Battenberg.

Jaipur, the capital of the northern province of Rajasthan, is known as the Pink City, because of the ornately decorated stucco buildings, which were painted to replicate the local red sandstone of Mughal architecture. One of the most photographed buildings is the Hawa Mahal (Palace of the Winds), a five-storey, red brick, honeycombed building, with screened latticework balconies. It was built in 1799, so that Royal ladies who observed strict purdah (covering of faces) could observe daily life, without being seen. There was certainly plenty for the ladies to see. From our hotel balcony, we spent happy evenings by simply watching the world go by; the highlight being a psychedelically painted, extravagantly decorated elephant, which casually strolled along the road, ridden by a mahout. No-one in the street gave it a passing glance, but we were fascinated.

The Janhari Bazaar and Badi Chaupar were superb for shopping, and we spent many happy hours browsing amongst ornaments, Mughal paintings, sandalwood carvings, pottery and the famous Jaipur quilts; called razais. Specialities included embroidered silk slippers made in Jaipur, and embroidered camel-skin slippers from Jodhpur (the origin of the name of the riding breeches). We went into a fabric shop which specialized in exquisite chintz, which originated in northern India and became very popular in England and France. We arranged to visit a local block-printing, textile factory; an attractive four-storey building, with internal balconies which overlooked a decorative central courtyard. Wooden blocks were carved by craftsmen in a design reminiscent of Paisley patterns, and these were later used to print lengths of cloth in a repeat-pattern. Yet another scene which will have changed very little over the centuries.

Heavy Metal

One beautiful, balmy evening, a group of us were out for a stroll around Jaipur and we found ourselves attending a heavy metal concert. I don't mean by a band like Metallica or Black Sabbath, the only head-banging I have ever done was in the Church of the Nativity in Bethlehem. I mean heavy metal in the literal sense. Down a side street, further into the dark shadows, we heard the sound of percussion-based music being played. Intrigued, we stopped out of curiosity and I decided to explore further. The others kept an eye on me and remained close to the street lights. Tentatively, I walked along the side street and discovered that the music was coming from a local scrap yard. As I approached the half-open double gates, I was spotted by a couple of men who immediately gave me a warm, welcoming smile and gestured for me to come over. Hesitantly, I stepped inside the yard and was amazed to see that there was a floodlit concert area with an audience of about thirty people sitting on rows of plastic chairs. The surrounding scrapyard was piled high to form a metal auditorium of cars, fridges, washing machines, mangles, rusty, farm implements and air conditioning units. The semi-circular wall of junk created, not surprisingly, a tinny reverberation of the sound, which echoed through the leaves of the surrounding trees. It was like a structure from a post-apocalyptic movie. On a small stage at the front, a band played instruments which had obviously been made from scrap material.

Imagine a 1950s British skiffle group performing on instruments made of tea chests, broom handles, washboards and dolly tubs. (Again, for younger readers, ask your Grandparents). Hold that thought, and now transpose it to an Indian group with makeshift instruments made of car bumpers, hub caps or wrought iron railings. The ingenuity was amazing, and some of the instruments looked like shiny works of art which would not have looked out of place as a modern piece of sculpture in an art gallery. A tea stall, operating from a small caravan, was doing a roaring trade. The performers seemed to momentarily miss a beat, as most of the audience turned to scrutinise this interloper who had just wandered in. For some reason, back-street scrap yards didn't seem to feature on tourist itineraries. Before I could say anything, a man sitting on the front row was unceremoniously removed to the back, to make room for me, as a plastic cup of steaming tea was thrust into my hand. Before I sat down I gestured that I was going back to the gate. They looked disappointed, until I signalled to Norma, Barry, Colin and the rest to come over. As they came into the scrap yard, sorry, concert hall, everyone had an expression of amused, slightly bemused amazement, and the band stopped playing. Every performer beamed a welcome smile, and a new front row of chairs was rapidly assembled from a spare stack. Tea quickly followed, and the band, which was called 'The Tin Men', struck up with renewed vigour.

The band was an eight-piece combo, to use the musical vernacular, and they were smartly turned-out in matching pale blue outfits over loose trousers, called churidars. Their embroidered tunics, called kurtas, were mid-thigh length, and collarless, in the early Beatles style. I should stress that any comparison with the Beatles ended there. They all wore small hats, similar to those worn by waiters at a fast food restaurant, and each player wore identical dark blue silk slippers, embroidered with gold thread, like the ones we had seen on the market stalls in Jaipur. They looked like a Nehru tribute band.

The members of the audience were even smarter in dress. It seemed incongruous that such a setting, a scrap yard down a dark side street, should stage a show for people who would not look out of place at London's Royal Albert Hall or the Opera House in Covent Garden. We were smart for the evening, but felt under-dressed compared to everyone else. Ladies of all ages wore dazzling saris of bright turquoises, reds and gold, all beautifully embroidered and complemented by stunning Indian jewellery; such as bangles, necklaces, bracelets and earrings in gold.

As I slowly sipped my very hot tea, carefully avoiding slurping a mouthful of tea leaves, I was able to study the band and the range of instruments in closer detail. The ages of the players ranged from mid-twenties, to a drummer who looked as though he was in his seventies. Still too young to qualify for the Rolling Stones, even then. Perhaps the Tin Men were a long-established group which had evolved over the decades and changed personnel along the way. Like the Temptations. Again, any comparisons to the Temptations end there.

The drummer sat surrounded by as much polished metal and gleaming chrome as a Hell's Angel on a Harley Davidson. His cymbals were wheel hubs of various sizes, and he had so many of them that he looked more like a juggler spinning plates. A set of hollow tubes of ascending length hung from a frame and were played with a hammer. I wondered momentarily if Mike Oldfield had passed this way a few years earlier, because the sound created was very similar to 'Tubular Bells'.

The English musician and entertainer Roy Castle came to mind. He was renowned for his ability to squeeze a tune out of anything fitted with a mouthpiece. He would have loved the Tin Men. The brass section, with a bit of copper thrown in, was made up of a hybrid of previously damaged and discarded instruments. One virtuoso performer even played a solo on an ornately decorated, cast-iron radiator, (see what I mean about heavy metal). The mouthpiece replaced the valve and a funnel was fitted at the other end.

"There must be easier ways to bleed a radiator," whispered Barry.

"We had radiators in our last house that made noises like that all on their own," I replied.

The music was, of course, of the Indian variety, which we enjoyed very much, and then, to our great surprise, they sang a song which they dedicated to us: 'Oh when the Saints go Marching in'. We joined in as loudly as we could, and it gave me brief pangs of nostalgia and homesickness because it is the song the crowd always sings to support St. Helens Rugby League team; the Saints. We had a great night and at the end of the show we mixed and chatted with everyone, including the band. We must have had an 'access-all-areas backstage pass'. We offered to pay for our seats and the endless cups of tea, but such was the generosity of our hosts that they wouldn't hear of it. Finally, we insisted on making a donation to their instrument fund.

During the walk back to the hotel, we were all in high spirits following our un-planned, unexpected, impromptu evening's entertainment. They often turn out to be the best nights out.

"It was great to have a sing-a-long here in India," said Nick.

"Well would it surprise you to know," replied Colin, "that karaoke was actually invented in India?"

"No," we all disagreed, more or less in unison, "everyone knows it was in Japan."

"No," insisted Colin, deadpan, "it was definitely in India… by a bloke called Gerupta Singh."

Colin laughed while the rest of us just groaned.

We joked about the Tin Men, with the predictable quips about the Tin Man in the 'Wizard of Oz'. We started to suggest alternative names for the band.

"What about the Junk Yardbirds?" suggested Colin, proudly.

"The Metal Gurus," exclaimed Ruth, excitedly

We all agreed, brilliant, even though she had to give away her guilty secret that she was once a Marc Bolan fan. Finally, after deep thought, Barry came up with, 'The Car Fender Strato Castors.'

Where There's Muck...

The following day we were up early to visit one of the most famous destinations in India: The Amber Palace. It is located within a hilltop fort a few miles from Jaipur, and impressive 16th Century buildings appear to grow out naturally from the hills. It was built by

Raja Mann Singh, one of Mughal Emperor Akbar's generals, and is an intricate blend of Hindu and Muslim architecture.

There is a ramp which hairpins its way up to the Palace, and we decided to travel from the Lion Gate entrance by taxi. An elephant taxi that is. I had visions of us having to climb aboard a kneeling elephant, using its trunk as a staircase before climbing over the top of its head and sitting in a straddle position behind its flapping ears, then hanging on for dear life as it rises to its feet. Well, that was how I had once mounted a camel in Morocco, so to speak. No such fun. From a raised platform Norma, Nick, Beth and I simply strode across a small gap, as if stepping onto a bus or a train, onto the howdah (a carriage of seats on the elephant's back). The mahout (driver) strapped us in and once the Elephant taxi, which was as bejewelled and brightly painted as an Afghan truck, got into its stride, we quickly adapted to the steady, sleepy rhythm of the movement.

Talking about movements, the activities taking place behind us distracted us from fully appreciating the magnificence of the surrounding views. A small, barefoot, nut-brown man followed our taxi, keeping a steady ten yards behind us. He wore a once-white cloth on his head wrapped around to form a scruffily-assembled turban, and a loin cloth draped over his shoulder, round his waist and gathered between his nether regions to leave his legs bare. I wondered if he was on his way to enter a Gandhi look-a-like competition. He had a friendly face, etched by a lifetime outdoors, and he constantly waved and smiled at us with a toothy grin of yellow teeth. His job-description would make interesting reading on his CV; A 'Pachyderm Cleansing Operative'. With his bare hands, he scooped up each pile of fresh steaming dung, placing them in buckets, strategically placed along the side of the road. We watched with fascination, combined with amusement and revulsion. During my time as a teacher, I came across the term 'career pathway' many times, but never in such a literal sense, involving an actual pathway and huge heaps of manure.

Perhaps this was the elephant man's chosen path in life. In Tudor England, 'the Keeper of the King's Stool' was a prestigious position in court, and I believe that in Ancient China the Emperor's morning ablutions were carefully monitored by courtiers, (or were they just going through the motions). Our Indian dung-man could have been an enterprising local farmer collecting fertilizer for his fields. But wait, I think I've got it. He was a supplier for the Turner Prize-winning artist Chris Ofili, whose modus operandi was to stick mounds of elephant manure to his canvases and paint them in bright luminous colours. As you do. I once went to see an Ofili exhibition, and, you know how the eyes of portraits seem to follow you around the room? Well, it is the same eerie sensation with a Chris Ofili painting. Only it is the smell that follows you. It's uncanny. We are familiar with Ming Vases and T'ang Horses, and I think future art historians will categorise Ofili's elephant paintings as his Dung period. I am joking of course; they were impressive paintings.

So let us return once again to the elephant man. We arrived at the palace, and as we dismounted from the howdah, he came over to greet us, still smiling. He gave his hands a superficial rub on his clothes, and then held them out to us. I dropped a couple of rupees into his palm, but deftly swerved his grateful handshake.

The Palace overlooks Maota Lake, and we had a beautiful panoramic view of the surrounding green countryside and the shimmering Pink City below us. We marvelled at gates, temples, gardens, courtyards, pavilions, palaces and huge ornate halls. We were dazzled by thousands of mirror tiles and coloured glass covering walls and ceilings.

The following morning, everyone was gripped with excitement as we left Jaipur for our next destination; Agra.

A Marble Teardrop.

Quote: *'Let the splendour of the diamond, pearl and ruby vanish like the magic shimmer of the rainbow. Only let this one teardrop, The Taj Mahal, glisten spotlessly bright on the cheek of time…'*

Rabandrannath Tagore, Indian poet and first
Nobel laureate from Asia.

The Taj Mahal, which means Crown Place, is arguably the most famous building in the world, and needs no introduction and requires no description. It was built in the 17th Century by Shah Jahan, (the fifth of the Mughal rulers), in memory of his wife Mumtaz Mahal, who died aged 39 in 1630. It was designed by a Persian engineer/astronomer called Ustad Ahmad, a resident of Lahore. Originally, it was envisaged that there would be twin buildings, with a second Taj Mahal built in black marble as a mausoleum for Shah Jahan himself. It was intended as a mirror image on the opposite east bank of the River Yamuna, a tributary of the Ganges. That would have made it even more awe-inspiring, but finances wouldn't stretch that far, even though the foundations were laid. So, like Elvis Presley, the Taj Mahal had a twin who died at birth, but went on to achieve adulation and enduring world-wide fame. Building materials were brought in from far and wide. White marble from Rajasthan, jade and amber from Asia, sapphire, topaz, and coral from China and Burma.

Shah Jahan was so delighted with the completed mausoleum, that he singled out the building workers for special treatment. According to legend, he ordered that their hands be mutilated so that they would be unable to replicate the building for anyone else. There's gratitude for you. No such thing as a bonus payment. I suspect that local builders would have been very reluctant to give him a quote for any more jobs. Shah Jahan grieved for his wife for a couple of years, spending most of his time secluded, alone and neglecting his duties. His son, Aurangzeb, assumed the Mughal throne during the period of mourning, and imprisoned his father in the Agra Fort. He must have inherited his father's sense of compassion and gratitude. From his prison, Shah Jahan could see the Taj Mahal. As he gazed out, ruefully, I wonder if he was aware of the words of William Shakespeare's 'King Lear' (written earlier in the same century): 'How sharper than a serpent's tooth it is, to have a thankless child'.

When Shah Jahan died, as a prisoner, he was laid to rest beside his wife. The tombs are encased in an incredibly elaborate marble screen and the interior of the Taj Mahal is lit through marble lattice work. A magical place to visit!

One evening, we went as a group to a highly recommended restaurant which specialized in sizzling platters, which steamed like a hot spring and hissed like a snake. They were hot metal plates on a square wooden platter, and the waiters carried them expertly to the diners while sidestepping and swerving other on-coming waiters with the nimble dexterity of a rugby player. The swing doors from the kitchen practically flew off their hinges, as a straight karate kick seemed to be the preferred method of opening them. Each waiter would emerge theatrically from the steam, a platter balanced precariously in each hand. It was fascinating to watch; an accident waiting to happen. Apparently, no mishaps had occurred in years. Norma, Barry and I decided to take a bicycle rickshaw back to the hotel.

"Hotel Grand, 137 Station Road please," we instructed the driver, as we squeezed into the seats.

"I wonder if he would let me pedal," Norma whispered, but not as quietly as she thought. He immediately pulled over to the side of the road, dismounted and gestured for her to take over. She started off quite well, with the Indian rickshaw driver jogging along by her side. We started to veer off alarmingly, and Norma managed to apply the brake to prevent us from ending up in a ditch.

"Careful with your steering, driver."

"It's difficult to concentrate on the road when this man is tickling my leg." The driver just laughed and got the rickshaw back on the road, as if tickling a female passenger's leg was the most natural thing in the world. Eventually, she delivered us safely back to the hotel, managing to steer the rickshaw with one hand while delivering the occasional slap with the other.

Half as Old as Time

Quote: *'Older than history, older than tradition, older even than legend, and looks twice as old as all of them put together'.*

Mark Twain.

In Varanasi (formerly known as Benares) we were booked into the Hotel de Paris, which was a former colonial building set amongst neat and colourful gardens. Our rooms were located along a cloister of arches edging around the lawn. Norma and I were the last to check in, and as we followed a porter we could hear the sound up ahead of footsteps on a gravel path. As we rounded the corner, the cloistered pathway in front of us was totally black, and as the porter stepped forward the gravel crunched beneath his feet. Only it wasn't gravel. He had stepped onto a carpet of large black cockroaches. Norma stopped dead in her tracks.

"There is no way I am walking through that lot!" she said strenuously, as if confronted by some medieval trial-by-ordeal.

"But it is the only way to get to your room, madam," commented the porter, with a tone of surprise; as if wading through a sea of cockroaches was the most natural thing in the world.

"Okay," I conceded, "I will give you a piggyback ride to the room."

The most piercing scream a few moments later was only because I couldn't resist pretending to stumble en route. The room was quite comfortable, and even the gecko on the ceiling seemed like nothing compared to a million cockroaches outside. The following morning, I opened our door silently and slowly, and I cautiously popped my head outside. Surprisingly, there was not a trace of cockroaches, apart from the black footprints leading to each room.

At dawn, we set off from the hotel to witness the ceremonies at the Holy River Ganges, the most important Hindu pilgrimage site in the world. The narrow maze of streets in Varanasi provided us with the now customary sights, sounds, smells and poverty that we had become accustomed to in the sub-continent. There was a light pall of grey smoke hovering, and, as we got closer to the river, it filled the streets as the burning smell combined with incense. Along the street were disabled beggars, street traders and piles of rubbish. Several funeral processions were taking place. Mourners were chanting, banging drums, playing cymbals, ringing bells and praying, as they carried the bodies of their loved ones, wrapped in cloth, towards the Ganges. Some fireworks were set off to awaken the Gods. Flower sellers offered us lotus blooms. As we emerged from the narrow alleyways between buildings we were able to look out across the River Ganges, as funeral pyres burned in front of us. It is believed that The Ganges, or Mother Ganga, is made from the tears and sweat of the Hindu God Shiva. If Hindus die there they break the cycle of death and re-birth. Bodies were draped in either turquoise or pink cloth, some covered in red hibiscus flowers, were placed on the pyres which were lit by a torch from a flame said to have been burning for a thousand years. The ashes were cast into the holy river. The deceased who are regarded as being pure; pregnant women, babies, sadhus (holy men) and, surprisingly to us, victims of cobra bites, are not burned, but weighted down and placed into the river whole. However, some became loosened from the ballast and floated down river. We noticed that some bodies were only partly cremated before being placed in the water. We were told that this was because some families could not afford to pay for enough wood to burn. Disturbingly, we noticed packs of dogs jumping into the water further down river.

The stone steps leading down to the river are called ghats, and these are the main focus of religious activity, as pilgrims bathe ritually and perform Puja (showing reverence and remorse for their sins) towards the rising sun across the river. It is believed that the Hindu God Shiva presides over Varanasi, and the Kashi Vishwanah Temple (Golden Temple) is sacred to Hindus, as Lord Shiva is enshrined there. The most significant of the ghats leading down to the river is called the Dasashvamedh Ghat (the Ghat of Ten Sacrificed

Horses), where another Hindu God Brahma made the sacrifice to pave the way for Shiva's return.

We were taken by small boat out into the River Ganges to fully appreciate the splendour and awe-inspiring sight of colour, bathed ephemerally in mist and smoke. Sadhus, standing motionless like statues meditating, others bathing to cleanse themselves of sin, women washing colourful saris in the holy waters, children playing and splashing in the river, while packs of dogs gathered on the banks. Worshippers would spend surprising amounts of time with their faces submerged in the water. None more so than a man who floated alongside our boat. I watched with fascination waiting for him to come up for air. I found myself holding my breath, almost testing myself to see how long I could last. Then our boat man prodded him with his paddle.

"He is dead," he announced, with an unconcerned shrug, and then calmly launched him out of the way. A unique and fascinating, if sombre experience.

Meditation; It's Better Than Sitting Doing Nothing

Norma is a great believer in the benefits of yoga, and one of her ambitions was to practise yoga in its spiritual home; India. She inquired at our hotel if there were any local yoga centres, and the concierge said that he would ring the yogi man, and arrange for him to come to the hotel. The following day, Norma recruited a class, including me, most of our group and several hotel guests. We assembled on the lawn, and the yogi man greeted us with lots of bows and praying hands. We responded likewise. He was a small, wiry man with a shock of dark hair and a brown face, patterned with more wrinkles than the craquelure on a Renaissance portrait. We sat on our towels in rows, waiting to be guided through a routine of gentle, stretching exercises, which Norma had described to us when she cajoled us into joining the class. However, the yogi man seemed to be more of a contortionist than a practitioner of yoga. His party-piece was to get himself into a stance similar to a sprinter in the start position, with his hands on the grass in front of him. Somehow, he threw his legs around his elbows (don't try this at home) which left him standing on his hands, with his bottom rocking between his arms. When he said, "Now you try it," none of us could move for laughing. Actually, one of our group, Reg, a thin but strong, sinewy rock-climber and mountaineer who was on his way to join a Himalayan trek, managed the position. I treasure the photograph.

The yogi man now gave us a demonstration of other anatomy-defying techniques, which we attempted with different degrees of success. Then, he produced a reed basket, which intrigued us until he lifted the lid and up popped a King Cobra snake. He asked if any of us would like to play his wooden flute in front of it to get it to sway. Not surprisingly, no-one had a great desire to get within striking distance of a cobra. We thanked him, paid him his fee and off he went, with the basket on his head.

After the mesmeric shock of being eyed-up by a cobra, we decided to have a nice cup of Indian tea on the terrace. A squadron of giant, colourful dragonflies hovered around us for a while. Unlike the cobra and the giant cockroaches, their attentions were welcomed as they flew in formation around us in the bright sunlight. We watched with fascination until our peace and tranquillity was disturbed by another visitor.

A local man, who looked remarkably like the yogi man, approached us, smiling and waving. However, we couldn't help but notice that there was one small difference; he happened to be carrying a ten-foot python. He held its head out towards us while its body, which must have been a foot in diameter, was draped around his neck and around his body. He wasn't so much carrying it as wearing it. Chairs scattered, as if someone had carried a lion skin into a film show. He assured us that we were perfectly safe, and asked if anyone would like to have a photograph taken with our scaly visitor, (the snake that is, even though its owner fitted the same description. You know, how dogs tend to look like their owners). Compared to this monster, the cobra looked like a grass snake, but at least the python didn't possess a deadly, venomous bite. So, (to quote another python), I looked on the bright side, and volunteered, with a touch of bravado. Before I could change my mind, I was being gently squeezed by this twelve-foot reptile. (I'm sorry, but it seems to get longer, like Pinocchio's nose, every time I tell the story. I'm sure any anglers reading this book will understand). I could feel the power of the snake; it was like being bear-hugged by a Turkish masseur. After much persuasion, Norma agreed to have a go. Being Australian, Mick was wary of snakes and declined the invitation, but he offered to hold Norma's hand throughout her ordeal. He regretted it later. Norma gripped his wrist tighter than the fourteen-foot snake (there I go again) was squeezing her. It was as if she was sitting in the dentist chair, her fingernails digging in as she held her breath in terror. The photograph is brilliant. Norma's facial expression is a combination of terror and laughter, wide-eyed and mouth wide open, while Mick is cringing with pain through his tears of laughter.

The journey north from Varanasi to Nepal made me feel quite sad in some respects because we were leaving India, which remains one of my favourite countries. Moreover, we were about to enter the final country on our overland trek. The bus had become our home over the past several months, our womb with a view, and our travelling companions had become close friends.

House of Snow

After the humidity of India, the first thing we noticed about Nepal was the clear air. The road climbed through dense sub-tropical foothills, as we made our way through the Seti valley towards the Annapurna Range. Incidentally, Seti is an acronym for the organisation: Search for Extra-terrestrial Intelligence. They took the name of this valley, because aliens are rumoured to have landed in this remote part of the world... 'The Truth Is Out There'. Don't believe a word of it; I have just created my own conspiracy theory. Hang on a second, what have I just spotted running across the road in front of the bus? Was it the Yeti?...

The drive became a re-run of our drive up to Kashmir, as we looked down the ravine at the River Trisulu, a tribute of the Ganges, flowing fiercely hundreds of feet below us. Monsoon rains had washed away sections of the embankment, and our bus ran the gauntlet of monstrous potholes and boulders the size of cars. En-route we passed villages which seemed to be clinging on for dear life to the edge of ravines. There were occasional tea stalls, but we decided to keep going.

Due to its inaccessibility, Nepal has never been colonized, and consequently there have been no outside influences on art and culture. Indeed, no road linked Kathmandu to the outside world until 1956. Just to think of the exotic destination of Nepal conjures up images of Mount Everest, the famous Gurkha Regiment, the Yeti, and not forgetting the 1911 poem by J. Milton Hayes: 'There is a green-eyed yellow idol to the north of Kathmandu'.

Add to that list one of the most famous men to have ever lived in the history of the world. In the 5th Century BC., Nepal was the birthplace of Prince Siddhartha, and to this day there are probably more statues of him throughout the world than of anyone else. If you are scratching your head wondering who this Prince was, perhaps I should mention that I am referring to none other than Gautama Buddha, the founder of Buddhism. As we have seen earlier in our travels, he taught the importance of morality, concentration and wisdom, to attain enlightenment and to achieve Nirvana. This is when Buddhists are released from the cycle of death and re-birth, a similar philosophy to that of Hinduism, which we had seen in Varanasi.

In Tents Arachnophobia

Driving through Nepal is a fairy-tale come to life, with jaw-dropping scenery at every turn. It is like the Rockies, Andes and Alps rolled into one. We passed through picturesque villages amongst pine forests, carpeted with rhododendron, patchwork landscape and banana plantations. We set up our camp in the town of Pokhara, where we were overlooked by a breathtaking backdrop of the Annapurna Range. We had a sensational view of the 22,956ft Machhapuchhare; popularly known as The Fish Tail Mountain. It is one of the most beautiful peaks in the world, and it reminded me very much of the Matterhorn in Switzerland. We were soon surrounded by local children asking for pens and sweets, which we happily supplied, and we joined them in a game of football. We were close to Phew Tal Lake, and one of the locals took us out on his flat-bottomed rowing boat, called a dungaa. It reminded us of our stay on Dal Lake in Kashmir, especially when flower sellers approached us in their boats.

I was fascinating to watch the Nepalese Sherpas, first-hand. The loads they carried seem to defy gravity; packages the size of a baby grand piano on their backs supported by a strap (called a namlo) across the top of their heads. They must have neck muscles stronger than a rugby prop forward.

We set off on the final leg of our overland trek the following morning. The mist coming off Phew Tal Lake formed an early morning dew on the branches of trees, and on spiders' webs, accentuated by the low light of the rising sun. But these were no ordinary spider webs. They were about 6 metres in diameter, stretching between the trees. Row upon row of them linked the trees like Christmas decorations in a tree-lined English village. The spiders were Golden orb weavers, one of the largest species in the world, which made the one that crawled up Sean Connery's arm in 'Dr. No' seem like a housefly by comparison. I shuddered to think that we had slept in a tent only a couple of hundred yards away. As we all gasped in astonishment, Mick laughed and said

"I thought that it would be better not to tell you about them last night. Anyway, they aren't poisonous."

"No," I shouted from the back of the bus, "but they look big enough to be able to drag us out of our tents!"

The drive to Kathmandu was a switchback of hairpins, with the occasional rock fall just to keep the driver on his toes. It is situated high up in a green fertile valley, which is surrounded by terrace hills similar to those we had seen previously in Kashmir.

Because It's There

Kathmandu was created due to its position on the trade-caravan route between Tibet and India, and, over the centuries, has acquired legendary, mythical status as a destination for travellers, hikers and mountaineers. Everywhere, there are shrines overgrown with bougainvillea, Buddhist prayer flags and the smell of jasmine. Himalaya, which means House of Snow, is home to Chomolungma, Goddess Mother of Mountains. This is of course Mount Everest, which was named after Sir George Everest, a 19th Century Surveyor General of India, who never actually saw it. Incredible as it may seem, fossilized sea creatures have been discovered high up in the mountains; evidence that the area was once a sea bed. The Himalayas and the Tibetan plateau have been pushed up, over millions of years, by the Indian sub-continent moving north due to continental drift. This geological process continues to this day, and the summit of Mount Everest (Chomolungma) is a couple of centimetres higher in altitude than it was in 1953, when Edmund Hillary and Sherpa Tensing were the first to conquer the mountain. It is still open to conjecture whether George Mallory and Andrew Irvine were the first to reach the summit in the 1920s. When Mallory was asked why he wanted to climb Mount Everest, he answered, famously, "Because it's there." He set off with a picture of his wife in his wallet, and promised to leave it at the summit. His body was found on the mountain over 80 years later. His wallet was still in his pocket, minus the photograph. Her picture did eventually reach the summit; their son climbed Everest many years later to fulfil his father's promise.

We checked into the Blue Star Hotel, not far from the centre. Durbar Square is at the heart of old Kathmandu, and the most distinctive building is the late 16th Century wooden temple known as Kasthamandap. Clustered around are ancient wood-carved temples and palaces in the multi-roof pagoda style. We also visited the Buddhist temple Swayambhunath, known as the Monkey Temple. (A domed stupor with giant eyes). Buddhist prayer wheels were at every temple, and were spun constantly by monks, pilgrims and members of the public. The wheels are cylindrical and are embossed in Sanskrit with Buddhist prayers, and it is believed that spinning the wheel is equivalent to reciting the prayers orally. So, as far as I understand it, the wheel does the praying on behalf of a worshipper. It is the same concept, I suppose, as Renaissance painting in Europe, where a wealthy benefactor would make a donation to a church and commission an artist, like Raphael, Botticelli or Giotto, to paint him on a wall or ceiling in the act of praying. That means that he can be seen praying constantly in the hope of booking his place in heaven. So a Buddhist Monk can spin the row of prayer-wheels at the temple and pray by proxy, to save valuable time. This begs the question; just how busy can a Buddhist Monk be? On a things-to-do scale of 1 to 10, where 1 is a new-born baby lying in a cot, and 10 is an army surgeon operating in a field hospital in a war zone, where would a Buddhist Monk be placed? I would suggest at about number 3, just above Steve McQueen in the cooler in The Great Escape, and one place below the secretary who takes down the minutes of every meeting of the Preston

Guild. The prayer-wheel concept is a brilliant idea. It would be a godsend (no pun intended… for a change) for students. Instead of having to revise for an exam, they could just spin the science wheel, or geography wheel or history wheel and, hey presto, it has done all your revisions for you. A stand-up comedian at the Edinburgh Fringe or the Hammersmith Apollo would merely have to walk on stage and spin his joke wheel. Any laughs would depend on the way he spins 'em. The audience would probably not be there anyway… they will have sent their laugh-wheels instead. I wondered why the Buddhist Monks of Kathmandu had not patented the idea, and syndicated it world-wide. They are all probably far too busy.

I bought a brightly coloured batik, in reds, oranges and yellows depicting this memorable place. Many temples were oddly adorned with erotic carvings, which were quite crude and even cartoon-like. By contrast, those in India were subtle and sensuous, which is to be expected from the country of the Karma Sutra. Apparently, it is all to do with the preponderance of wooden temples in Kathmandu and, according to legend, the Goddess of Lightening was a shy virgin who wouldn't dare strike a temple with such goings-on. I suppose it is the same idea as the grotesquely ugly gargoyles on European Gothic churches, which were intended to frighten away evil spirits.

The everyday life on the streets was similar to everywhere else on the subcontinent; the dust, smells and colours. Sadhus, holy men that we had seen in Varanasi, sat on blankets in the dirt, half-naked, smeared in dust with matted hair and beard. Brightly dressed local women carried large wicker baskets on their backs, full of anything from vegetables, fruit or firewood, carried by a namlo in the same way as the Sherpa. Buddhist monks in their saffron robes seemed to be everywhere.

Romanza

Most of our friends were on their way to Australia, a few to New Zealand, while for some, Kathmandu was their ultimate destination for climbing and hiking expeditions. Our friend Nick was on his way to stay in a Tibetan Monastery for a couple of months. We didn't have one farewell meal, as people were leaving on different days. Our goodbyes were more like Haydn's 'Farewell Symphony', during which members of the orchestra gradually exit the stage, one by one, during the performance. We all exchanged contact details, and in our case, by the time we arrived in Australia we had a ready-made circle of friends.

Norma and I stopped at a little roadside stall to try a local dish called Tama, which is Nepalese soup made from dried bamboo shoots. As we were eating, we heard some familiar music coming from an upstairs room across the road. Over the clamour of Kathmandu street-life, we could pick out the sound of 'Romanza' being played on a classical guitar; the music which had under-scored our overland trek. We thought that it was quite a coincidence, and that perhaps it was coming from a radio or cassette player. We soon realized that it was being played live by a musician because the music kept stopping and then starting again. Either that, or someone's cassette player was on the blink. Curiosity got the better of us so we strolled over and pushed open the door, which was slightly ajar. We climbed some rickety old wooden stairs, which creaked with every step, and we were ready to apologise in case we had walked uninvited into someone's house. Not that the friendly Nepalese people would have minded… they would probably have put the kettle on. We reached a second-floor, sparsely-furnished room where, sitting on the bare wooden floor, where a small group of local men listening to the guitarist play.

"Clarry?" I said, as the music stopped abruptly and he turned round.

"Norma? John? What are you doing here?"

"Oh, we just happened to be passing, so we thought we would pop in to say hello." As you do in Kathmandu old town.

It transpired that Clarry was in the process of selling his guitar to a local man, because the next stage of his journey was by air and checking a guitar through an airport would be an unnecessary expense. He had a prospective buyer interested, and was demonstrating its tone and clarity (no pun intended). It was a sad reminder that we were at the end of our overland adventure.

Dave, the co-driver, was booked to take the bus back to England. Mick was at the end of his contract, and his next destination was Bangkok. The three of us decided to travel together. We booked a flight through a travel agent in Kathmandu, who also booked our accommodation. The clerk in the shop handed us our hotel details, written in English in a spidery scrawl. We were booked into the Hotel Metro... something-or-other, as the handwriting of the Nepalese travel agent trailed off illegibly. At the airport, we were amused to see a booking desk for Yeti Airlines. (I didn't notice one for Seti Vertical-Take-Off Airlines). We flew out on Thai Airways (Royal Orchid), which was superb. We had a magnificent view of Mount Everest, and, as we marvelled at the highest point on earth, we reminisced about our trip and remembered that we had also been to the lowest point on earth; The Dead Sea. Perfect symmetry.

Chapter Four

On a Far Eastern Promise

What a Carry On

Mick, Norma and I took a taxi from the airport to Bangkok city centre. The driver gave a cursory glance at the sheet of paper on which was written the name of our hotel. He nodded in recognition, and we drove off precariously, as he expertly negotiated us through the Dodgem-car mayhem of Bangkok traffic. We pulled up in front of a colonial-style building, which displayed a large Metro sign. As we were taking our bags from the boot of the taxi, we couldn't help noticing that there was a long queue waiting to go in.

"This must be a very popular hotel," I mused, to no-one in particular. The driver gave me a furtive, sideways glance as his brow furrowed with confusion.

"I don't think this is our hotel," observed Norma, dubiously, "it's a *cinema.*"

The long line of excited local people was waiting to see the latest blockbuster movie. If I gave you a thousand guesses as to which film was being shown, I would be surprised if anyone would even come close; 'Jaws'? 'The Towering Inferno'? 'James Bond'? No, it was a 'Carry On' film. 'Carry On England', appropriately enough. Apparently, they were very popular in the Far East. Charles Hawtrey,

Sid James and Kenneth Williams were the George Clooney, Brad Pitt and Clark Gable of their day.

The driver asked for a second look at our hotel booking. He gave us an apologetic gesture, and put our bags back into the taxi. As we drove away, Mick joked, "Actually, I wouldn't have minded seeing that." All three of us laughed, and, with perfect, un-rehearsed synchronicity, we quoted, theatrically, the most famous line from all of the 'Carry On' movies: Kenneth Williams, as Julius Caesar, when he proclaimed, 'Infamy, infamy... They've *all* got it in for me.'

This made us laugh even more. The driver joined in, more out of courtesy than humour, I suspect. Eventually, we arrived at the Metro Hotel and paid the driver extra bahts as a tip.

Unfortunately, the hotel reception desk had no record of our booking. In those pre-computer days, the receptionist double-checked different surnames in his file, and also to see if it had been booked under the name of the travel agent in Kathmandu. All drew a blank.

"What a carry on," muttered Mick, but this time without the laughter.

However, the hotel did have vacancies, so we were able to book two rooms. Even though it was in the budget category, the hotel was quite sumptuously appointed; lots of red velvet upholstery, flock wallpaper and mood lighting. The general decor reminded me of the bars at Butlin's in Pwhelli, circa 1964: names like; The Blue Parrot, or The Tropical Lagoon, festooned with plastic parrots and palm trees. The bars were probably designed by someone who had never travelled further than Brighton. Until, that is, he moved to Bangkok.

We were quite tired after the flight, so we decided to have an evening meal at the hotel restaurant. This was my first experience of Thai food and I had steamed jasmine rice with chicken green curry. To this day, Thai cuisine remains one of my favourites; right up there with Wigan pies.

We went into the hotel bar for a few Singha and Chang beers. Most of the tables were located in small booths and were totally enveloped by the plush seating. It was like sitting on the Waltzer at a fairground in the early sixties, when a leather-clad greaser would spin you round, to the sound of delighted female screams, and Dion and the Belmonts singing 'The Wanderer'.

As the evening progressed, the three of us chatted jovially, while the bar gradually became more crowded. Different nationalities seemed to come and go. The atmosphere was reasonably friendly, but no-one seemed willing to engage us in conversation. We started to feel a little self-conscious, and as the bar emptied, we decided that it was time for a good night's sleep before sight-seeing the following day.

Due to the proliferation of canals, Bangkok in the 19th Century became known, inevitably, as the 'Venice of the East'. This epithet has been conferred on a number of cities: St. Petersburg and Amsterdam are often described as the 'Venice of the North'. Nowadays, areas of Bangkok tend to attract a similar demography to that of the Red-Light District in Amsterdam. Perhaps, in view of the fact that Bangkok was originally known as Bang Makok, it would be more appropriate to call the city: 'The Amsterdam of the East.' Just a thought.

Shall We Dance

We bought tickets for the River Taxi on the Chao Phraya River, and this gave us fantastic views of the beautiful city. The Grand Palace was built in the 18th Century, as home to the Royal Family, and it was the setting for Margaret Landon's 1944 best-selling novel, 'Anna and the King of Siam'. This tells of the experiences of Anna Leonowens as a teacher to the wives and children of King Mongkut in the 1860s. In the movie, starring Yul Brynner, and also the stage musical, there is a scene in which the children are being sent off to bed. To the accompaniment of the tune, 'March of the Siamese Children', each child takes it in turn to say goodnight to their father. This touching scene finishes with the youngest, and cutest, child invariably invoking 'sighs' and 'ahs' from the audience. Well, in real life, this scene would require the music to be on a continuous loop, since there were 82 of them. That's right, 82 kids (and 39 wives). If Anna Leonowens went to Siam to escape the over-size Victorian classes created by the likes of Dickens' Mr Gradgrind, then she must have been in for a shock.

At the risk of sounding pedantic, and getting my pronouns in a twist, I wonder why Rodgers and Hammerstein didn't call their 1951 hit musical ‘The King and Me’? Surely, that would be grammatically correct. I feel like asking, “Yes, ‘The King and I’... what?”

This brings me nicely to the subject of Wats. (I must apologize for that excruciatingly tenuous link. I couldn’t resist it).

Wat means temple, and they are ubiquitous throughout the region of Indo-China. The Grand Palace complex is surrounded by a huge white wall, and at the entrance on Na Phra Lan Road, visitors who happened to be wearing shorts or insubstantial tops were issued with very unflattering one-size-fits-all clothes. The most striking building within the grounds is Dusit Throne Hall, with its famous four-tiered roof.

Built in the 16th Century, Wat Pho is Bangkok’s oldest and largest temple. It is still home to resident monks, and the large complex comprises a school, pavilions, mosaics, statues and stupas. The Reclining Buddha can be viewed here. It is 46 metres long, 15 metres high, and made of brick, plaster and gold leaf. The reclining posture symbolizes his arrival at Nirvana.

The floating markets, such as the Ton Kem Market, reminded me very much of life on Dal Lake in Kashmir. Square-ended rowing boats, called sampans, competed for custom, selling everything from flowers, fruits, vegetables, and crafts. We were even served a hot meal from a noodle boat, which pulled-up alongside ours.

The Chatuchak Market is the biggest in Thailand, with 15000 stalls and a vast array of products. We were particularly impressed by the quality of the silk, and a stall-holder explained to us that it was known as Ring Silk. It was so delicate and sheer that a length of cloth could actually be pulled through a wedding ring. Norma bought a length of silk, which she had made-up into a dress at a local tailor's shop, which offered twenty-four-hour service.

After a fascinating, if tiring, day amongst the hustle, bustle and vibrancy of Bangkok, we decided to take a Tuk-tuk back to the hotel. We arrived red-eyed from petrol and exhaust fumes, ready for a drink. We asked the desk clerk for our keys, and, as he handed them over, he signalled to a man who was sitting reading a newspaper in the foyer. Immediately, this man dashed over to us with quite a concerned look etched on his face. "Mr. Meadows?" he asked, glancing at some documentation he was carrying.

"Yes. Is there a problem?"

"My name is Tadashi. Could I have a quiet word?" he whispered, furtively, while ushering us towards a table booth.

Norma, Mick and I looked at each other with an air of confusion as we sat down. Tadashi told us that he worked for the booking agency which had arranged our hotel reservation.

"I have spent hours trying to track you down," he announced, with a look of relief and a faint smile. He managed to confuse us even further when he told us that our hotel manager had become concerned when we didn't check-in yesterday. "I checked the airline company and traced you via the police register of visitors to Bangkok."

"Hang on a second," I interrupted, amidst all this confusion, "The hotel manager is over there, behind his desk."

"But Mr. Meadows, this is *not* your hotel."

He confirmed this by showing us documentation for the Metropolitan Hotel, *not* the Metro Hotel. I shrugged and told him, reassuringly, "This hotel seems fine, there is no need for you to be so agitated."

He then leaned forward, conspiratorially, and whispered, "But, *this* hotel is, as I think you would say in England, *a Knocking Shop*!"

Collectively, our mouths dropped open; none more so than Norma's.

"It is a place of ill-repute, and *not* the type of hotel that we would book our clients into."

To his obvious relief, the three of us burst out laughing spontaneously. It went some way towards explaining the bordello-themed decor.

"You mean to tell me," I announced, with mock indignation, "that I have spent a night in a glorified brothel... with my *wife*!"

By now, Mick was helpless. Furthermore, the sly smile and a glint in his eye was as if he was a fox who had been given the keys to the hen house. (Always assuming, of course, that a fox is cunning enough to be able to open a door with a key).

"If you would like to collect your luggage, I will arrange a transfer to the Metropolitan Hotel."

After a day touring the city, the last thing we felt like at that moment was the disruption of packing and traipsing across town to another hotel.

"For the sake of just two more nights, is it worth the trouble?" Mick suggested, with a hint of pleading in his voice. The final word had to go to Norma. We looked at her as she sat there, non-plussed and contemplative.

"After months of sleeping in tents, caves, by the roadside, in the desert and in communal rooms," she announced, with a woeful look, "I suppose I could add a brothel to that list."

We all laughed and Mick joked, "You never know, Norma, you might even get an offer."

She smacked him playfully and replied, "Don't be cheeky, and don't forget, John was offered *ten* camels for me at the market in Kabul!"

Tadashi shook hands and waved goodbye, and we ordered some drinks.

"I feel as though we *really are* in a 'Carry On Film," I joked, taking a welcome sip of cold beer.

"Yeah," laughed Mick, "Carry On, Bang Makok."

Bamboozled

For our final day, we booked on a tour to Rose Gardens, just outside Bangkok. It is a sort of microcosm of Thailand, and we were able to see various cultural activities, all brought together in one complex. It is a similar concept to that of, say, The Tivoli Gardens in Copenhagen, or the Epcot Centre in Florida. We were given a demonstration of working elephants, who lifted and moved huge tree trunks with ease. The elephants seemed very well looked after, and being highly intelligent animals, seemed to relish an appreciative audience.

The performance of traditional Thai dancing was elegant, and dazzlingly colourful. The costumes were sumptuous and some of the headdresses being worn were like miniature golden models of Bangkok temples. They would be a sensation at Royal Ascot. Rabam Lavo was a very elegant style of dance while Khon was the most stylised. The Thai fingernail dance (Fawn Lep) was also up to scratch. I was particularly fascinated by a Bamboo Dance. This involved long, heavy bamboo poles, a few inches in diameter, being held at each end in pairs, a few inches off the ground. They were rhythmically banged on the floor, and then against each other, in time with traditional Thai music. The dance comprised a hopping, jumping technique, as the girls, all beautiful and dressed in Traditional Costume, stepped in and out of the colliding bamboo poles. I watched with fascination and cringed at the thought of one false step, since delicate ankles would certainly be crushed between the bamboo. To me, it was more of a trial-by-ordeal rather than an aesthetic experience; like watching a Victorian circus performer put his head in a lion's mouth, with an audience hoping he would survive. Or perhaps not. We secured ringside seats at a Thai boxing match. I felt as though I was feeling every punch, knee and roundhouse kick. If I had the choice, I think I would prefer to risk the Bamboo Dance.

Our brief stopover in Bangkok was fascinating and memorable, to say the least. Later that night when we were packing our bags, I realized that I had left my camera case in Mick's hotel room. I nipped along the corridor, gave a quick knock and went in. The image that confronted me has been engrained in my mind's-eye forever. For the benefit of readers of a delicate disposition, all I will say is that, if I had owned a bike, I would have been able to park it in the crack of Mick's gluteus maximus. He looked over his shoulder and laughed, without missing a beat. His companion looked over his shoulder and gave me a broad smile and a wave, as if I was forming a queue. I picked up my camera case and made a quick exit.

"That was quick," remarked Norma, as I got back to the room. The look on my face required no further explanation.

On the flight to Singapore, we were mysteriously up-graded to first-class and offered champagne. I don't know why. Perhaps it was another breakdown in communications, or, more probably, it was by way of apology from the booking agents. Not that Mick would be likely to ever make a complaint.

So there we were, reclining in sumptuous luxury, quaffing champagne; Norma and I... Sorry, Norma and Me.

Singapore Sling

In Singapore, we checked into the plush Hotel Miramar. The foyer was impressive; plenty of polished marble, a fish pond, a waterfall and an open, stone staircase, with not a plastic parrot or hooker in sight.

Modern Singapore was founded in 1819 by Englishman Sir Thomas Stanford Raffles, of the British East India Company. The British Empire was looking to set up a trading post in the region and, from his ship 'The Indiana', Raffles recognized the potential of the small swampy island. Little is known of the earliest history of the island, but there is evidence that Chinese sailors of the 3rd Century called it Pu-Luo-Chung, which means, 'island at the end of the peninsula'. Its present name derives from the 16th Century, when a Sumatran Prince was sheltering from a storm, and he thought he saw a lion. Subsequently, he founded a city there, and called it Singapura; Lion City in Sanskrit.

When Raffles landed, the island was inhabited by locals known as Orang Laut (Sea People), and Chinese traders. He negotiated a treaty and began the trading post. Due to its strategic position, business expanded rapidly and exponentially, and attracted workers and merchants from all over Indo-China.

Just three years after its founding, Singapore's first architect, George Coleman, arrived to design the Residency House for Raffles. Coleman also created many Palladian-style houses; that most ubiquitous architectural style which incorporated all the elements of classic Graeco-Roman architecture. Today, there is a pleasing mix of styles as these original buildings nestle amongst the high-rise glass and steel towers.

It is fortunate that these older buildings have survived. When Singapore achieved independence in 1965, the economy was weak, and it was felt that modernisation was essential to revive prosperity. As a consequence, many historic buildings were demolished, and much of the character and culture were swept away in the clearance. In the 1980s, conservation became more important and some were saved. (This reminds me very much of a similar scenario in Miami Beach, when the 1930s Art Deco Buildings were saved in the nick of time).

Many of these traditional buildings are centred on the site of Raffles' original landing; the Colonial Core. These include the City Hall, St. Andrew's Cathedral, Singapore Cricket Club, Old Parliament House and the Victoria Theatre. A statue of Raffles stands proudly at his original landing place.

The Singapore River snakes through the centre of the city; passing Clarke Quay (named after the second Governor), under Elgin Bridge to widen into The Boat Quay, before opening into Marina Bay. The Boat Quay comprises rows of old trading houses, which have been restored and renovated into bars and restaurants, in the same way as the Albert Dock in Liverpool. Incidentally, we returned to Singapore twenty years later and were astounded at how the cityscape on the north side of the Boat Quay had risen. The earlier office blocks were now dwarfed by the new generation. It was like visiting a family after a few years to find that the children were now head and shoulders taller than their parents.

We visited Chinatown and happened upon The Buddha Tooth Relic Temple, which, as the name clearly suggests, is a temple containing an *actual* tooth of the Buddha. There is nothing unusual in this, since many different religions have built places of worship dedicated to relics: body parts, items of clothing or artefacts. But, here is the thing: there appears to be enough teeth of the Buddha scattered around the world to make a full set of dentures, and I have seen some of them. In Sir Lanka there is the Temple of the Sacred Tooth in the city with the sweetly ironic name of Kandy. There is the Lingguang Temple in Beijing, one in Japan and, bizarrely, one in California. The Buddha seems to have left a trail of his teeth. Perhaps there is a hidden message waiting to be discovered by Dan Brown or Indiana Jones. The Buddha could have pulled out his own teeth without anaesthetic because, being Buddha, he was able to... *transcend dental medication.*

Food is an important aspect of Singaporean culture and social life, and not surprisingly, it seemed as though there were restaurants representing every part of the world. In fact, we had our first experience of a food-hall concept in Singapore: a communal eating area, encircled by different restaurants. These are very common nowadays in Britain; Manchester's Trafford Centre spring-rolls to mind.

Despite this maelstrom of gastronomic influences, Singapore has still managed to develop its own signature dishes. I gave the fish-head curry a miss on the grounds that I don't like eating anything that is looking at me. I did eat a sheep's eye when we were in Iraq, but only because I was starving and I thought that it would see me through the day. Incidentally, I celebrated my birthday a few years ago at a restaurant in Peru. I ordered the National dish; guinea pig. Fortunately, it was not served prostrate with its eyes looking up at me from the plate. Actually, the hardest part was catching it in its exercise wheel. (Joke, honest). When anyone ever asks what an unusual meat tastes like, the stock answer is, (no pun intended, for a change), usually chicken. However, cuy (as guinea pig is known in Spanish) was more like a rabbit in taste and texture. A few weeks after we got home, my 10-year-old nephew, Ben, asked us if we could look after his pet while he went on holiday with his parents. How many guesses do you need? Right first time; it was his pet guinea pig; Rocky. I think succulent Rocky must have had an inbuilt instinct as he looked up at me warily from inside his cage. We were like Sylvester and Tweetie Pie.

Anyway, after that impromptu dash to the other side of the Pacific, let's get back to Singapore before our meal gets cold. We tried the Hainanese Chicken, which was poached in stock, served with rice, steamed with garlic and ginger, washed down with a few Tiger and Anchor beers.

One of the most famous hotels in the world is the Raffles Hotel, built in 1887. Mick had an Australian friend who worked in Singapore, and he arranged for us to have a guided tour of the hotel. In the lobby is the Writers' Bar, in which photographs of celebrity guests are proudly exhibited; Noel Coward, Somerset Maugham, Rudyard Kipling and Charlie Chaplin. We viewed the Empire Cafe, Palm Court, the Ballroom and had something to eat at the Raffles Grill.

Of course, no visit to the Raffles Hotel could be complete without sampling a Singapore Sling in the world-famous Long Bar. It was first created in 1910 by Chinese bartender Ngiam Tong Boon, and it is made with gin, cherry brandy, Cointreau, pineapple juice and fresh lime. One drink led to another. It is a tradition that discarded peanut shells cover the floor of the bar. No-one seems to know the reason why. It seems so incongruous in such a meticulous, pristine city, where littering is a serious offence. The uniqueness of Raffles Hotel seems to have been diluted, as franchises have now opened in different parts of the world. A few years ago, we went into a branch in Kuala Lumpar in Malaysia, but it didn't have the same feel to it, and the Singapore Sling wasn't quite the same. I felt exactly the same about Harry Ramsden's Chippy in Yorkshire. As students in Leeds, we would often treat ourselves to a massive serving, on newspaper, of course, of fish and chips at the original Harry Ramsden's in Guiseley. It was established in1928, but these days they are to be found at Motorway Service Stations. Sacrilege. Napoleon once said, 'It is but a small step from the sublime to the ridiculous'. I think my last comparison, from Raffles to Harry Ramsden's, is more of a quantum leap into the surreal.

We visited the Botanical Gardens of Singapore, and felt at home immediately as there was an English-style, Victorian octagonal bandstand where concerts are performed. For a moment, I thought I was back in Victoria Park in St. Helens. The Gardens were founded in 1859, and it was there that the seeds, brought from Brazil, were nurtured to begin the massive rubber plantations of Malaya. Today, the Gardens are famous for orchids, and the Orchid Garden has the largest display in the world, with over one thousand species. The orchid-growing programme was started in 1928, which, by startlingly coincidence, was the exact same year that Harry Ramsden opened his chippy. I would like to claim, here and now, that I must be the only person in the history of the human race to recognize that monumentally historic connection. Perhaps they should name a new orchid; 'Harry Ramsden'. Or better still, open a fish and chip franchise in Singapore and call it 'Harry Krishna's'.

A Pride of Merlions

The signature emblem of Singapore is the Merlion, which I assumed was an ancient symbol of historical significance. Surprisingly, this is not the case. It was dreamed-up by the Tourist Board, as recently as 1964, as an instant mythical creature; similar in concept to a gryphon, a centaur or Pegasus. Singapore's name, in the Javanese language of Temasek, means Sea Town. Presumably, it didn't take a great leap of imagination to combine a fish with a lion to create a lion-mermaid. There are now five in total, so I suppose we could call them a Pride of Merlions. The original designer/sculptor appears to have been influenced by the Chinese ceremonial faces of a lion. Personally, I felt as though he had taken the amorphism too far in the direction of Disney. Older readers might remember Lenny the Lion, ventriloquist Terry Hall's dummy, who was popular on television in the 1950s and '60s. Once I had made that connection I couldn't get it out of my head.

We took a cable car across to Sentosa, which is an island off the southern tip of Singapore. It was actually a British military base until 1967, and it has been transformed into a complex of museums, theme parks and nature trails. Sentosa was once known as Pulau Blakang Mati, which is Malay for; Island at the Back of Death. It was so-called because of frequent outbreaks of fatal diseases that killed nearly all of the original settlers. When the island was turned into a leisure playground for tourists, it was decided, for some reason I cannot quite understand, to change its name to Sentosa, which means, The Isle of Peace and Tranquillity.

When we returned to Singapore twenty years later, a monorail, the Sentosa Express, now links Singapore to the island and all the attractions. Lenny, sorry, Merlion had an addition to the pride: the 37 metre-tall Merlion Tower. This version has undergone a laser-eye operation which gives it a penetrating stare: a laser light from the eyes.

In my opinion, Singapore could be an example to the rest of the world: a tiny country in which different religions, diverse cultures, cuisine and architecture all exist harmoniously. Mosques, temples, churches and synagogues exist in close proximity, as Christians, Muslims, Hindus, Buddhists, Jews and countless others live in peace. There are the Sri Krishnan Temple, St. Andrew's Cathedral and Maghain Aboth Synagogue. The Sultan Mosque is fantastic, with its minarets and magnificent golden onion-dome, topped with a crescent moon and stars. What was most astonishing, though, was that the Mosque was designed by... an Irishman! (Denis Santry). Mick was booked on a different flight to us, so we said our goodbyes in Singapore. We just *had* to have a farewell photograph taken in front of Fuk Tak Chi Temple, which could just as easily have been the name of our hotel in Bangkok.

Chapter Five

A Land Down Under, Where Women Glow and Men Chunder

A few years ago, with calm assurance, I answered the one-million-pound question on Who Wants to be a Millionaire. Such was my confidence that it was not necessary for me to phone a friend, or to opt for 50:50. "What is a resident of Sydney called?" asked Chris Tarrant. The four options were: Sydnesian, Sydonian, Sydneysider, and Port Jacksonian. I knew the answer immediately; I used to be one. I could not believe my luck, a question as easy as *that* for one million pounds. I answered, "Sydneysider," and, after the briefest of pauses, added, "Final answer." Chris Tarrant maintained a poker face as he looked directly into the camera. "Let's take a break," he prevaricated, with a mischievous twinkle. Two minutes later, I was an instant millionaire. Perhaps I should mention at this point that I was actually watching television. Nevertheless, it gave me the same feeling of satisfaction and intellectual fulfilment as if I had been sitting on the studio high chair. (That is the only false statement written in this book.) Besides, I am not sure how many of the previous fourteen questions I had answered correctly to get me to the ultimate jackpot.

Anyway, after that flight of fantasy, it is time to get back down to earth, literally. As we approached Sydney airport, the two iconic symbols dominated the cityscape below us: The Opera House and the

Harbour Bridge. Being Australia, nicknames are inevitable, and respectively, they are known as Nuns in a Rugby Scrum, and the Coathanger.

As we taxied across the apron towards the airport terminal, the passengers were instructed to cover their eyes. We were then sprayed in much the same way as 19th Century immigrants arriving on New York's Ellis Island. "Sheep dip next," I spluttered.

Our visas allowed us to work temporarily in Australia. The rules of entry were nowhere near as stringent as they are today. My greatest concern was my haircut. As I caught a glimpse of myself in a plate glass window, I could not believe that I had allowed a street barber in Singapore to cut my hair. I must have been his first customer, *ever*. The style he had gone for could only be described as '12th Century English peasant'. In the era when the feathered mullet was king, I arrived looking like the village idiot, or an extra in a Robin Hood film. In the 1930s, I believe my new look was known as a pudding-basin cut.

The passport control officer had a friendly, easy-going manner as he perused our passports with interest. As he flicked back and forth through several pages, he studied some of the stamps judiciously.

"We have travelled overland from London to Kathmandu," I elaborated, wondering if there was a problem, since adjacent queues seemed to be moving along smoothly.

"Yes, I assumed as much," he answered, seemingly unimpressed, "It's a popular route with Australians and New Zealanders, but we don't get too many Brits making the same journey."

We just nodded and waited patiently for him to stamp us through.

"Any problems on the way?" he inquired, almost pointedly.

"No, none at all."

"Was it a good trip?"

"Fantastic, thank you for asking."

We were beginning to wonder if this was standard procedure, or if we were about to be detained.

"Is anything wrong?" I enquired, by now expecting to be put on the next flight home. I was convinced it was my haircut.

"Oh, not at all," the officer answered, seemingly oblivious to the line building up behind us. "It's just that my son is currently touring Europe in a camper van, and he has just written to let us know that he is going to come home overland. Having spoken to you two, I can now reassure my wife and tell her to stop worrying." He stamped our passports and wished us a pleasant stay in Australia.

We picked up our bags at the carousel and made our way to the Customs Desks. The officer unzipped Norma's holdall and a whiff of yak permeated the air. He unrolled and held aloft her Afghan coat, holding it at arm's length.

"I have brought it all the way from Herat," she explained, in a pleading tone while maintaining a disarming smile, "I hope you aren't going to confiscate it." The customs officer just shook his head and answered good-humouredly, "If you'll wear it, you can keep it."

With that, we had cleared all the formalities and made our way towards the main exit. Before we leave the airport, it is worth mentioning that the official title is Kingsford-Smith Airport. Charles Kingsford-Smith was an Australian veteran of Gallipoli, who later became the first person to fly across the Pacific Ocean. In 1928, he flew the aeroplane, Southern Cross, from California to Australia, via Hawaii and Fiji. It was a monumental achievement which attracted worldwide attention, and it is surprising that he is not as world famous as pioneers such as Amy Johnson, the Wright Brothers or the most famous aviator of them all; Charles Lindbergh. In fact, Lindbergh became the most famous individual in the world following his momentous, historic flight across the Atlantic in 1927. If I told you that his flight was with Ryanair, would you believe me? It *is* true. Well, almost: his aeroplane, The Spirit of St. Louis, was built, in San Diego, by Ryan Airline (near enough, which, I hasten to add, is not Ryanair's mission statement).

As the bright sunshine filtered through the main concourse of the airport, the huge Christmas tree reminded us that it was actually early December. We emerged from an air-conditioned comfort zone into the shock of searing heat, under an uninterrupted blue sky. We quickly jumped into the first available taxi, which, thankfully, was air-conditioned.

"Where to, mate?"

"Bondi Beach, please."

A former colleague and good friend, had contacted a New Zealand couple, Phil and Heather Jones, who were his friends. They had a room available in their apartment, and that is where we were now heading. As we took in the sights of Sydney for the first time, both of us experienced strangely ambivalent feelings. We were, of course, excited at the prospect of living for a while in Australia, but on the other hand, it was time to face up to responsibilities. We had just spent something like six months with nothing at all to concern us, apart from what we would be having for the next meal, or what fascinating places we would be visiting next. We had no house, rent, mortgage, car, or job. At twenty-seven years of age, all of our worldly possessions were in two zip-up holdalls. Without exception, all of our family and friends thought that we were out of our minds to give up everything and go off travelling. To us, it was a cathartic experience and, in some respects, we did not want it to end. As we sat in the taxi, lost in our thoughts, inevitably, we had returned to reality.

In Australia, they drive on the left, and I noticed that the driver kept slowing down to allow cars to filter in from road junctions on the right.

"You are very courteous," I remarked to our driver. "We don't get that level of consideration in England," I added, superciliously.

"It's the law, mate," he answered, making eye contact via his rear-view mirror. "We have to give way to the right."

“It sounds like an insurance scam waiting to happen,” I observed with just a hint of cynicism. The driver smiled sardonically, nodding in agreement, as he slowed down yet again. (I believe that the law has subsequently been changed; too many accidents).

The taxi dropped us at Phil and Heather’s apartment block in Hastings Parade. To our great relief, they were expecting us, give or take a day or two. They welcomed us warmly, as if we were long-lost friends and led us into the lounge. Phil was a big bloke, every inch a rugby player. He had red hair, a pale, freckled complexion and a face which looked as though it had experienced, first-hand, a few seasons of rucks and mauls. Heather was also quite tall, with dark luxuriant shoulder-length hair, a healthy, tanned complexion and beautiful large eyes, the colour of burnt umber. Following a brief conversation, consisting mostly of trivial small talk, the four of us got on well as we all laughed, crucially, at the same time, and at the same things. Over a very welcome cup of coffee, Phil told us that he worked as a printer and that he played for the Eastern Suburbs Rugby Union club. Heather worked in an architect’s office in Sydney city centre. They were spending some time in Australia before going off travelling around Europe for a couple of years. Then came the bad news... Our room for the first few nights was to be the kitchen, not the lounge, because a rugby mate of Phil’s had commandeered the sofa for a few nights. An Australian couple occupied the second bedroom, but Phil assured us that they would soon be leaving.

How can I describe the apartment? It was clean and dry, but I would not have been surprised to find out that the owner of the property was called Rigsby. The balcony was particularly interesting, accessible through a wooden sash-window in the lounge, leading on to the flat roof of the garage. The outdoor furniture consisted of a battered old sofa overlooking Hastings Parade.

Our first night's sleep in Sydney was in sleeping bags on the linoleum floor. Our heads were near the oven door, not that we were feeling suicidal you understand. Phil warned us that the oven door was faulty, and the system he employed for preventing it from flying open was to wedge it with a one-pound claw hammer. There was no such thing as a bedside light; we had to make-do with candles. Compared to this, sleeping in a cave in Petra had been the height of luxury.

We had enough funds to sustain us with food and rent for only a few weeks, so finding a job was our number one priority. While Phil and Heather were at work we decided to spend our first day familiarising ourselves with the city. We took the bus from Bondi and went for an aimless stroll. We noticed that there was a proliferation of familiar English names such as Kings Cross, Paddington, Hyde Park, the Queen Victoria Building and the Strand Arcade. By contrast, there were also many other road signs and names derived from the indigenous Aboriginal population: Woolloomooloo, Parramatta, Wollongong, Bennelong Point and indeed our new home of Bondi.

The second thing I noticed was quite alarming; I was beginning to show symptoms of anxiety, palpitations, and shock. Frequently, I gasped for air, which made me stop dead in my tracks, momentarily. Furthermore, I had developed an exaggerated twitch in my right arm. I didn't need to see a doctor as I was able to self-diagnose my ailment: I christened it 'Overland Backpackers' Involuntary Reflex Syndrome'. Having subsequently spoken to other long-term trekkers, I have discovered that it is a very common affliction. I had just spent the best part of six months joined at the hip to a leather pouch for twenty-four hours a day. It contained our passports, visas, cash, travellers' cheques and tickets. I had it with me at all times, secured with a strong leather belt. Even during the night, I wore it around my shoulder. We had heard stories about travellers who had placed their valuables and essential at their feet *inside* a sleeping bag, only to find out the following morning that thieves had sliced the sleeping bag open. Whether walking through Middle Eastern bazaars, or the back streets of dusty desert towns, it became second nature to regularly tap the pouch for constant reassurance. To lose all our money and documentation in most of the countries we had travelled through would have been an unimaginable disaster. It was in the era before internet banking, email, text or social media, and intercontinental telephone communication was, at best, unreliable. Only once did this nightmare scenario *almost* happen to us, when I went to a primitive, fly-infested, corrugated-tin-roofed toilet in some desert outpost in the middle of Iraq. They were, of course, the Arab-style squat toilets, which comprised two footprint mouldings on which to place your feet, with a hole in the porcelain over a disgustingly indescribable tank of sludge. By then, we had all perfected the technique of holding your breath for an almost suicidal period. (I increased my lung capacity to such an extent that I could have qualified as a pearl diver in Fiji). Unfortunately, on that particular day, I had made a monumental error and put my precious leather pouch on the wrong end of my belt, not next to the buckle. As I undid my pants, the weight of the pouch pulled the belt through the loops of my trousers, and, to my horror, it started to fall towards the hole below me. Everything seemed to go into slow motion, but I managed to grab it just before it disappeared into the abyss. I was never any good at cricket, but at that moment, I somehow managed to summon up the speed and reflexes of an international slip-fielder. If I had not caught the pouch in time I would have, quite literally, been in deep shit. We could have been interred forever.

Hopefully, that gives you some insight into the temporary trauma experienced by intrepid travellers who have recently been surgically separated from their conjoined belt pouches. Like leprosy and the Black Death, this particular affliction seems to have been eradicated throughout the world. Cheap flights and increasing political instability have resulted in overland treks such as ours being practically impossible these days. No longer do we see people on the streets of Sydney, or Auckland or Earl's Court in London approaching each other 'going for their guns', like trigger-happy gunslingers of the old West.

Haggling over prices is another habit that travellers need to be gradually weaned off. We wandered into Grace Bothers in Sydney. (Yes, there *really* was a large department store of that name).

"Are you being served?" asked the assistant in the menswear department. I was tempted to ask, with devastating, original wit if John Inman or Trevor Bannister was free, but I was determined not to pass any comment. I did not wish to risk being answered, in a condescending tone, "Congratulations sir, you are the one millionth customer to ask that question."

Norma chose a couple of shirts for me. (Even to this day she doesn't trust me to go out on my own to buy clothes. Just because I used to think that Fashion Faux Pas was a clothes shop in Wigan). I began to haggle over the price as I seamlessly began my well-rehearsed routine, honed to perfection in countless souks and markets. However, the shop assistant gave me a woeful look; more bizarre than bazaar. Norma gave me a penetrating stare, as if to say, 'We are in Australia, not Afghanistan'. I just thought, 'How can anyone develop a look that says so much'? We bought the shirts, and for the rest of the day I concentrated on overcoming my haggling obsession.

We made our way down to see the Opera House, and, even though it had only been open for about four years, it was already one of the world's most photographed buildings. The visual impact is enhanced by its location on a prime setting, in a similar way to that of the Statue of Liberty in New York, or the statue of Christ the Redeemer, which stands majestically on the summit of Corcovado in Rio.

The harbour bridge, which opened in 1932, is situated only a couple of hundred yards from the Opera House, and together, they complement each other to create a signature of a vibrant, modern city. It was manufactured in England following the design of the Tyne and Runcorn bridges.

The site of the original settlement is now a popular tourist area, known as The Rocks Centre, which is similar in style and ambience to other waterfront places such as the Fishermen's Wharf in San Francisco, or the Victoria and Alfred Quay in Capetown. We were still officially tourists, before we had to succumb to that dreaded four-letter word: work. Therefore, we decided to act like tourists and had a Victorian sepia photograph taken at a small studio. They dressed us up in period costume and we then posed in a Victorian setting, feeling like The Sundance Kid and Etta Plaice. I sat on an antique, upholstered chair, with Norma standing dutifully at my side. It was, after all, Victorian times.

"Try to exude an air of pomposity, mate," the photographer advised. This caused us to burst out laughing as I hammed it up for our small audience of onlookers. I was wearing a top hat, cravat, waistcoat and three-quarter length velvet jacket. Norma wore a huge hat of ostrich feathers and a bejewelled full-length dress, held together with a row of plastic clothes pegs down her back. We were told not to smile because cameras in the 19th Century required a long exposure, and hence, the stern, unsmiling faces of Victorian photographic portraiture. Today, we live in a large Victorian house and our picture looks at home in such a setting. When friends or visitors have asked about it, we tell them that they were my great, great grandparents.

"I can see the family resemblance between you and your great, great grandfather," is the usual comment, followed by, "But how come your great, great grandmother looked remarkably like Norma?"

"Ok, I will admit the truth. We are time-travellers!"

Daisy, Daisy...

A few months before we sold up and left Runcorn, we had posted letters to various establishments in Sydney to inquire about employment possibilities. Norma had been told by colleagues in the world of beauty therapy that English-trained therapists were highly sought-after in Australia. She had received an encouraging letter from a Mr. Simmons, the owner of a city-centre Hair and Beauty Salon, inviting her to contact him when she eventually arrives in Sydney. We decided to go on a reconnaissance mission, and made our way to the city centre. Norma didn't have the letter with her, but she could remember that the salon was called 'Daisy Bates' and was located in a precinct known as Centre Point. Incidentally, Daisy Bates was an Irish-born Australian who championed the rights of Aborigines in the 19th and 20th Centuries. The English fondness for excruciating puns as the name of a salon, had not reached Australia. If it had been English-owned, no doubt the salon would have had a name something like 'Didgeree Hairdo' or even 'Waxing Down Under'.

We went into this plush, air-conditioned world and found the salon, which was large, double-fronted with a marble-clad reception area.

"Wow, I would love to work there," exclaimed Norma, clearly impressed. "I will ring the owner tomorrow to inquire if there are any vacancies."

"Why not go in now?" I suggested, eager to become a kept-man, but careful not to appear to be *too* enthusiastic in encouraging my wife back into the world of work.

"I can't go in unannounced and dressed like this," she replied, while looking at a reflection of herself in a shop window.

"You look fine, and besides, Aussies don't stand on ceremony the way they do in England."

"Okay, I will just go to the reception desk and ask for an appointment."

"G'day, may I help you?" asked the receptionist, pleasantly.

"Good afternoon. Would it be possible to make an appointment to speak to the owner?" inquired Norma. The receptionist seemed slightly taken aback by this request, as if anticipating a complaint.

"Is there a problem?" she asked defensively.

"No, not at all. My name is Norma Meadows and Mr. Simmons wrote to me in England earlier this year inviting me to call in to see him."

"Oh, I see. Please take a seat while I ring him."

Almost immediately, a tall, immaculately dressed man swept flamboyantly through the salon. His gregarious manner and friendly word with staff and clients left us in no doubt that he was the owner. He came over, beaming a warm smile and greeted Norma with open arms as if he had known her for years.

"You have finally arrived."

"Yes, nice to meet you. Mr. Simmons, I presume?"

"Please call me Leonard."

"This is my husband, John."

He greeted me with a firm handshake, while glancing almost imperceptibly at my hairstyle. I use the word 'style' in its loosest sense, you understand.

"I wasn't sure if you would remember me," Norma remarked.

"Oh yes. I was impressed by your C.V., and jealous of your overland adventure."

"We only arrived yesterday, and I thought I would try to make an appointment to see you."

"No time like the present, come through to my office." Norma looked momentarily startled, but quickly regained her composure.

I resumed my seat and started to flick through some newspapers and magazines. I didn't even know the name of the Australian Prime Minister until I came across an article and photograph. It was Malcolm Fraser. Even though it was the cricket season, the sports pages still found space for football, (the Phillips Soccer League), and of course rugby league.

"Are you next?" asked a female voice, just as I was engrossed in an article about a change to the ferry times to Manly, wherever that was. When the same question was repeated, this time preceded by a deliberate cough, I looked up sharply as I realized that someone was speaking to me.

"Er, no I haven't got an appointment, but I think I need something doing with this," I answered, while pointing at my hair with a woeful expression. She checked at the reception and came back to tell me that she could fit me in now. We chatted congenially as she gradually transformed my hair back to something approaching normality.

An impressive sound system filtered music at a tolerable volume to underscore the general chit chat and clicking of scissors. Then something happened which surprised me and caused me to spin round in the swivel chair. Leo Sayer came on the radio, singing his latest chart hit; 'You Make Me Feel Like Dancing'. A row of half a dozen hairdressers, male and female, instantly stopped what they were doing and each picked up a hairbrush. There followed three minutes of singing, with a hairbrush for a microphone, and choreographed dancing of which a Motown group would have been proud. Looking around, I seemed to be the only client surprised by this impromptu show. After an appreciative round of applause, my hairdresser, Michelle, returned to the task in hand. She told me that they choose a particular song for a week or two and work out a routine. Looking back, if it happened these days the performance would be recorded on numerous i-phones and tablets before going viral on social media; whatever all that means.

Norma emerged from the office, accompanied by Mr. Simmons, just as I was getting up from the chair. She gave my haircut a nod of approval, and the three of us went to the reception area. Mr. Simmons shook hands with Norma and went back to his office after saying, "See you in the morning."

"So, you've got an appointment tomorrow?"

"No, I've got a job! I start tomorrow."

"Welcome to 'Daisy Bates'," said the receptionist.

I took out my wallet to pay for my haircut. "Do you give a staff family discount?" I inquired, without feeling the slightest pang of impertinence. I hadn't quite kicked my haggling habit just yet.

The following morning Phil and Heather and the others were up and gone by seven thirty.

"Good luck in your new job," I said to Norma, as she was about to leave the apartment.

"I'm looking forward to it," she replied cheerily, before adding pointedly, "What are *you* going to do today?"

"Oh, I thought I would take a stroll along Bondi Beach," I replied, quickly adding, "And I will put out a few feelers for a job."

Even though the beach was beginning to come alive with surfers and picnickers, I began to feel strangely alone. I realized that it was the first time I had actually been on my own since we departed London all those months ago. Norma and I had been in each other's company for twenty-four hours a day. Nobody along the beach gave me a second glance, but one or two gave me a wide berth when my right arm went into involuntary spasms. I felt as abandoned as Robinson Crusoe as I looked out across the ocean.

Back to School

Earlier that year I had also sent off speculative letters to some schools in Sydney. They included a brief curriculum vitae and an outline of our travel plans. I did receive a very nice letter from a Mr. Mark Bishop, the Headmaster of Cranbrook School. He wished me luck on my overland trek, and stated that he would like to meet me, and he invited me to contact him when I eventually arrive in Australia. I had packed his letter at the bottom of my bag, and furthermore, I had compiled a pocketsize photo album of my own drawings and paintings, together with a selection of my pupils' work.

I rang the school and asked the Headmaster's Secretary for an appointment to see Mr. Bishop. The secretary very politely, but firmly, inquired as to the reason for my request. I explained to her that the Headmaster had written to me in England, and that I was ringing at his invitation. That seemed to do the trick; I had managed to get past the gatekeeper. "Please hold," she instructed officiously. I waited patiently, expecting her to come back on the line with an appointment time. I was momentarily taken aback when she said,

"The Headmaster will speak to you now." A friendly voice then said,

"Mr. Meadows, so you finally made it to Sydney."

"Hello Mr. Bishop," I answered, "I wondered if you would remember me."

"I do indeed, and I have asked my secretary to retrieve your letter from her filing system." He invited me to visit the school the following morning.

That evening, Norma flopped down onto the sofa on the garage roof (or should I say patio?)

"How was your first day?" I asked.

"Exhausting."

"Too many clients?"

"No. Learning the moves for 'You Make Me Feel Like Dancing!"

Phil and Heather joined us, with a very welcome bottle of wine from a case they had purchased on a recent trip to the Hunter Valley. We toasted Norma's first day, and I was able to tell them that I had arranged an appointment at Cranbrook.

The following morning, I caught the bus from Bondi Beach to Double Bay, and walked a short distance to Cranbrook School. I was immediately impressed by the imposing building, which was beautifully situated with views of Sydney Harbour.

The Headmaster, Mark Bishop, was a smallish man with dark, thinning hair. His half-moon glasses and academic gown, gave him a studious appearance. This was enhanced by his timeless, oak-panelled study, which was furnished with polished wooden furniture, glass-fronted bookcases and leather-upholstered chairs. A trophy cabinet of cups, shields and pendants proudly displayed achievements in a wide range of activities such as athletics, cricket, rugby and inter-school debating competitions. I felt as though I had walked into the pages of R. D. Denderfield's novel 'To Serve Them All My Days'. The Headmaster greeted me with a firm handshake as he made immediate eye contact. His warm smile lit up his face and he put me at ease straight away. Over coffee, we chatted as he bombarded me with questions about the overland trek. He was genuinely interested and laughed when I told him one or two stories. However, the subject of a job was not mentioned, and it did not seem appropriate to blurt out 'Gis a job', like Yosser Hughes in Alan Bleasdale's 'Boys from the Blackstuff'. I broached the subject by showing an interest in some of the pupils' paintings hanging in his study, and I took out my pocketsize album for his perusal. Again, Mr. Bishop showed genuine interest and asked questions about my various paintings and drawings. I had been in his study about twenty minutes when he announced, "Right, let's get down to business. You are a young man looking for a teaching post and I will try to help you. At the moment there are no vacancies here at Cranbrook, but I will give you a couple of phone numbers and addresses, and you can mention my name." I informed him that my current visa allowed only temporary employment. Mr. Bishop dismissed this with a sweep of his hand, explaining that it would not be a problem.

My first feeling was one of disappointment, because I was hopeful during our conversation that there might be a vacancy. At the same time, I was grateful to Mr. Bishop for giving me his valuable time and pointing me in the right direction, which was, unfortunately, towards the door. I gave him my address and phone number and he came outside to the school driveway to shake hands and wish me luck. As I walked away, I looked back wistfully at the school, but at least I had some contacts to follow.

That evening Phil and Heather looked at the list of schools.

"A couple of these are north of the harbour. You would have to catch the Manly ferry every day."

"At least I know the new timetables," I responded wryly.

The following day I went for an aimless stroll to consider my options. I stopped at the Bondi Junction Hotel for a schooner of Toohey's, which was so cold that it gave me instant neuralgia. Being temporarily numb from the neck up seemed to crystallize my brain, and my thoughts focused on a North of England maxim: 'When in doubt, do now't'.

I have always been a great believer in fate, and something was telling me to hold back. Often in the past when I have waited, Micawber-like, for something to turn up, in most cases it has worked. Call it instinct, luck, a gut feeling or even a guardian angel. I decided not to make any telephone calls that day.

The very next morning, something *did* turn up. The phone rang, and as I picked up the receiver, I stretched over for a pen and notepad to take a message, naturally assuming that it would be for Phil or Heather. I was surprised when a female voice asked to speak to Mr. Meadows, in view of the fact that I had only been in the country for two days.

"Yes, Mr. Meadows speaking."

"Good morning, it's the Headmaster's secretary at Cranbrook School. Mr. Bishop wants to know if you have acted upon any of the contacts he gave you yesterday?"

"I have looked at the location of some of the schools, and I have started to compose a letter of application," I answered.

"In that case, could you come into school this afternoon to see Mr. Bishop regarding a last-minute vacancy?"

There is a story that when the 19 year-old Elvis Presley received a phone call at home from Sam Phillips' secretary at Sun Studios in Memphis, he was round there before she had put the phone down. My enthusiasm was not quite at that height, but you get the picture. I took the liberty of borrowing one of Phil's ties from his wardrobe. He was a lot bigger than me, but his tie fitted perfectly.

I turned up at Cranbrook expecting to be one of several candidates for interview, but the secretary was alone in the outer office. Mr. Bishop emerged from his office and greeted me warmly, inviting me to join him. After a few minutes of pleasant, inconsequential small talk, he told me that, the previous day, a female member of the Art department had been to see him to offer her resignation, with immediate effect. Spookily, I felt that it must have been at around the time that I was having my gut-feeling over an ice-cold beer. Mr. Bishop went on to tell me that the teacher's husband was in the Australian Air Force and that he was to be transferred, at short notice, to Queensland.

The Headmaster said simply, "Follow me, I will show you round the school." Everywhere was quiet because the school had 'broken-up' for Christmas, which, Down Under, also means the long summer holidays at the end of the academic year. The Art department overlooked an impressive cricket oval, with Sydney Harbour as a backdrop under a flawless blue sky. It was a world away, physically and metaphorically, from my previous school: a glass and steel rectangular building at the edge of a council estate in Runcorn.

As we walked around Cranbrook, I still presumed that this was a prelude to a formal interview in front of a panel of school governors. Mr. Bishop knocked politely on the door of the Bursar's Office before entering.

"Mr. Lloyd, I would like to introduce you to John Meadows, who will be joining our Art Department next term," he said matter-of-factly.

"Will I?" I asked with astonishment, while still shaking hands with the bursar.

"Yes, we will regard our chat the other day as your interview." He shook my hand vigorously and added, "Welcome to Cranbrook. I will leave you here to sort out all the formalities with the Bursar."

I spent the next half hour filling out a variety of forms, contracts and documents. I was signed-up to Medibank, Australia's Health Service, and the Bursar asked me for details of my, still non-existent, bank account. He recommended a branch in nearby Double Bay, an affluent area nicknamed Double Pay.

"So that's everything covered. You will be paid from the beginning of the academic year, January 1st, and we will be in touch with you with details about the beginning of the new term, which is in February."

"Hang on," I said, bemused, "Are you telling me that I will be paid for a month, before actually starting work?"

"Yes, provided you don't forget to let me have your new bank details. Have a great Christmas."

A great Christmas is exactly what we *did* have. Several of our Australian friends from the overland contacted us to invite us to office or house parties. Leonard Simmons, Norma's new boss, invited us to a party at his penthouse apartment, which had a panoramic view of Sydney Harbour. On Boxing Day, we joined a group to picnic in the glorious sunshine at Watson's Bay, at South Head at the mouth of Port Jackson, to watch the start of the annual Sydney to Hobart yacht race. The North and South Heads are dramatic sheer cliff formations that frame the gateway to the natural harbour, and the flotilla of yachts sailing through into the open Pacific is one of the most awe-inspiring spectacles in world sport.

After Christmas, Norma and I enjoyed exploring and getting to know our new home. Sydney is a city that has grown naturally, and evolved organically, as opposed to cities such as, say, Washington or Canberra, which have been planned and laid-out deliberately. The twisting streets of Sydney developed from random paths created by convicts and soldiers during the early days of the colony.

Port Jackson is the official title of the more commonly used name of Sydney Harbour. The first European to discover this huge inlet of the Pacific Ocean was Captain James Cook, who, surprisingly, did not enter the harbour, but simply sailed past the North and South Heads in 1770. Cook named it after a fellow Yorkshire man, Sir George Jackson, an Admiralty administrator who had mentored him and helped to further his career. European settlement started as a penal colony when the First Fleet arrived, under the command of Captain Arthur Phillip, on the 26th January 1788. This date is regarded as the birth of the nation, and today the 26th January is celebrated as Australia Day.

We now regarded ourselves as bona fide Sydneysiders. We could just as easily have been called Townshenders, since the city was named after Thomas Townshend. (That should be a *Two Million* Pound question). He was an 18th Century British politician who also happened to hold the title of Viscount Sydney.

As a build-up to the beginning of term at Cranbrook, Norma and I were invited to several functions and garden parties. Mr & Mrs Bishop were the perfect hosts and we were made very welcome by all the staff. Someone mentioned to me in conversation that my predecessor, one of only three female teachers at an all-boys school, just happened to be a former beauty queen; something like 'Miss Queensland'. Not much of an act to follow; like coming on after the Beatles at the Royal Variety Performance.

I quickly settled into the school routine. It was apparent immediately that the history and traditions of Cranbrook play an important part in the ethos of the school. The building was originally a grand house built in the 1860s and owned by Robert Tooth. (Not *another* House of the Tooth). He was a member of a family of brewers, and he named his house Cranbrook, after his birthplace in Kent. It changed hands a few times until 1901, when the Government of New South Wales acquired the building, to provide a residence for the State Governor. Some of these Governors, for example, Sir Harry Rawson and Sir Gerald Strickland, are remembered today as the names of Houses within the school. Cranbrook was sold in 1917 to a group who became founders of the school. The Reverend Fredrick Perkins, a Church of England clergyman, was appointed as the first Headmaster, and, in July 1918, the school was declared open.

The general ethos of the school was one of an all-boys English Public School, the Founding Fathers having been pupils at several such schools. There were marble busts, statues and countless historic photographs. I even spotted one of our old friend Charles Kingsford-Smith visiting Cranbrook in 1928.

The boys were either boarders, who lived in dormitories or study bedrooms during term time, or day boys who travelled into school from miles around. The rows of freestanding roll-top baths, antiquated showers and Edwardian tiles looked like a ready-made film set for the movie 'Chariots of Fire' (which actually became the case at one of my future schools; Cowley in St. Helens, which was used for location filming).

It would seem appropriate that a Victorian building such as Cranbrook, with its Hitchcockian setting on a hill, should have an obligatory ghost. (Especially in view of the fact that a certain P. T. Frankenstein appears on the school register of 1943). The ghost of the second owner of the house has been sighted. He was Robert Towns, who died at Cranbrook in 1873, and his ghost is said to have appeared in his bedroom weeks after his death. During my time at the school, this room was a shower room in Rawson House, directly above the Master's Common Room. I distinctly remember that the shower was not used at all one day. 'Psycho' had been on television the night before.

Dreamtime

The art department had a reasonable collection of objects and artefacts for observational studies. I was glad that I had collected some of my own during my travels and I was able to start off projects based on Indian, Thai or Arabic cultures. The boys produced some excellent kites, lino and silk-screen prints in addition to drawings and paintings. Inevitably, Aboriginal Art featured prominently and I enjoyed finding out more about the subject.

Research has estimated that Aborigine Art dates back thousands of years, possibly from 30,000 to 50,000 years. Conversely, it is one of the most recent styles of art to be developed commercially; as recently as the early 1970s. Today, this form of art can be found on ties, scarves, table mats and the ubiquitous boomerangs for sale in the tourist craft shops. The price of authentic contemporary paintings on canvas, stone or bark has risen exponentially in recent years. A few years ago, an Australian Aborigine, Sid Domic, played with distinction for Warrington and Hull Rugby League Clubs. In his spare time, he pursued his hobby as an artist, following the traditions of ancient Aboriginal Art. He was featured in a BBC Television documentary, making a painting and explaining his work, which was in the distinctive dot style. Subsequently, he sold his entire collection and was inundated with commissions. From what I remember, he was a top quality player, but his hobby soon financially outstripped his rugby league career. Rather than sign a new contract along the dotted line, he decided that it was more lucrative and less painful to actually *make* dotted lines instead.

This distinctive style of Aboriginal dot painting originated in the desert regions, while other different styles came from other regions. For example, the small paintings on bark and rock came from Western Australia, while the crosshatching style, known as rarrk, is from Arnhem Land in the Northern Territory. The importance of painting to the Aborigine people is due largely to the fact that they never developed their own *written* language.

Consequently, other forms of communication, such as dance, storytelling, song and art, take on much greater significance in recording their heritage. The history and culture of the Aborigine people have been handed down over millennia through these art forms. The stories, called Jukurrpa, focused on 'The Dreamtime', the period when the world was created.

In addition to teaching art, I was asked by the Master in charge of rugby, Martin Pitt, to coach the under 15s rugby union team. This was mainly due to the fact that in my letter of application I had mentioned that I had played for England in the historic first-ever Universities Rugby League International a few years earlier. The score line had a touch of irony, as France beat us 18-12. I enjoyed coaching and organising the Cranbrook team, which had some talented players, and we had a good season. Being involved in rugby resulted in fate guiding me once more. I have mentioned previously that certain incidences of fate, or pure good luck, has often happened to me. Like being in the right place at the right time to be appointed a master at Cranbrook, or, just before Norma and I got married, I secured a teaching job, a lucrative summer job and a house; all in one day. Martin invited me to join the rugby staff for a weekly get-together, after school on Fridays, in the bar of the nearby Eastern Suburbs Rugby Union club. It was an opportunity to get to know colleagues and relax at the end of a working week over a few midis or schooners of Tooheys.

After a few weeks, Martin asked me, "John, are you still looking for a flat?"

"Yes, we are still sharing with a New Zealand couple in Bondi Beach."

"An old boy of the school has been in touch to inquire if any Cranbrook teacher is looking for accommodation. Apparently, he has to go to England on business at very short notice, and he wants someone honest, reliable and respectable to take over his house." Martin paused for comic effect, before adding, sardonically, "I couldn't think of anyone who fits that description, so I thought I would ask you."

I rang the number that Martin had given me, and I spoke to Mr. Mike Preston to arrange a meeting.

"Kent Road? Rose Bay?" exclaimed Phil and Heather when I showed them the address, "That's definitely at the posh end of the market."

Number 28 was half-way along a tree lined cul-de-sac, situated opposite the Indonesian Embassy. I rang the doorbell, a huge ship's bell on the front porch, which I had to quickly grab with my hand to dampen the sound. It was loud enough to bring in ships through the Heads. Mike Preston greeted us gregariously and welcomed us inside. The house was a beautiful, half-timbered, 1930s English-style, detached building with mature gardens of bougainvillea, poinsettia, azaleas, and begonias. A well-tended lawn had a path, which led to a hexagonal-shaped summerhouse. Paradoxically, beautiful gardens such as this are still referred to in Australia as the *back yard*.

The house had been redeveloped a few years previously into three apartments: Mike owned the ground floor, an elderly couple lived on the top floor, and a lady in her early sixties lived alone on the lower ground floor, accessed by a steep driveway.

As he showed us around his large two-bedroom apartment, Mike enthused about his time at Cranbrook and told us that he had maintained regular contact with the school. He had to leave Australia almost immediately, and wanted to simply walk out and hand the keys over. I began to realize that it was likely to be way beyond what we wanted to pay in rent.

"We would love to live here," said Norma, "but it depends on what you are asking for rent."

"How does fifty dollars a month sound?" he asked matter-of-factly. It was about a quarter of what we were expecting. "You are a teacher at Cranbrook, so that's good enough for me from a security point of view, and after all, you will be looking after all my worldly possessions." We shook hands on the deal and he asked me to visit his solicitor's office in Double Bay to pick up a rent book and sign the relevant forms.

"Let's have a drink to celebrate. I will ring Nita, who lives downstairs, to come up to meet you."

She was a very elegant, silver-haired lady who greeted us with a warm smile. She christened me Johnno straight away. We didn't see Mike again, and we moved in a couple of days later, not that we had much to move.

Scrummaging Nuns

We settled into our new home very quickly, and over subsequent months we became very good friends with Nita. We got to know her daughter, son-in-law and grandchildren, who were regular visitors, and they invited us out many times. A memorable evening was a visit to Sydney Opera House to see the classical guitarist John Williams perform with The Sydney Symphony Orchestra. The acoustics inside the concert hall were impressive, but achieved, I feel, at the expense of aesthetics. I was surprised to see plain, stark concrete walls, when I expected modern avant-garde design to match the exterior of the building.

The Sydney Opera House is a meeting place of ancient and ultra-modern. It stands on a promontory, which has the Aborigine name of Bennelong Point, named after an Aboriginal senior man called Woollarawarre Bennelong, who lived in the area and watched the First Fleet arrive. The equivalent today would be like watching an alien spacecraft landing on earth. Eventually, Bennelong came to live amongst the settlers and he learned to speak English. Bizarrely, he became a friend of Governor Phillip, who had a house built for him on the site where the Opera House now stands.

In common with numerous other iconic, revolutionary buildings throughout the world, the Sydney Opera House had a long tortuous, gestation period. The project was first proposed as long ago as the 1950s and a design competition was launched. Over two hundred architectural designs were submitted in 1956, and Jorn Utzon, a Danish architect, was announced the winner. Inevitably, if history teaches us anything, the estimates of time and costs escalated exponentially. Seven million Australian dollars exploded to over one hundred million, while four years expanded to fourteen. Work commenced in 1959 and it finally opened in 1973. After the first seven years of building, the Government became so exasperated that payment to the architect stopped. Unsurprisingly, Utzon resigned and left the country. Comparatively speaking, fourteen years seems to me to be quite reasonable when compared to the building of the (still to be completed) Cathedral of Familia Sagrada in Barcelona. Furthermore, compared to the Gothic Cathedrals of Europe, the Sydney Opera House was thrown-up overnight.

Antiques Roadshow

Not long after moving into the apartment, we invited a few friends round for a drink, as a low-key housewarming. Also, we had a guest to surprise our overland friends; Nick had arrived after his stay at a Tibetan Monastery. It was an opportunity for Phil and Heather to meet some of our overland friends and pick-up some travel tips for their forthcoming tour of Europe. They were leaving a few days later, and it was a sad day when we said goodbye. They were excited to be flying to London for the Antipodean rite of passage: touring Europe in a VW Campervan, culminating in a pilgrimage to the Munich Oktoberfest. They couldn't wait to get to Earl's Court in London to buy a van. Their departure gave us itchy feet, and made us look forward to our own future travels; once bitten by the travel bug, the only cure is to get back on the road again. Margaret, who was an Antiques Dealer, was particularly fascinated by some of Mike's furniture and ornaments. She carefully handled one or two pieces and gave us an impromptu lecture on the history and value of Mike's possessions. Colin volunteered to drive over to Conn's Chippy in Bondi for fish and chips, not forgetting of course their famous battered king prawns. We dished up the food in the traditional English manner; on a newspaper. Oh yes, we certainly knew how to treat valued guests. As Norma handed out the cutlery, Margaret's mouth dropped open and her eyes bulged as she scrutinized her knife and fork assiduously.

"What are these?" she exclaimed.

"They are called *knives* and *forks*," I interjected, in a mock condescending tone. "Do you not have such implements in your house?"

Everyone laughed, but Margaret put down her fish and chips and concentrated on the cutlery.

"Do you realize," she announced, with slow deliberation and a disbelieving smile, "that *this* is William IV cutlery? It is solid silver and worth an absolute fortune!"

So there we were, tucking into fish and chips from a page of The Sydney Morning Herald, using extremely valuable, hallmarked-silver William IV knives and forks.

"Can I get anyone another drink?" I asked, whilst screwing up my newspaper.

"Yes, please," replied Margaret, whimsically, "I don't suppose you have a bottle of Chateau Mouton-Rothschild, 1945 vintage of course. A snip at a mere £5000 per *glass*."

"Certainly, madam," I responded sniffily, in my best English butler accent, "Would you like it served in a midi or a schooner?"

Three Petrified Sisters

During a school holiday, Norma and I decided to visit the Blue Mountains, about 30 miles from Sydney. We took the train to the town of Katoomba and booked into the Carrington Hotel, which was perfectly situated as a base for walking and sightseeing. The surrounding landscape was dramatic, with sandstone cliffs, deep gorges and dense woodland. Eucalyptus trees release their oil into the air, giving the mountains a blue haze, from which the name is derived. The area has been popular with tourists for many decades, and it was interesting to see sepia photographs of visitors in the 1920s. They reminded me very much of similar photos of Windermere in the Lake District.

We walked to Echo Point for a stunning view of the iconic landmark of the Blue Mountains: The Three Sisters. This is a ridge of sandstone peaks, at Jamison Valley, which has been formed by erosion over thousands of years. There is also a smaller peak at the end, which we were told is called The Little Brother. The name derives from an Aboriginal legend, which tells the story that the pillars were once three beautiful sisters, Meehni, Wimlah and Gunnedoo, who were turned into stone. They had fallen in love with three brothers from another tribe, but were forbidden to marry. The brothers decided to capture the three sisters, resulting in a tribal battle. An elder of the women's tribe turned the three sisters into stone for protection, intending to reverse the spell when the battle was over. Unfortunately, he was killed so the sisters remain as stone monuments forever.

The most fabulous view of all was from the Scenic Skyway, a glass-bottomed aerial cable car across the gorge, which provided a sensational view of Wentworth Falls.

Twenty miles west of Katoomba are the Jenolan Caves, which are the oldest in the world (340 million years). More than 400 limestone caves have been discovered since 1830, and further exploration continues to this day. They are awe-inspiringly spectacular, and the only other caves I have been in which can compare are the Cango Caves in South Africa. Each of Jenolan's caves has a different quality.

My favourite was The Lucas Cave, which contains the Cathedral Chambers; famous for superb acoustics, and is used regularly as a concert venue, including international concert pianists.

"I wonder if Mr. Sweeney has ever performed here?" Norma mused, superciliously.

Echo, Tango, Foxtrot

Yes, we had our very own concert pianist at home: our neighbours, in the apartment above us, Mr. & Mrs. Sweeney. They were far more elusive than Nita. There was the occasional sighting of Mr. Sweeney lurking amongst the shrubbery, and neither of us can ever remember seeing Mrs. Sweeney. I often wondered if his reclusive wife was kept upstairs, like Mrs. Rochester in 'Jane Eyre'. Mr. Sweeney was a keen pianist, and we had been warned by Nita that he liked to play every Sunday between six and seven. We could set our clocks by it. Those of you who have read my previous book will perhaps remember that I described the lady who played the piano at school assemblies as a cross between Les Dawson and Thunderclap Newman, playing 'all the right notes, but not necessarily in the right order'. Well, compared to Mr. Sweeney, she was Rachmaninov. Between six and seven o'clock on Sundays, everything was overpowered by sounds from above, vibrating through the floorboards and rattling the crockery in the kitchen. Television or radio was out of the question, and any conversation could only be conducted by 'mee-maw', as if in a Victorian textile mill. Following the adage; 'If you can't beat 'em, join 'em', we decided to dance to the music. Every Sunday, we pushed back the furniture and practised the foxtrot, tango, waltz and quickstep. Our dancing was about as accomplished as Mr. Sweeney's playing, so we made a good team. Even Mike Preston's china figurines joined in the dancing, as they vibrated along the mantelpiece. Figures magically came to life as if it was Tchaikovsky's 'Nutcracker', or Rossini's 'La Boutique Fantasque'. We tried our best to keep from laughing, and, with mock-seriousness, we exaggerated head positions and body posture. Actually, I think we became quite good. Perhaps not. Our personal pianist had a limited repertoire, which we called, 'Mr. Sweeney's Opus'. Perhaps 'Mr. Sweeney's Hopeless' would have been a more accurate description.

One Sunday evening, and without a word to Norma, I went into our bedroom and emerged right on cue as the music began, spot on six. I coughed extravagantly to get her attention, and Norma lowered the Sunday paper she was reading. I stood proudly, formally dressed in a black jacket and trousers, wearing one of Mike's black velvet bow ties. (It was the 1970s after all). Norma laughed out loud, but, when I turned round to reveal a white card with a competitor's number pinned to my back, she almost drowned-out Mr. Sweeney.

Ned Kelly and a Pair of Old Boots

For the benefit of my exam classes, I organised a school trip to the NSW Gallery in Sydney, to view a visiting exhibition: The American Photo-Realists.

The gallery, the fourth largest in Australia, is located in a beautiful setting in parkland at the Domain, with panoramic views across the harbour. It seems incongruous that such a traditional, Graeco-Roman building, with a portico and Ionic columns, should share a landscape with the Nuns and the Coathanger. It is as if London's National Gallery has been tele-ported like an 18th Century Italian Capriccio painting.

Even though our school trip was specifically to view the work of American Photo-Realist, we also found time to look at some of the permanent collection. I was particularly interested in Australian paintings. As we will discover later, when we move on to the South Pacific, the earliest paintings of newly-discovered lands were either topographical, scientific or botanical. They were usually the work of a ship's artist or botanist.

Basically, they were European paintings transposed to an alien environment. Cloud formations and trees tended to be almost a pastiche of Turner, Constable or the Dutch landscape painter Ruisdael. Eventually, an Australian style of painting emerged, and the gallery of NSW has superb examples. In the 1880s and 90s a distinctive style evolved; Australian Impressionism. Artist Tom Roberts returned from Europe greatly influenced by the French Impressionists. His oil painting, called 'Bailed-up', depicts a stagecoach robbery by bush rangers in the parched outback. It glows with light and atmosphere, and the snapshot, informal pose of the horses reminded me of Dega's racehorses.

A1947 oil painting called 'Sofala', by John Drysdale, tends towards the surrealistic, as the bleak, desolate town of Sofala radiates heat, light and the despair of a drought-stricken, eroded area. I felt the heat just standing in front of the painting.

One of Australia's most famous painters was William Dobell. Often, his portraits were satirical and slightly out of proportion. His subject matter and technique were influenced 19th Century French painter Daumier and his famous painting, 'The Cypriot', reminds me of El Greco.

The first Australian to achieve real international stature in painting was Sidney Nolan. In 1946 he painted the Ned Kelly series of pictures in which he depicted the Australian landscape boldly, in brilliant colour. In the movies, Ned Kelly was portrayed, by, of all people, Mick Jagger. Has there *ever* been a greater miscasting in the history of the movies? It is as if our old friend Charles Hawtrey was given the role of 'Rocky'. Ned Kelly must have been spinning in his armour.

After lunch we moved on to the modern exhibition.

"Sir, what is the point of this?" asked two of the boys scornfully, as they looked down their noses at a pair of well-worn, old brown shoes being displayed on a plinth. "How can they pass *this* off as art?" they added rhetorically.

"This is merely following a tradition dating back to the early twentieth century, when artists presented ready-made objects as works of art," I explained.

The boys rolled their eyes and gave me a woeful look, which made me determined to persevere. A couple of other boys joined us around the plinth, and, in my peripheral vision, I sensed that one of the uniformed attendants was eavesdropping our conversation.

"For example, Pablo Picasso put together a bicycle seat and handlebars and called it 'Bull's Head'." My class remained expressionless and unimpressed. By now, the gallery attendant had sidled over to join our group. He gave me a faint smile and nod of approval as I proceeded with my impromptu lecture.

"In 1917, a French artist named Marcel Duchamp shocked the art world by taking a white porcelain urinal, and signing it with his nom de plume: R. Mutt. He called his ready-made sculpture 'Fountain'." The boys looked at me in a collective disbelief.

"A *urinal*?" someone finally blurted out, "Like the ones in the *Dunny*?"

The boys turned to the gallery officer and said, "Fair dinkum?"

"Fair dinkum, mate," he replied.

I was determined to win the group over, and as I began to give further examples, such a Duchamp's 'Bottle Rack', the attendant stepped forward and took out a pen from his top pocket. He leaned forward and tapped one of the old boots, but instead of the expected sound of a dull thud of plastic on leather, it was a 'ping, ping' sound. Everyone, me included, stood wide-eyed as we realized that the battered, creased, leather shoes and laces were actually made of pottery. Suddenly, as if by magic, the object of such ridicule had been transformed into something fantastic and unbelievable, as the boys enthused about the shoes on the plinth. It was a perfect example of trompe l'oeil, or trick of the eye. It certainly fooled us, and the attendant had, rather playfully, allowed me to soldier-on about 'found objects' and 'ready-mades'. I could have taken out my crystal ball, (they come free with the flux capacitor and the De Lorean time machine,) and shown my class the future: unmade beds, calves sawn in half and pickled sharks. I think it would have resulted in not so much rolling eyes, but rolling in the aisles.

The rest of the exhibition included examples of American Photorealism: pictures of such meticulous airbrushed detail that they are indistinguishable from photographs. Subject-matter tended to be mundane; pick-up trucks, gas stations and diners, but these were reproduced with such accuracy that they become compelling. The viewer cannot help but scrutinise things which would have otherwise been ignored or taken for granted; rust, reflections in chrome, refractions through glass. Personally, they put me in mind of oil paintings by the 15th Century Flemish artist Jan Van Eyck, who remains unsurpassed in my view.

As we left the gallery, I was intrigued by the antics of some couples in the park. (No, it's not what you think). They were standing in pairs, facing each other, a few feet apart, with hands held out at waist height. I wondered if it was some form of oriental meditation, like Tai Chi; the kind of thing you see in parks in China and Japan. They all stood, smiling and motionless, while being photographed from the side. My confused expression caused some of the boys to come over to me.

“Sir, do you know what they are doing?” asked one of the boys, with a knowing smile.

“Not a clue,” I confessed.

“Follow us, and we will show you what is going on.”

We walked across the grass, and the boys positioned me behind one of the photographers. The optical illusion was fascinating. I was looking at a real life, trompe l’ oeil: two people were ‘holding’ Sydney Opera House, as if it was a model resting on their hands. There are other examples of this kind of photographic trickery in various parts of the world. The most famous example is in Pisa. Look at any photograph of the Leaning Tower, and I guarantee that on the surrounding lawns you will see people posing with their hands up to prevent it from falling over.

My class thoroughly enjoyed the exhibition. Back in the art room at school, it led to some debate about the paintings and sculptures we had seen. What previously could be dismissed as just faithful copying, could now be seen as a means of enabling the viewer to appreciate the aesthetic qualities found in mundane, everyday objects.

“Sir, can I go to the toilet please?” asked one of the boys, towards the end of the lesson.

“Can’t you wait until the bell goes?”

“No, sir, I need to look at the urinals for some artistic inspiration.”

Hair on a G-string

The front door of our apartment opened into a reception room, which Mike had converted into a library. Floor-to-ceiling bookshelves covered the walls. Mike had told us that many of the books were quite valuable, including one or two first editions, and he obviously liked to display his collection of leather-bound volumes. It looked like a stage-set for a play such as 'Sleuth'. I would often sit in there playing my guitar, wondering if Mr. & Mrs. Sweeney were upstairs dancing, while trying to stifle their laughter. Clarry had given me one of his old guitars so that I could practise some of the chords, songs and techniques he had taught me at numerous camp sites across the world. Also, I had been given some lessons at Cranbrook from one of the music teachers: A Spaniard, named Tony Guitarra; which, coincidentally, is Spanish for guitar. A man born to the job.

One Sunday afternoon, I was trying to master a particular chord sequence when I detected a slight movement at the outer limits of my peripheral vision. Instinctively, I turned my head towards the bookshelf on my right. I couldn't see anything, and assumed that it must be my imagination, or, perhaps, the sunlight flickering through the window. Barely half a minute later, I sensed the same feeling, and, while continuing to strum, I casually looked over again. My blood turned cold, and a shiver ran down my spine as I felt the hair on the back of my neck stand up. A *huge* tarantula was emerging from the top of a row of books. It's long, hairy legs were beginning to edge over the front as I froze and stopped playing. The spider also froze, as if it knew that it had been spotted. My hands felt as cold as a corpse's, but I decided to resume strumming gently, while making sure that I didn't lose sight of our unwelcome visitor. Sure enough, the tarantula crept along 'The Complete Works of William Shakespeare', before beginning its descent. It made its way down the spine of 'The Mayor of Casterbridge', and headed towards 'Bleak House'. That would be an apt description of our house, if it had escaped. Earlier, I described the room as being like a stage-set for 'Sleuth'. Well, change that to 'Deathtrap'. The tarantula was the size of my fist, and reminded me of the ones we had seen in Pokhara in Nepal. I continued to play the guitar in the belief that a sudden silence would cause it to adopt a motionless stance, before making a sprint for cover.

My big worry, apart from a tortuous, excruciating death, was that I must not lose sight of it. It was like a scene from a James Herbert horror novel. As the tarantula slowly made its way across the carpet, it seemed to grow bigger. Perhaps it was my imagination, but it was starting to take on the dimensions of the aliens in 'War of the Worlds'. It reminded me of the giant spider in the James Bond movie 'Dr No', which was set in Jamaica. Sean Connery was asleep in bed and he was woken-up by a stirring under his sheets, as it were. A terrifying, hairy tarantula crept along his hairy, terrified body as he lay motionless, sweating profusely. So, what did he do? He waited until it crawled onto the pillow, and then he flicked it on to the floor. He hit it with his shoe in a dramatic sequence, with each blow accentuated by musical accompaniment. What was good enough for James Bond, was good enough for me. Slowly, very slowly, I used the heel of my foot to push my shoe off the other foot. Thank goodness for slip-ons. The tarantula slowly crept by, and I continued playing as if I was one of the snake charmers we had seen in India. My heart was thumping and I was starting to sweat like Sean Connery. It came within range and I could not delay any longer, as it would soon start to move away from me towards the bookshelf on the other side of the room. I would only have one chance. If it escaped and disappeared, I am afraid that going to bed that night, or any other night, would have not been an option. Extreme arachnophobia tends to result in severe insomnia. I stopped playing, and the tarantula instantly stopped dead in its tracks. I swiftly threw down the guitar, picked up my shoe, and leapt forward. He was away at incredible speed but I managed a glancing blow, which slowed him down, momentarily. Fortunately, I caught him clean with the second blow and then followed up, James Bond-style, with a couple more to finish him off. All that was missing was the musical accompaniment, although the wooden floorboards amplified the sound. I sat down on the chair and wiped my brow. The door to the lounge opened very slowly, and Norma hesitantly popped her head round. I was too exhausted to speak. I pointed at the massive 'splat' on the carpet and held up the bottom of my shoe. An explanation wasn't necessary.

"I thought someone had burst in and attacked you," she exclaimed in horror.

"If I had the choice, I think I would sooner confront a burglar."

First Name on My Team Sheet

At Cranbrook, I had made it clear from the outset that I had entered Australia on a temporary visa. No one at the school seemed overly concerned, and there were several foreigners on the staff, I just hoped that I could sort something out before our visas expired. One afternoon, I was sitting in the Masters' Common Room selecting my rugby team for that weekend's match. Martin came over to me and asked casually, "John, have you made any progress with your residency application?"

"Er, no," I replied hesitantly.

In addition to being Head of Rugby, Martin was also Deputy Headmaster, which caused me to wonder if his question was an official inquiry on behalf of the school.

"Do you know who his father is?" he asked me, pointing to the scrum-half

on the under 15s team sheet in front of me.

"No." I replied, intrigued.

"He just happens to be a Member of Parliament in Canberra, representing the Eastern Suburbs district of Sydney."

I raised my eyebrows and nodded, trying to look impressed by this revelation.

"What's more," continued Martin, with a knowing smile, "He is a member of the Government, with special responsibility for... Immigration."

Now this did make me sit up.

"I have known him for years. I saw him in Sydney the other day and I mentioned you during the course of our conversation. He is coming to the match on Saturday, and he is going to have a word with you to offer his help."

"That's great, thank you." Just as Martin was opening the door to leave, I held up my team sheet and said, "Martin, I think the scrum-half position is sorted for the rest of the season."

During half-time of the rugby match, the MP introduced himself, and following a brief chat about the game, he assured me that he would look into my application, Norma and I were granted permanent residency status not long after.

A Gold Medallist... at Après Ski

Colin and Barry invited us to join them on a skiing holiday, suggesting that four of us could drive to Thredbo, in the Snowy Mountains. We had never been skiing before, so we eagerly accepted.

The roads were largely empty and the landscape was open and panoramic. We took turns driving, and my only instruction was to beware of kangaroos; not something that features in the English Highway Code. At regular intervals, there would appear yellow warning signs which featured the distinctive silhouette of a kangaroo.

We stopped at a popular tourist destination on the coast, where kangaroos would emerge from the shelter of Eucalyptus trees and approach us. They were used to being fed, and had almost childlike human traits as they gathered round us. Norma was feeding a small group, and talking to them as if they were pets. One smaller kangaroo even tapped her on the forearm and gave her a look as if to say; 'What about me?', when she inadvertently missed him out.

The Snowy Mountains are the highest range in Australia, and the highest peak is Mount Kosciusko, discovered by a Polish explorer who named it in honour of a Polish politician. Thredbo is built in the style of an Alpine village, and we had booked into a chalet-style hostel. On our first morning, we were met with blizzard conditions, and I have never been so cold in my life, which probably sounds surprising for a country like Australia.

Before I even had a chance to reach the nursery slopes, I fell off the ski lift and broke my finger. I had watched carefully, as I stood in the queue, trying to study the technique of how to sit on the continuously moving chair-lift. Nothing to it, I thought. When it was our turn, we were instructed by the attendant to stand side-by-side on our skis, and watch out for the chair-lift as it approached. We sat down together, but unfortunately I wasn't quick enough raising my feet, and my skis got stuck in the snow. This propelled me forward, causing the chair-lift to hit me on the back of the head, knocking me face down, spread-eagled in the snow. As I fell, I took Norma with me. Just as we started to stand up, I heard a loud shout from skiers in the queue, "Look behind you!" Yes, it really was turning into a pantomime. The next chair-lift was rapidly approaching, so we quickly threw ourselves to the side. I hit the barrier, and felt a sharp pain in my left hand. I had managed to break my left index finger. I stood up, caught a glimpse of my reflection in a plate glass window; the abominable snowman came to mind. The people in the queue all started to laugh, which was only to be expected from a bunch of Aussies watching a Pom fall from grace, even though two of them were our friends. All I could do in response, was to bow theatrically, as if I was Raymond Briggs' 'Snowman'.

"You okay, mate?" asked the lift attendant, as he handed me my skis and poles. He then lined us up for the next lift, even though I was ready to give up there and then. This time, I lifted my feet so high that I almost fell over backwards. My broken finger started to throb as I tried to support my hand in the hope that the freezing air would numb the pain. Every time we went over a pylon the vibration reverberated directly to my finger. Fortunately, Barry, being a doctor, was able to put on a temporary splint and bandage my hand at the ski lodge at the top of the run.

I made a valiant attempt to master the nursery slopes, but I had to concede defeat. I spent the rest of the day in front of the log fire enjoying hot Glühwein, while watching through the huge plate glass window as the others had fun in the snow. Every snow cloud has a silver lining; over the next six weeks I mastered bar chords on my guitar.

The Grave Robbers?

"John, I am organising an expedition for Cranbrook's outdoor-pursuit group, and I was wondering if you would design a logo for the Landrover," asked Roger, a colleague at school.

"Yes, I would be happy to help. Let me have some details."

"We are going to follow, partway, in the footsteps of Burke and Wills."

"Burke and Wills?" I replied, somewhat perplexed.

"You *have* heard of them, haven't you?"

"Yes, I think so. Weren't they grave-robbing, body snatchers in Edinburgh in the 19th Century?" I answered vaguely, dredging up factual trivia from the deep recesses of my memory bank.

Roger's brow furrowed as he scratched his head. "I think you must be confusing them with Burke and Hare," he eventually responded, with the merest hint of condescension, "Burke and Wills were outback explorers."

"Of course they were," I laughed, with a touch of bravado, hoping to bluff my way out of my general ignorance of Australian history. I don't think I was too convincing. To be honest, I thought that perhaps Burke and Hare could have been transported to a penal colony in New South Wales, and re-tracing their footsteps could have been along some escape route. Since body-snatching and grave robbery would not be my specialist subject on Mastermind, I thought that trying to justify my lack of knowledge would be pointless.

Besides, mentioning things like convicts, transportation and penal colonies could be the wrong subject to bring up in conversation with a Sydneysider.

Roger gave me a little information booklet, which outlined his proposed school expedition. I learned that Robert Burke, an Irishman, and William Wills, an Englishman, were the first men to cross Australia from south to north, in 1861. They were sent by the Victorian Government to travel from Melbourne to the Gulf of Carpentaria. They completed the journey successfully, but in all other respects, the expedition was a disaster. They both died of starvation at Cooper's Creek on the return journey. It is surprising that Burke was ever chosen as leader of the small party. He had no experience in exploration, and he had little knowledge of bush craft or how to live off the land. Furthermore, his man-management and decision-making skills left a lot to be desired. They died due to a combination of incompetence and bad luck.

I produced a design for a logo, which was displayed on the Landrover. Channel 10 Television loaned the school an expensive TV camera to record the expedition. It seems an extremely generous gesture, but the owner of the TV company just happened to be the father of one of our pupils. He was Australian's richest man, Kerry Packer, whose son, James, was in the Cranbrook Prep School.

Courtesy of the Road

Nita's daughter, Robyn, picked me up from home one day, to take me down to Sydney Harbour to go water skiing with her husband. The children, Jenny and Mark, who were four and seven respectively, were in their seats in the back of the car. They gave me a beaming smile as I climbed into the front passenger seat. At the bottom of Kent Road, Robyn signalled to turn right onto New South Head Road. She waited for the next car to slow down in order for us to join the traffic.

"Give the nice man a wave," she suggested cheerily to the children.

They duly obliged by leaning over and giving him *the finger*. They followed up by gesticulating vigorously with clenched fists pumping in an up-and-down motion. Their grotesquely contorted facial expressions completed the performance. I caught a brief glimpse of this out of the corner of my eye, but Robyn witnessed the full display in her rear-view mirror. She gasped in horror as she pulled over and slammed on the brakes. As the car shrieked to a halt, she turned to her children and screamed.

"What on earth do you think you are playing at?!!"

The children were momentarily stunned by this outburst from their mother. They sat there in wide-eyed bewilderment, and Jenny's bottom lip started to quiver as tears welled up. I managed to keep a straight face, but it was difficult.

Finally, Mark answered, timidly, "But you told us to wave at the man."

"Yes, but you do *not* wave to other drivers like *that.*"

"But mummy," he pleaded, innocently, "*That's* how Grandma *always* waves."

Britannia Waives the Rules

1977 was a memorable year in many ways, and, in Australia, the Queen's Silver Jubilee was the most significant event. When The Royal Yacht Britannia was due to arrive in Sydney, our Australian friends booked tickets on one of the harbour ferries, which were open to private hire for the day.

As we approached the ferry terminal, huge crowds were everywhere: around the Rocks Centre, in front of the Opera House, along the Harbour Bridge and along the north and south shores of Sydney Harbour. Everyone, without exception, was decked out in Union Jack scarves and hats, while waving Union Flags of all sizes. The panorama made the Last Night of the Proms seem almost unpatriotic. We sailed out towards the Heads as part of a flotilla of hundreds of vessels of all shapes and sizes. It seemed as though anything that could float had put out to sea, Dunkirk-style. There were kayaks, canoes, rowing boats, powerboats, small dinghies, ocean-going yachts in full sail, and multi-million-dollar luxury cruisers. As the Royal Yacht entered Port Jackson through the North and South Heads, she gave a blast of her horn in acknowledgement as she sailed majestically towards her destination at Circular Quay. The welcoming flotilla sailed alongside on both sides, and our ferry managed to sail much closer than security would normally allow.

"I hope I don't chunder in front of the Queen," remarked Colin, patting his stomach.

"Chunder?" I responded.

"Yeah, haven't you heard that one before? It means throwing up!"

As Colin leaned over the side, Barry took over and explained further:

On the long sea voyages from England, frequent bouts of seasickness would cause passengers and sailors alike to lean over the side of the ship and shout, 'Watch under!'. This was eventually truncated to 'chunder'. In the 1980s, the word became widely used after the Australian band 'Men at Work' made the record 'Down-Under'. You remember; 'I come from a land down under, where women glow and men chunder'. That's right, a worldwide, number-one hit about throwing-up and vegemite sandwiches!

The wake and swells caused by so many vessels in Sydney Harbour created a soaking spray, and the white water accentuated the cerulean blue of the sea and the cobalt blue sky. Together with the proliferation of red, white and-blue, it created a never-to-be-forgotten sight. The Queen and Prince Phillip came on deck to wave their appreciation. (Chunder-free we hoped, since we were directly below). I doubt if Henry VIII would have had a more colourful reception as he travelled on the Royal Barge down the Thames from Hampton Court. I felt as though I was part of a modern day painting by the 18th

Century Venetian painter, Canaletto. It was reminiscent of a painting I had seen in London's National Gallery called 'Regatta on the Grand Canal'.

That night there were Jubilee Parties and firework displays everywhere, and we enjoyed a few scoops of the amber nectar. The Australian Republican Party seemed to have taken that day off.

Dancing Queen and The King

Elizabeth II wasn't the only queen to visit Australia that year; the 'Dancing Queens', Abba, attracted comparable crowds when they visited Sydney. They were probably even more popular in Australia than they were in Britain or Sweden. Even today there are numerous Abba tribute bands throughout the world, with names like Voulez-Vous, and Bjorn Again. The stage musical 'Mama Mia', which is great fun, has become a world-wide hit that looks set to run for many years. The movie of the same name even managed to secure the services of multi Oscar-winner, Meryl Streep. You are probably wondering why I am writing so much about Abba spin-offs. Well, in Australia, in 1977, a character called Norman Gunston probably set the ball rolling with a string of hits covering Abba songs. But here's the thing: he was so appallingly bad that he became morbidly fascinating. The modern day equivalent would be the deluded 'singers' who appear on The X Factor and Britain's Got Talent. Invariably, the huge audience gives them a massive round of ironic applause, which only cranks up their delusions of greatness.

Today's audiences would go wild for Norman Gunston. He was tall, lanky and ungainly. He wore a shiny, mohair, blue suit, circa 1961, and a Cliff Richard bow tie. His thinning, greasy hair was fashioned into a comb-over, and his gimmick was to have several pieces of slightly bloodied tissue paper stuck to his face, as if he had cut himself shaving. Even to this day, I cannot listen to Abba singing 'Fernando' without smiling and cringing at the memory of Norman's strangulated version. I believe (hope) that he was somebody's alter ego, but I am still not sure. I remember watching a documentary about Wings' world tour of the 1970s. In Australia, our old friend Norman, who had managed to cut himself shaving yet again, interviewed Paul McCartney. Paul's confused, slightly wary demeanour indicated that he wasn't quite sure if Norman Gunston was for real.

As far as I am concerned, the most momentous event of 1977 was the death of Elvis Presley. I still vividly remember listening one morning to Radio Station 2UE when the disc jockey announced the sad news. I was just about to leave for work and was stunned. I walked to school, head bowed, with shoe suede blues. It highlighted my disappointment at, idiotically, not taking the chance to see Elvis in concert in Las Vegas when I was touring America by Greyhound Bus.

We Wuz Robbed

I went to see a couple of rugby league matches, and the biggest of all was the World Cup Final between Australia and Great Britain, at Sydney Cricket Ground. Jubilee year must have intensified my patriotic fervour as I belted out 'God Save the Queen' with gusto. The British supporters had every reason to feel confident since Great Britain had actually won the Rugby League World Cup only five years earlier, in Paris. However, despite my optimism, my day at Sydney Cricket Ground was to end in disappointment. Australia won a tough, tense game with the agonisingly close score of 13-12.

The 1972 Rugby League World Cup win in Paris gives me a convenient link to my next story: the victorious Great Britain team included a certain Mike Stephenson, the Dewsbury hooker. (For the benefit of any American readers, I should point out that a rugby hooker is not the same as a hooker in your country). By 1977, he was playing for Penrith in the Sydney competition, and his name had been inevitably Australianised to Stevo. We will be meeting him soon, in his capacity as a rugby league co-commentator for Sky Television in the UK.

Time-Travelling Pom

At this point, I need to interrupt my space-time continuum and take out my flux capacitor to go 'Back to the Future'. We will be instantly transported from Sydney to Wigan, where my future -self is a teacher at the Deanery High School. (This must be the only case in the history of Australia of someone being transported *from* Botany Bay to Wigan).

In an instant, I am now back in Wigan and my flux capacitor indicates the year 1990. The following story will take us all the way back to Sydney...

Year Eleven pupils were on Work Experience, a programme which gives them the opportunity to sample life in the world of work. Teachers volunteered to supervise several students each, which involved visiting the workplace to monitor progress. Pupils were required to submit a professional report. Over the years, I have visited factories, offices, hospitals, undertakers, shops, and galleries. One of the most memorable was when I visited a student who worked for Wigan Borough Council in the Social Housing Department. When he returned to school, he handed in an impressive, well-presented report. The title on the front-cover was: 'My Work Experience as a Wigan Rent Boy'.

One of my students, Andrea, was working as a sales assistant at an electrical retail shop in Wigan town centre. At the time, I was considering buying a satellite television receiver, so I thought that I would buy one at the same shop, while on a work-experience visit. I should explain at this point that my track record when buying electrical gadgetry was not good. For example, two of my less-than-astute purchases were a Betamax video recorder, and an eight-track cartridge player for my car.

There were two satellite formats available at the time: a round dish, which received signals from the Astra Satellite, or, alternatively, a square dish (known as a squarial), which was served by the Marco

Polo satellite. My mind was made up for me when it was announced that Sky Television had signed a deal to broadcast rugby league, via Marco Polo. That was the clincher. It was a squarial for me.

With cash in my wallet, and my work-experience documentation in my briefcase, I went to see Andrea in the electrical shop. I chatted to the manager and was able to negotiate a good price for a squarial and a receiver box. I felt quietly smug that my overland haggling skills had paid dividends. I don't think I will ever kick that habit. However, a mere three months later, it was announced in the press that the Marco Polo Satellite was to be discontinued. The squarial on the roof of my house would soon be obsolete and about as useful as an ashtray on a motorbike. I shook my head in dismay while mumbling to myself, 'Bloody typical, wrong choice *again!*'

The following week at school, I decided to put a poster on the general notice board in the staff room:

For Sale

Square Ariel (squarial) one owner. (Relatively new.

Would make a terrific plant pot stand, or modern sculpture)

Betamax Video Recorder.

Eight-Track Cartridge Player.

(Fantastic quadraphonic sound in your car, provided you never get fed-up listening to 'Quadraphenia').

Will deliver in my Sinclair C5

No time wasters please.

This light-hearted list caused some amusement in the staffroom. A couple of days later I was teaching a class in my art room, when a member of staff, whom I knew vaguely, came in.

"Hello Mr. Meadows, I'm Roy Coulson of the Geography Department, and I wondered if I could have a brief word."

"Of course," I replied, suspecting that it was another member of staff asking for paper and paints for a classroom display.

"I've come about your ad on the staff notice board."

"Oh yes?" I responded, thinking that he was about to ask me to remove it now that the joke is over.

"I'm interested in buying one or two things," he continued, deadpan.

An Eric Morecambe aside came to mind, when he used to look towards the camera and say, "This man's a fool."

I decided to humour him. "Certainly, which ones in particular?"

"Well, I thought the squarial would look good as a sculpture on my front lawn," Roy continued, but by now was unable to maintain a straight face. At this point, we both found it difficult to suppress laughter any longer. This caused everyone in my class to look up from their works of art wondering what the joke was. Roy explained that he had found the notice very funny, and couldn't resist playing along with the joke. He was a Liverpudlian, with a Scouser's sense of humour, and from then on we became, and remain, the best of friends.

When I said that the squarial was the wrong choice, it is not *strictly* true. I did manage to have the last laugh. As part of the SKY Television's rugby league coverage, they announced a competition called 'Timeless Tries', which required entrants to choose, in order of preference, six great tries. The competition was sponsored by Australian Airline QANTAS, and the prize was a trip to Sydney to see the Australian Rugby League Grand Final, at the Sydney Football Stadium. Accommodation for the winner, and a guest, was in the 5-star Regent Hotel, perfectly situated between the Harbour Bridge and the Opera House. It was a dream prize, and I entered the competition in a systematic way: of the six alternatives shown on television, I chose what I thought would be the best two, the middle two, and the worst two. Based on these categories, I worked out a permutation and sent six entries on postcards, each blessed with a silent prayer as I put them into the post box.

The day of the draw finally arrived and we sat in front of the TV. The presenter started to announce the winning order of tries, as decided by a panel of experts. Excitedly, I sat with copies of my six alternatives in my hand.

"In reverse order, at number six..."

I was scanning and marking my cards with the zeal and professionalism of a seasoned bingo player. Gradually, each of my entries fell by the wayside, but I had *one* winning entry.

Then came the draw. The presenter, Gary Rhodes, announced, "Out of thousands and thousands of entries, we have a few hundred correct ones, and here they are." On the desk was a large goldfish bowl containing cards and envelopes, in a variety of colours. David Oxley, Chairman of the Rugby League, was invited to make the draw, and he plunged his hand into the bowl. After a couple of swirls, he pulled out a card, gripped between his index and middle fingers.

"It's a white postcard. *Mine* is a white postcard," I shouted, my excitement building to a crescendo. Mr Oxley then looked at the card and said,

"It's another win for Wigan," as he handed the card over to the presenter.

"Wigan, it *must* be me."

Then came the moment of truth... The announcement:

"The winning entry is from John Meadows of Wigan."

At that point, everything seemed to go into slow motion.

"It *is* you," exclaimed Norma, in disbelief.

"Well, congratulations, Mr. Meadows," said Gary Rhodes, as he spoke directly to me straight from the television.

"Thank you very much," I replied idiotically, as if it was a two-way conversation.

It is a very strange experience to have someone speak to you, and you alone, personally from a television screen. Remember, this was way before Skype, Instagram or smart phones.

"Well, Mr. Meadows," continued my new best friend in television cyber space, "you and a guest will be jetting off to Australia for the Grand Final. Well done, and we will be in touch."

"Well, it looks like you are coming with me to Australia," I said to Norma, almost nonchalantly.

"Fantastic," she replied. "Do I have to actually go to the match, or could I go shopping instead?" I think she was joking.

The phone rang almost immediately, and I had picked it up before it could reach the second ring.

"Hello," I said eagerly, expecting to hear from someone from SKY TV.

"Are you watching the rugby on Sky Sports?" asked my friend Bill from St. Helens, "You've won the 'Timeless Tries' competition, you jammy bastard!"

This was the general gist of several subsequent telephone conversations from various friends and relatives, always finishing with me saying, "I'd better hang up now, because I am expecting a call from SKY TV."

Eventually, one of the many calls was from someone with an unmistakable Aussie accent. "G'day. I'd like to speak to Mr. John Meadows please."

"Yes, speaking."

"I'm Neville Smith, producer of SKY Sports Rugby League. I presume you saw the draw?"

"Yes, it's great news. I can't believe it."

Neville explained that his office had been trying for over an hour to get through, and he laughed when I told him that there had been a succession of people ringing to call me a jammy bastard.

One small problem now occurred to us; we needed leave of absence from our jobs. The following morning was A Level results day, so I knew that the Headmaster, Mr. Williams, would be in school. I told him about my good fortune and said,

"As you know, Headmaster, the Aussie Final is in mid-September, so I would like to request term-time leave of absence."

He shook my hand vigorously to congratulate me on my win, and said that he could not foresee a problem, but he would need to speak with the School Governors. The following Monday was a Staff Day, prior to the beginning of term. Traditionally, it always begins with a service at Wigan Parish Church, conducted by the Rector, who also happened to be the Chairman of Governors. It was a bright and sunny September morning when I arrived early. I was sitting on a bench when the rector, Canon Forest appeared from the church wearing full regalia and looking resplendent as the bright sunlight reflected off his gold trimmings. He strolled over to me and said, "Good morning John, we had a Governors' meeting this morning. Well done, what a fabulous trip. We certainly wouldn't want to deny you taking up your prize." The Principal of Norma's college also gave permission.

The local press took a great interest in my win. Also, I was interviewed by SKY television on the pitch at half-time during a Wigan match at Central Park. As the SKY commentator, Eddie Hemmings, held the microphone and we stood in front of the cameraman, it was a little off-putting to hear Deanery pupils start shouting from the crowd, "There's our teacher on the pitch."

When we arrived at Sydney Airport, we were met personally by Eddie Hemmings and Neville Smith, the producer whom I had spoken to on the phone a couple of weeks earlier. We were taken straight to the Regent Hotel, where Eddie's co-commentator Mike Stevenson (universally known as Stevo) was waiting to greet us. The marble clad foyer was a joy to behold, decorated with luxuriant tropical plants and fresh flowers. A string quartet played as we checked in.

We had been allocated to best suite in the hotel, with a view of the Harbour Bridge to the left and the Opera House to the right. We were overwhelmed by the hospitality and generosity of our hosts, who made us feel very much a part of their team. Channel 10 TV in Australia made us feel like VIPs, and Eddie even gave us a mention during his commentary of the match: "Friends of Norma and John Meadows will be pleased to know that they are having a great time." An understatement.

The match itself was a great occasion at the Sydney Football Stadium. It was more Superbowl than Wembley Cup Final, the presentation and atmosphere influenced more by America than Britain. The cast of 'Grease' performed the half-time entertainment, as 1950s pink Cadillacs drove around the perimeter of the pitch. I couldn't help but to wind up all the Aussies sitting near us in the stadium.

"This is an awful lot of trouble to go to just to decide who plays Wigan at Anfield in two weeks' time for the World Club Championship," I announced, as loudly as possible. There was plenty of friendly banter, as you would expect from the Aussies. Supporters sitting near to us were impressed to find out that we had won the trip, but even more impressed when I told them that I would be going to Anfield for the World Match. Penrith beat Canberra to win the Australian Grand Final. Wigan beat Penrith at Anfield two weeks later to become World Champions. I supported Wigan that night, albeit through gritted teeth. I am from St. Helens after all.

Spending time in Sydney was indeed a trip down Memory Lane. We took a bus to Rose Bay, and, unannounced, called to see our former neighbour, Nita, who had waved us off at the airport fourteen years earlier. As we walked past her kitchen window, we casually tapped on the glass and waved, as we had often done before. She looked up, waved back and continued washing-up for a few seconds, until she realized it was no longer 1977. She welcomed us with a look of shock on her face. The first thing I noticed when we went into her apartment was that the portraits I had drawn of her grandchildren were still proudly on display in her lounge.

"What are you doing here?" she exclaimed, delightedly.

"It's a flying visit. We are only here for a week."

"What? You've come all this way to Australia for just a *week*?"

"Yes, I have won the trip in a competition."

"You always were a lucky Pommie bastard!"

Somehow, that statement, when spoken by an octogenarian with a strong Australian accent, seemed like a sincere compliment.

We went over to Bondi Beach and had a stroll along Hasting Parade. Since we had left, it had certainly gone up-market. (Perhaps it was *because* we had left). We stood outside the apartment we had shared with Phil and Heather, and noticed that, instead of a battered sofa on a garage roof, it now had a *proper* balcony with patio doors.

We called in at Cranbrook School to say hello to anyone who might remember me. The Headmaster was long-retired, but the same secretary was still there. She welcomed us warmly and invited us to walk around the school. The interior of the main house had changed very little; with the same historic photographs and marble busts on plinths. I was pleased to find that there were quite a few members of staff who had been colleagues all those years ago.

Winning the television prize has brought us conveniently back to Sydney, so it is an appropriate time to climb aboard the time-machine and resume our round-the-world trip.

Chapter Six

Some Enchanted Evenings

The Long White Cloud

Aboard the Air New Zealand flight from Sydney to Auckland, I was able to relax and enjoy a drink. I had given my farewell speech at Cranbrook at lunch time, before going directly to the airport. I was a little shell-shocked, feeling as though I had left Australia quicker than Ronnie Biggs had done on his way to Brazil. As we approached New Zealand, the view below illustrated, quite graphically, why the country is also known, in Maori language, as Aotearoa; 'The Land of the Long White Cloud'.

Many airports around the world showcase their country by welcoming visitors with exhibitions of arts, craft and culture. We were used to the usual array of murals, sculptures and gift shops; be it the Yellow Submarine at Liverpool Airport or the statue of Lief Ericson at Keflavik in Iceland. Maori Art was prominently displayed in the concourse at Auckland Airport, and it whetted our appetite for our brief stay in the city.

Our city-centre hotel was very comfortable and traditional; circa 1950s. There is a cliché that going to New Zealand is like stepping back in time. (Something we time-travellers are well used to). I don't know if that is true, but the television in the lounge was showing

Coronation Street; Ena Sharples, Minnie Cauldwell and Martha Longhurst were drinking milk stouts in the snug of the Rovers Return, and Ken was still a student. I felt as though I must have used my flux capacitor by mistake.

There were plenty of tourist pamphlets on display at the front desk, and we browsed over a drink in the hotel's intimate bar. We planned our excursions and read some history. New Zealand can claim to be the youngest country in the world, as it was the last place to be colonised by human beings. It is open to debate, but research indicates that this happened only about 1,000 years ago, and it closed the circle which began when the earliest humans started to migrate from East Africa. The first New Zealanders came from the Polynesian Islands to the north, having migrated to there from South East Asia over a couple of Millennia.

Maori culture has evolved from these Polynesian ancestors, and New Zealand now takes great pride in this heritage. The Maori excels at carving wood, bone and stone, and a particular speciality is nephrite, a form of jade. In New Zealand, this is known, imaginatively, as greenstone. We visited a factory, and it was fascinating to watch the stone being polished; using just water and bare hands. We browsed in the factory gift shop and settled on a greenstone souvenir Tiki. I paid the asking price, since a year in Australia had cured me (almost) of my haggling compulsion. The term Tiki is applied to carved human figures throughout Polynesia.

The historical origins of Tiki are unclear; fertility symbols are the most likely explanation.

The Maori had the country to themselves for something like 500 years, until the first Europeans arrived. Dutchman Abel Tasman, (after whom the Tasman Sea and Tasmania are named), arrived in the 17th Century, on behalf of the Dutch East India Company. He received a hostile reception from the Maori, who killed some of the sailors. Not surprisingly, Tasman decided not to explore further and ordered a hasty withdrawal.

Over a century later, Captain James Cook charted New Zealand, and this opened the door for European whalers, seal hunters and timber traders. As with other indigenous civilisations, for example; the Inca, Maya, Aztecs and North American Indians, the traditional way of life of the Maori was up-turned. The Europeans brought disease, in particular measles and smallpox, which caused devastation.

Warlike instincts had been infused in Maori culture for centuries, and inter-tribal battles had become part of their history. Consequently, the introduction of guns was disastrous: in the 1820s, at least 20,000 Maori were killed in the inter-tribal Musket Wars. Today, this warlike heritage has become ceremonial and manifests itself as a challenge to visitors or sporting opponents. Even Queen Elizabeth has been welcomed by half-naked, tattooed warriors with their tongues out. (No, I don't mean the Wigan Warriors). New Zealand's most famous team in any sport is the rugby union All Blacks. The fearsome, traditional Haka, performed before test matches, must be worth a few points start, even before kick-off. Perhaps the English should respond with a ferocious Morris Dance. Black has become the traditional colour for nearly all New Zealand National Sports Teams, and some have jumped on the All Black bandwagon: the cricket team is known as The Black Caps, and the basketball team is, wittily, The Tall Blacks. Following the corporate trend, the New Zealand badminton team name was The Black Cocks. Sadly, this was changed after a year. There were some complaints; I can't imagine why.

A notable exception to the black national identity is the New Zealand Football team; The All Whites. How do you compete with the All Blacks? The answer is; you don't. This reverse psychology reminds me very much of the Beatles. How do you follow Pop Artist Peter Blake's iconic album cover of 'Sgt Pepper's Lonely Hearts Club Band'? Answer: a plain white album cover called simply 'The Beatles', embossed in white. This was designed by another famous Pop Artist, Richard Hamilton. I wonder how much he charged for presenting a sheet of plain white paper? This album cover has received critical acclaim. Perhaps they should have called it 'The Emperor's New Clothes'.

Auckland has the largest Polynesian population of any city in the world, and this culture is reflected in the names of surrounding bays, harbours and natural features. On the other hand, English names proliferate in the city centre: Albert Park, Victoria Park, Nelson St.,

Liverpool St., Wellesley St., to name but a few. Bizarrely, there was also Khyber Pass Road.

We booked on a coach trip to sample wine-tasting in the nearby Henderson Valley. We stopped for a photo opportunity to view the panorama of the city. It is situated on a narrow isthmus between the Manukau Harbour on the Tasman Sea, and the Waitemata Harbour on the Pacific Ocean. I wasn't surprised when our coach driver told us that Auckland has the largest boat ownership per population of any city in the world. It is known as The City of Sails, as was clearly evident from the view below us.

A Day So Good, We Lived It Twice

The flight from New Zealand to Tahiti took us across the International Date Line, which meant that we had a Groundhog day. I still find it difficult to fully understand this concept. Even Phineas Fogg forgot about it. A day has to begin and end somewhere, and the International Date Line is that place. It threads its way from pole to pole through the Pacific, carefully avoiding any land. If, for example, it had been plotted through any island, it would be possible to time-travel in your own house: Wednesday in the lounge, Tuesday in the kitchen. It would play havoc with meal times, bed times, television schedules and birthdays. So there we have it. I hope I have cleared up any confusion.

In 2011, Samoa applied to have The International Date Line moved in order to be on the same side, and day, as neighbours and trading partners Fiji, Tonga, Australia and New Zealand. I don't know who one applies to for such a move, but perhaps I could request that the tropics be dragged further north, a little nearer to England. Samoa's request was granted and now, in the history of that country, the 30th December never existed. Samoa used to be twenty-three hours behind Auckland, and is now one hour ahead. I am beginning to confuse myself again, but I am not alone because many Samoans thought that they had been robbed of a day of their lives.

A similar thing once happened in Great Britain. Here is a quiz question: What happened in Great Britain between the 2nd and the 14th of September, 1752? Answer: Nothing at all! Those eleven days do not exist because of the change from the Julian to the Gregorian calendar. Not surprisingly, this caused much confusion amongst the population, as many people genuinely believed that their lives had been cut short by eleven days.

One spin of the earth is a day, and one orbit of the earth around the sun is a year. These have been fixed for over 4 billion years and even the human race cannot change them. To quote that famous scientist of the future, Scotty, 'Ye canna change the laws of physics, Captain.' However, other measurements of time, such as weeks and months, are human innovations. I believe that the Romans actually experimented with eight days a week, as did the Beatles... 'I guess you know it's true'.

We booked into the Holiday Inn in Papeete, Tahiti's capital. During check-in, we were invited to buy tickets for a Tahitian Feast, which was taking place the following day. After eating airline food across the Pacific, we eagerly accepted. We were certainly ready for a good night's sleep. It had been a long day, or was it two days?

I have seen some all-you-can-eat buffets in my time, but this was something else. It continued for twelve hours as we were entertained by traditional local singers and dancers. Norma was asked to join in, and she readily agreed, accompanied by local musicians playing traditional instruments. She was festooned with garlands of flowers and dressed in local costume. The meal was cooked in an 'ahimaa', a pit filled with heated stones, and we enjoyed suckling pig, fish and clams. Still one of our best meals ever, even though some of the French restaurants in Papeete rivalled any we had been to in Paris.

The following morning, we negotiated with a local driver, Manua, to take us on a guided tour of the island. He told us that his name means 'the bird messenger of happiness'. It was like driving through a kaleidoscope of colour as our driver pointed out hibiscus, bougainvillea, and poinsettia, to name just a few, set against a turquoise Pacific. Manua told us that flowers play an important role in the life of Tahitians. Both men and women wear a tiare bloom (the national flower, a fragrant white blossom), behind one ear to send out signals; on the left, (the side of the heart), to show that they are married, or on the right side if they are single and available.

"Or married, but open to suggestions," added Manua, with a mischievous grin.

He was very knowledgeable and he outlined the history of his country. There have been several theories as to the origin of the original settlers of Tahiti. The Norwegian explorer, Thor Heyerdahl, proposed the theory that early settlers sailed from Peru in South America thousands of years before Christopher Columbus crossed the Atlantic. In 1947, Heyerdahl proved that such a voyage was possible, by making the perilous journey on the famous Kon-Tiki reed raft. However, recent research suggests that the original Tahitians were Polynesians who sailed from the east.

Incidentally, the English word tattoo is derived from the Tahitian word tatau. In Polynesian culture, tattoos are traditionally considered signs of beauty. This particular art form has spread virally to Britain and throughout the world in recent years, and lavishly embellished acres of flesh parade along every high street, like human advertising-boards. Being a former teacher, I studiously resist any temptation to point out a spelling mistake to a passing stranger.

Tahiti is part of a group of islands called the Society Islands which, together with four other groups, make up French Polynesia. The first European to land there was Samuel Wallis, a British Captain of HMS Dolphin, which arrived in 1767. It was a chance encounter and he didn't stay long because he was actually searching for Terra Australis Incognita, a theoretical southern continent. So-called experts of the time postulated that it must exist to counterbalance the northern land masses; otherwise the earth would surely wobble off its axis. The Flat Earth Society had never heard of anything quite so ridiculous.

The following year a French explorer, with the gloriously colourful name of Louis Antoine de Bougainville, arrived and later wrote a best-seller glorifying Tahiti.

In 1767, Captain James Cook arrived on the HMS Endeavour. His mission was to plot the transit of the planet Venus across the sun so that the distance from the Earth to the Sun could be calculated. This would solve a navigational problem and finally enable sailors to accurately determine longitude as well as latitude. A fort was built at the northernmost point of Tahiti and called, appropriately, Point Venus. (It's just as well he wasn't plotting Uranus).

Ultimately, Cooke failed because he didn't have the sophisticated optical equipment to track Venus, and it could not be done with the naked eye. He had, quite literally, lost the plot. Back in Britain, a competition was launched with a prize for anyone who could come up with a means of measuring longitude. It was won by a watchmaker named John Harrison. Whenever that question crops up on a pub quiz I always remember it. He was my father-in-law. (I told you I was a time-traveller). Perhaps you remember a classic episode of 'Only Fools and Horses', when Del and Rodney *finally* became millionaires. A watch in their possession sold at auction for something like £9 million. It was a John Harrison watch.

As we toured the island, inevitably the subject of the 'Mutiny on the Bounty' would crop up, as Manua would point out Fletcher Christian's island, and a small waterfall as Fletcher Christian's shower, and so on. Being a volcanic island, the beaches are dark, but that was not good enough for Hollywood movie executives, who insisted on white sand. Manua pointed out specks of white sand which were imported for the Marlon Brando version of the movie in 1962.

Captain William Bligh, who had previously served under Captain Cook, was sent in 1789 on HMS Bounty, with Fletcher Christian as second in command. The mission was to collect breadfruit trees, which were intended as a cheap source of food for slaves in Jamaica and St Vincent. Also on board was the botanist Joseph Banks, the President of the Royal Society, who recorded and collected exotic flora.

Initially, The Bounty attempted to navigate around South America's notorious Cape Horn, but adverse weather conditions forced Captain Bligh to reset a much further course, via South Africa's Cape of Good Hope. Consequently, the arrival in Tahiti was delayed and they had missed the breadfruit harvest. This meant that the ship's company had to wait, and this is when Captain Bligh's problems began. The sailors began to enjoy the delights of Tahiti, and discipline started to break down. The local Tahitian beauties displayed, exotically, their natural charms. Sex was offered generously, and the sailors would give the women a variety of trinkets, picked up on their travels. The islands did not have any iron, and their boats were lashed together with rope. Consequently, and somewhat bizarrely, iron nails became a popular gift, and the Tahitian women would accept any size, length or shape. Nails as well. The ship's carpenter's supplies were soon exhausted, as were the sailors.

They even resorted to serrupticously prising nails from the Bounty, and the Captain had to deploy sailors, armed with fixed bayonets, to protect the ship from disintegrating.

Being an upstanding figure who was conscious of his position (which I suppose could also describe his crew, but in a rather different context), Captain Bligh declined to partake of the local favours. Obviously, he did not wish to harm his future prospects of promotion. With supreme irony, in 1814 he attained the rank of *Vice*-Admiral.

Two American writers, Charles Nordhoff and James Norman Hall, wrote the book 'Mutiny on the Bounty' in 1933. It became a best-seller, and was made into at least three major Hollywood movies: Charles Laughton and Clark Gable starred in the 1935 version, and in 1962, it was re-made, starring Trevor Howard and Marlon Brando, whose English accent gives Dick Van Dyck a run for his money as the worst in cinema history. A third movie was released in 1984, starring Anthony Hopkins and Mel Gibson.

Many of the descendants of the mutineers still live on Pitcairn Island, their final refuge. As a post-script, here is a touch of trivia: In 1972, the New Zealand Rugby League team, The Kiwis, toured Britain and were captained by a certain Roy Fletcher Christian, MBE. So, Fletcher Christian could rest in peace knowing that one of his direct descendants would return to England as a Captain.

Paintings of Another World

The first European artist to paint Tahiti was William Hodges, the official artist on Captain Cook's second voyage. In addition to portraits, sketches and detailed studies of botanical specimens, he also painted several canvases which captured the glorious colour and light of Tahiti. A particularly impressive canvas is the painting of Cook's ships, The Resolution and The Adventure, anchored in Matavai Bay. The drawings and paintings caused a sensation back in England, and were looked upon with awe and amazement. It was as if they were pictures of another world, and looked at in the same way that today we look upon photographs sent back from distant planets. Tahiti became a popular stop for whaling ships in the 19th Century, and this is how Herman Melville arrived on the island. He lived in Tahiti in the early 1840s and based his novel 'Moby Dick' in the South Pacific.

In 1888, Robert Louis Stevenson, the author of 'Treasure Island', arrived in Tahiti. Somehow, the island inspired him to write 'The Master of Ballantrae', which was set in Scotland, as far removed from Tahiti in every possible way. The eponymous star of the movie was Errol Flynn, whose shaky Scottish accent is right up there with the aforementioned Brando and Van Dyck.

Another writer, Somerset Maugham, visited Tahiti in 1916 and wrote 'The Moon and Sixpence'. This enigmatically-titled book is based on the life of Paul Gauguin, an artist who has become inextricably linked with Tahiti. Gauguin was a colourful character in more ways than one; his life and his paintings. Whereas the traditional paintings by William Hodges accurately captured the colour and atmosphere of Tahiti, the modern, radical independence of colour employed by Gauguin captured the essence and spirit. He is regarded as one of the Fathers of Modern Art, alongside Cézanne, and his primitive style, using colours in an unrealistic way, first began to develop in his paintings of Breton peasants in Brittany. The way of life and the colour of Tahiti were made for him.

As part of our tour with Manua, we visited the Gauguin Museum, which had a beautiful location in the grounds of the Harrison W. Smith Botanical Gardens. He was an American professor who moved to Tahiti in 1919 and cultivated lush tropical plants. If there is a more picturesque gallery in the world, then I would love to see it. Actually, it was more of a memorial than a gallery, since there was only a small collection of minor works, augmented by lots of photographs, sculptures, engravings, documents, artefacts and some of his furniture. Most of Gauguin's paintings are in the great galleries of the world; such as the Hermitage in St. Petersburg, Musée D'Orsay in Paris, as well as galleries in London, New York and Edinburgh. I believe that, at the present time, the Gauguin Museum in Tahiti is now run-down, or even closed. This is a great pity because Tahiti without a Gauguin would be like Salford without a Lowry. I wonder if those two places, Tahiti and Salford, have ever shared a sentence before?

Paul Gauguin's curriculum vitae makes interesting reading. He began his working life as a Parisian stockbroker and was well on his way to becoming wealthy when, in 1883, he decided to leave his

Danish wife and six children to become an artist in Brittany. His next career move was to work as a navvy digging the Panama Canal, before returning to Paris via the Caribbean island of Martinique. Famously, he went to stay with Vincent Van Gogh at the Yellow House in Arles, in the South of France. They did not get on, and he thought that Van Gogh was mentally unstable. This, remember, is from a man who had given up a lucrative business career and left his large family to become a labourer. After Van Gogh threatened him with a cut-throat razor, Gauguin fled the house and decided to get as far away as possible. As I mentioned earlier, Tahiti really is as far away as possible.

The movie 'Lust for Life' is based on this story, and Kirk Douglas and Anthony Quinn were perfectly cast as Van Gogh and Gauguin respectively. Indeed, the latter won an Oscar for his performance. As a denouement, let us fast-forward in my time-machine to the mid-eighties, when I was teaching art at Cowley School in St. Helens. At the end of the summer term, after the exams had finished, schools were able to adopt a more relaxed regime with trips to Alton Towers, lessons out on the lawn, quizzes and films.

"Sir, can we watch a film?" asked my class of hopeful fourth-year pupils, as they settled down for their final art lesson of the school year.

"I think so," I replied, "Let me see what I have got." I delved into my desk drawer and took out two videos.

"You can choose either, 'The Agony and the Ecstasy' or 'Lust for Life'." Eyes bulged and mouths dropped open, followed by giggles of anticipation. I quickly realized that this group of fifteen-year-olds had totally misinterpreted the titles.

"Don't build your hopes up," I said, holding up the videos, "This one is the life of Michelangelo, and this one is about Vincent Van Gogh."

A vote didn't take place. Everyone decided to do some painting instead.

Time to leave St. Helens and go forward to the past; Easter Island next stop.

The Navel of the World

Of all the islands on Earth with a permanent population, Easter Island is generally regarded as the most isolated. We flew 2,500 miles from Tahiti, and, as we approached the island, it looked as though a triangular chunk of Wales or Cornwall had been dropped into the Pacific Ocean. It seemed a bleak landscape; more like moorland than the luxuriant, colourful, palm-tree enriched flora we had enjoyed in Tahiti.

The first recorded European visitor to the Island was a Dutch explorer, Admiral Jacob Roggeveen, who arrived on Easter Sunday in 1722. He named it Paaseiland (Easter Island) to commemorate the day. Today, it is popularly known as Rapa Nui, a name given by Tahitian sailors in the 1860s, because it reminded them of an island called Rapa, near Tahiti. Personally, I like the name which was given to the island by its first inhabitants, who called it Te Pito o Te Henua, (The Navel of the World). This begs the question: where on earth is the anus of the world? I can think of one or two places which could compete for the title.

Thor Heyerdahl arrived by Kon-Tiki raft, and he spent some time excavating and studying on Easter Island. He noticed certain similarities with his earlier research in South America, such as sun worship and advanced stonemasonry. This convinced him even more that the first settlers had sailed across the Pacific from the east.

As we discovered in Tahiti, more recent evidence suggests that the first inhabitants came from the west. A group arrived around the 4th Century AD, led by a Polynesian ruler, called Hoto-Matua, who became the first King of Rapa Nui. To put this into some kind of historical context, it was at about the same time that the Romans were withdrawing from Britain.

An absence of historical records only adds to the intrigue of the island, and many theories have been suggested: they are survivors of the lost continent of Atlantis, or, inevitably, they are descended from aliens.

This tiny volcanic island, approximately 64 square miles in area, (about half the size of Malta), is world famous for one reason: the mysterious giant statues, called Moai. Easter Island must be the original 'mysterious island', because we are not certain what these were for, where the original settlers came from, or, indeed, the history of events on the island.

There are over 800 of the giant statues scattered throughout Rapa Nui. Some are trapped in the hillside, the carving of the soft volcanic rock having been abandoned. All the statues follow the same basic design; heavy foreheads and long pointed chins, while the hand positions are typical of carvings to be found throughout Polynesia. At an average height of twenty feet, the statues originally had eyes made of coral with pupils of black obsidian. The Moai were thought to represent deceased chiefs or revered ancestors, who protect ceremonial areas.

There have been many theories to suggest how primitive people were able to transport the massive statues from the quarry site, at the Rano Raraku volcano. Tree trunks were probably used as rollers, but this means of transport became impossible after all the trees had been cut down. It seems as though the most likely new method was to walk a statue, with teams pulling ropes in a synchronized sequence of rocking movements. Anyone who has tried to move a fridge/freezer or a wardrobe will understand this principle.

The Moai culture declined, and a new cult of 'The Bird Man' developed on Easter Island. The ritual is recorded in carvings on cliffs, and the aim was to find the first egg of spring, laid by the sacred Manu Tara bird. A representative of each tribe would swim across dangerous waters, to the tiny island of Moto Nui, to collect an egg. The leader of the winning tribe became 'Bird Man' for that year; a very important status.

When I was at school, I can't remember ever being taught anything about Easter Island. In fact, I don't think it was ever even mentioned in geography, history or any of my other subjects over seven years. I learned lots of useful things such as: the hinterland of the port of Valparaiso, the survival techniques of the Bushmen of the Kalahari, and Disraeli's foreign policy. As a retired teacher, I suggest that a study of Easter Island should become a compulsory part of the curriculum in geography, history, environmental studies, social sciences, anthropology, sociology, and politics. Winston Churchill said, 'The farther back you can look, the farther forward you are likely to see.' The history of Rapa Nui is a salutary warning to the human race; a microcosm of the future of the earth.

Pollen samples have shown that the island was heavily forested when humans first arrived, but all the trees were gone by the beginning of the 19th Century. As the forests were felled, soil eroded limiting food supplies, and, as there was no wood to build boats, fishing was severely limited. There were no means of leaving the island and over-population and hunger resulted in civil war, and even cannibalism. Statues were toppled and broken in anger, in the belief that the ancestors had forsaken the people. Two main ethnic groups were the Long Ears and the Short Ears, which sounds like a fantasy by Tolkien. But this was no fantasy. The Navel of the World had turned into hell on earth. As we stood in front of a row of Moai, we could almost sense the sadness in their hollow eyes.

I mentioned earlier that certain theorists have suggested that aliens were responsible for erecting the Moai on Easter Island. These people are probably followers of Erich von Daniken, author of 'Chariots of the Gods', who believed that the Nazca Lines in Peru were landing sites for alien spaceships. I have seen some very impressive airbrushed Photorealist paintings which show, in minute detail, spacecraft lowering the giant statues into place. It is known as Fantasy Art, and that is exactly what it is; fantasy. Or is it? If a spaceman came travelling looking for a place to land, where better than the world's most isolated island? There is a denouement to this: In 1988, the airport on Rapa Nui was extended specifically for one purpose; to accommodate the American Space Shuttle as an emergency landing site. Such a landing has not been necessary up to now. If it ever happens, then artistic fantasy will become photographic reality, as a real spaceship comes into land, witnessed by 800 inscrutable Moai: The Stone Age welcomes the Space Age.

Chapter Seven

Latin American Rhythms

In the Shadow of the Andes

Imagine a country which is not much more than the width of Britain, but is stretched in length to the same distance between London and New York: this is Chile. Before the advent of air travel, Chile was more like an island; squeezed between the Pacific Ocean to the west and the impenetrable Andes range to the east. We were surprised to be waived through passport control without any checks, until we realised that we had actually entered Chile on arrival at Easter Island, 2,500 miles to the west.

We stayed at a small, family-run hotel in Santiago city centre. The check-in desk was located in a tiled, open courtyard and we were welcomed warmly by the receptionist, who offered us a very welcome glass of Chilean red wine. The antiquated lift was a cage of decorative wrought iron, with a floor-numbering system in the form of a large clock. A rickety ascent took us up to the fourth floor. The room turned out to be a suite, with double doors leading to the bedroom.

The following morning, I woke up with a start as I heard the door open and could see the outline of a figure through the frosted glass of the bedroom doors. Cautiously, I popped my head around the door only to find the maid laying out breakfast. "Buenas dias," she greeted me, with a beaming smile. “Desayuno es aqui,” she continued, gesturing towards the table. Norma and I enjoyed breakfast at a small table on the wrought iron balcony, overlooking the busy street below. We were looking forward to our first day, not only in Santiago, but in South America.

We bought a map of the city at a little newsagent’s booth and, over a cup of coffee at a pavement cafe, we planned our itinerary. The layout of Santiago reminded me of New York; a grid system bisected by a diagonal thoroughfare which followed a similar line to Broadway. In Santiago, it has the more exotic name of Avenida Libertador General Bernado O’ Higgins, the Chilean - Irish founder of the Republic of Chile. At the time when we were there, in 1977, Chile was under the dictatorship of General Pinochet, who had taken over after a violent military coup d’ état. As tourists, we did not have any regulations placed upon us, but we were careful to strictly observe any instructions, and, in particular, to ask permission before taking photographs.

We decided that a panoramic view of the city would be a good way to start, and we walked to the funicular railway. This took us up to the Parque Metropolitano on Cerro San Christopher; named after the patron saint of travellers. The view of the city with the backdrop of the snow-capped Andes was simply sensational.

Here is an interesting little item I came across in Chile. When I was training to be an art teacher on a post-graduate course at Reading University, I studied stages of visual awareness and cognitive ability of young children. Rhoda Kellogg was a leading researcher in this field. (Yes, her books made up a serial). All over the world, children go through similar stages at similar ages: large circles become faces and then figures develop. Everyone, I am sure, will be familiar with the standard house, with mum and dad bigger than the house (because they are the most important). The sky is a strip of blue across the top, and the sun is a huge, yellow ball with rays radiating out; a scene which has been displayed on millions of kitchen memo boards and fridge doors. Chilean children's paintings are no different, apart from one thing. Invariably, there is a wavy or jagged line right across the page above the house and just below the sun and a strip of sky. It is a young child's interpretation of the Andes, something they see every day. I found that quite fascinating, and not something which I had come across before.

This snow-capped, backdrop to the city changes throughout the day, as the light changes. The sun rises over the mountains which bathe them in morning lilacs and purples, until the Andes picks up the rose coloured evening light as the sun sets over the Pacific.

There is a definite European feel to Santiago. Not surprisingly, there is a strong Spanish influence, and many of the grandiose 17th Century Baroque buildings are reminiscent of Madrid. Old buildings in the city centre were designed by European architects, inspired by Paris and Rome. We visited the principal art gallery, the Museo National de Bellas Artes, a beautiful, sumptuous sandstone building in the Baroque style, based on the Petit Palais in Paris.

As we strolled around Santiago we came across an open-air chess tournament. I watched with interest as I remembered Charlie Rosewall, the cockney patient whom I knew at Rainhill Psychiatric Hospital in St. Helens. (Where I worked as a nurse, I hasten to add, for the benefit of those readers who haven't (yet) read my first book). If I had played Charlie more often, I would have had the confidence to join in.

The central market, with its impressive intricate wrought-iron roof, reminded me very much of the markets at home. I found out, subsequently, that this ironwork was indeed manufactured in England.

As we walked along a back street, my attention was drawn to a dusty little curiosity shop. The window was crammed with all kinds of sun-faded crafts and children's wooden toys. In the middle, standing on a plinth, was a simple carving of four mop-topped figures, and an inscription 'Los Beatles'. In those days, way before the internet, social media and multi-channel televisions, there they were in the bottom south-west corner of the world. 'That's what I call true world-wide fame,' I thought to myself, with a feeling of national pride.

After a couple of very enjoyable days in Santiago, it was time to head over the Andes to Buenos Aires. The view from the aeroplane was spectacular, but I was slightly un-nerved by Norma's choice of in-flight reading matter; 'Alive'; the story of the Uruguayan Rugby Team that had crashed in the Andes. "It must have been somewhere about there," she observed matter-of-factly, while looking out of the window. "It's like reading 'Psycho' in a mid-west motel," I replied sardonically, as I sat next to her, white knuckled. Mind you, a few years ago we were on a cruise, and one evening there was a double bill on the television. It was (I kid you not) 'Titanic', followed by 'The Poseidon Adventure'. We could only assume that the Entertainment Officer had a somewhat perverse sense of humour, or perhaps he was working his period of notice.

It Takes Two…

On arrival at the airport, we were shepherded through a maze of chipboard temporary walls and hanging wires. The hard-hatted workmen were trundling around with about the same level of urgency as a Mexican donkey. Renovations were underway in preparation for the World Cup; a mere six months hence. Our original plan had been to stay in Australia for a few more months, to arrive in Argentina for the tournament. Unfortunately, our plans were scuppered by England, who failed to qualify. Norma was truly devastated, as I am sure you will appreciate. I consoled myself with the thought that England would have been drawn, inevitably, in 'the group of death'.

Buenos Aires means 'good air' in Spanish. Presumably, it was given this name before the main road, Avenida 9 de Julio, was built; the widest in the world, with sixteen lanes. It takes its name from the date, in 1816, when Argentina declared its independence from Spain.

Our city-centre hotel was perfectly situated, literally around the corner from Plaza de Mayo, which is overlooked by the famous Casa

Rosada (Pink House) at the far end of the rectangular plaza. A church choir, resplendent in red cassocks and white ruffs, sang Christmas carols in the shade of an arched walkway at the end of the plaza. The building provided superb acoustics, and it heightened our Christmas mood, even though the temperature was 28 degrees centigrade.

As we walked around the city, I made sure that I kept my camera in its case until I was given permission, or at least a nod of acknowledgement, from any uniformed guards, soldiers or police. We were pleased to find that we were always met with a positive friendly response.

Buenos Aires is laid out in a basic grid system. The Avenida de Mayo is named in memory of the May Revolution of 1810, which sparked anti-Spanish feeling, which led to independence six years later. It is a straight, tree-lined thoroughfare with pavement cafes, artwork and entertainment. It was intended to emulate of the boulevards of Paris, but, to me, it was more reminiscent of Madrid's Grand Via or Las Ramblas in Barcelona. We enjoyed a leisurely stroll along the Avenida, punctuated with a couple of coffee stops, until we arrived at the Plaza del Congreso, which is dominated by the magnificent dome of the Palacio de Congreso; the seat of Government. It was inspired by the Capitol Building in Washington, albeit a slightly elongated version, that follows the much-copied, familiar template of Graeco-Roman architecture. It was finished in 1906, and, incidentally, there is an almost identical version in Havana, Cuba.

Don't Cry for Me Argentina

Argentina is celebrated in the stage musical 'Evita', by Andrew Lloyd Webber and Tim Rice, and this has resulted in posthumous world-wide fame for the eponymous lady.

Evita is actually a nickname. When she was a young girl, Eva Peron was affectionately called Evita; a Spanish diminutive of her name, meaning Little Eva (but more tango than locomotion). She was the second wife of Juan Peron, President of Argentina. She died in 1952, at the tragically young age of 33, but, in her short life, she made her mark on Argentinean history. She is remembered with great affection in her own country, and the sympathetic portrayal of her on stage and in movies, (Faye Dunaway and Madonna), has brought her to greater world-wide attention. Evita was, herself, an accomplished and successful actress, and these skills probably helped her to persuade, cajole and charm, as she ceaselessly pursued many causes. I would describe her as being a combination of Emmeline Pankhurst and Princess Diana, with a touch of Mother Theresa thrown in for good measure. She campaigned for female suffrage, and, largely due to her efforts, women voted for the first time in a National election, in 1951. Gratifyingly, Evita lived to see this happen. Furthermore, she was energetically committed to helping the poor, hospitals, orphanages and workers' groups. She could be determined and ruthless with her enemies, so let's throw Margaret Thatcher into the mix.

Argentinean-born Che Guevara also owes much of his lasting fame to the 'Evita' musical. That and the famous photograph of him, which has achieved iconic status over the years. It was taken by Alberto Kordo, in 1960. It wasn't a posed portrait, but an impromptu snapshot. Subsequently, it has been called; 'the symbol of the twentieth century', and the 'world's most famous photographic image'. The Victoria and Albert Museum in London has stated that it has been reproduced more than any other photograph. It has been painted, sculpted, screen-printed, digitized and tattooed, to name just a few media. Once the photo had been given the Andy Warhol treatment, Che Guevara was right up there on the pantheon of celebrity with Marilyn Monroe, Elvis Presley and Campbell's soup. No student bedsit would be complete without a Che Guevara poster covering a damp patch.

However, the actual facts about Che Guevara don't seem to match up to this persona. He was a doctor whose first name was Ernest, and his wife's name was Hilda. His mode of transport was a motorbike, but, somehow, I cannot quite picture a visor displaying: Ernie and Hilda. When I say motorbike, what I actually mean is a bicycle with a small motor attached. The type favoured nowadays by expat British pensioners in Spain. (I'm thinking of buying one). It's hardly Marlon Brando in 'The Wild One'.

The name Che was actually a nickname: a word, often used in Argentinean Spanish, that Guevara often said out of habit. It is an affectation roughly equivalent, if you will, to Aussies and Kiwis over-use of 'mate', or a Jamaican saying 'man' at every opportunity.

Che Guevara was part of Fidel Castro's rebels who overthrew Batista's Government in Cuba, in 1959. Later, Guevara exported his revolutionary ideals to Bolivia, but he was killed by the army in 1967.

Viva Estancia

The concierge at our hotel spoke faultless English. He was immaculate in his dress-code, and he oozed charm and conviviality. He strongly recommended to us that we must visit a ranch, to experience the traditional way of life at an Estancia. He booked us on a coach tour, which also included a stopover at a waterfront café on the Rio de la Plata. As we enjoyed mid-morning coffee on a terrace overlooking the river, we both felt as though we had been instantly transported back to England. The clear, cerulean blue sky, bright sunshine and steadily-increasing temperature were the only reminders that we were *not* actually sitting by the Thames. The panorama was more Henley on Thames than the River Plate outside Buenos Aires. The immaculate gardens and manicured lawns of Mock-Tudor houses rolled down to the water's edge. Weeping willows dipped into the water as a rowing-eights glided by. It was idyllic, and yet, a month earlier, Norma and I were quite apprehensive about travelling to the great unknown of South America. We would have been happy to sit there all day.

At the Estancia, one thing has remained ingrained in our memories ever-since: we were served the best steak, *ever*. (If you are a vegetarian, look away now). It was the biggest, thickest, juiciest, freshest barbequed steak imaginable, and both of us have resigned ourselves to the fact that we will never taste the like of it again. I would go so far as to say that it could tempt a vegetarian, even more than a bacon butty.

Local gauchos gave us a demonstration of their world-famous equestrian skills. The ranch-skills on show were similar to those of mid-west American ranches, except that a cowboy uses a lasso and a gaucho throws a boleadoras. I was invited to ride one of the horses. I should stress that this was *before* lunch, in case you are feeling sympathy for the poor horse. The saddle was a western - style, and was as comfortable as a leather armchair. A sheepskin blanket under the saddle provided extra shock-absorbing suspension.

Health and safety seemed to be an alien concept. I wasn't given a hard hat to wear, just a traditional gaucho beret. I tilted it at a rakish angle and shouted to Norma, who was sitting on a five-bar gate.

"Hey, does this make me look like Che Guevara."

"No. More like Frank Spencer," was her acerbic response.

After lunch, there was a never-ending supply of Argentinean wine, as the carafes along the rows of trestle tables were topped-up regularly by the waiters. We enjoyed an energetic and colourful demonstration of different styles of traditional Argentinean dancing and music. Inevitably, the show was closed with a dramatic, sultry performance of the tango. All too soon, it was time to go. As we made our way back to the coach, I looked back on a scene of devastation. Paper table cloths were torn and re-patterned with random stains of red wine. Spare ribs were festooned like the aftermath of a kill by a pride of lions. Amidst this post-apocalyptic scene, two older ladies had become totally oblivious to the chaos surrounding them. They sat opposite each other, leaning forward with their heads resting on the table, fast asleep, snoring in perfect synchronicity. They were well-upholstered German ladies, who had enjoyed themselves immensely by joining in the singing, dancing and laughter. I couldn't resist a photograph.

The multitude of museums and galleries in Buenos Aires could rival in quality, quantity and diversity, those of Paris, London, Rome or Madrid. There are museums dedicated to modern art, decorative art, architecture, theatre, children, cinema, natural history, currency, rugby, sculpture and transport, to name a very small selection, purely at random. We always try to visit as many galleries or museums as possible wherever we go. In Buenos Aires we were spoiled for choice, so we opted for the Museo Nacional de Belles Arts, a neo-Classical building, the colour of terracotta. We spent a tranquil couple of hours looking at some modern pieces by Argentinean artists, and also the international collection, which included paintings by Rubens, Rembrandt, Monet, Van Gogh and Picasso.

For our final evening in the beautiful, vibrant city of Buenos Aires, there was only one choice for us: A Tango Bar. Our helpful concierge recommended one within walking distance of our hotel. We were welcomed warmly, and seated at a small table-for-two, at the edge of the dance floor. A seven-piece dance band performed from a tiled alcove, which facilitated great acoustics.

Not surprisingly, the meals available on the menu consisted predominantly of meat. We decided *not* to order steak or mixed grill, mainly in deference to the supreme steak at the Estancia. We chose Locro, a rich stew of beef, pork and vegetables, which was delicious, and not dissimilar to a Liverpudlian pan of scouse. For dessert we had pancakes covered in Dulce de leche; a creamy sauce, which was bottom- clenchingly sweet. Over a few beers and glasses of wine, we enjoyed watching, at close quarters, an intensely dramatic tango, performed by professional dancers. During the interval, several couples, who seemed to be regular customers, took to the floor and strutted their stuff. To my untrained eye, most of the couples seemed to be very good, and I sensed a certain level of unspoken competitiveness on the dance floor. The drama, unsmiling intensity, and occasional sideways glance at other couples, was fascinating to observe. As we downed a few drinks, I could sense the sexual tension generated by the very nature of the tango. It was probably the same for the dancers.

We were momentarily taken aback when a couple came over to our table and invited us to dance. Our tango partners were very kind and generous towards us, as they guided us through the moves. I found the most stressful aspect, apart from keeping a straight face, was the flicking of legs. I dreaded kicking my partner in the shins. After a couple of dances, Norma and I were reunited on the dance floor, and we tried our best for the rest of the evening. It transpired that we were the only non-Argentineans in the restaurant, and everyone made us feel very welcome. We had a great night, and it was handshakes all round as we left. As we walked back to the hotel, we were thinking the same thing as we turned to each other and said, simultaneously,

"Thank God for Mr. Sweeney and our Sunday evening dancing in Sydney."

Flying Down to Rio

Rio de Janeiro, one of the most beautiful and most photographed cities in the world, is actually a misnomer. The first Europeans to arrive, a Portuguese voyage of exploration, thought that the huge Guanabara Bay must be the mouth of a substantial river. They landed in January 1502, and, imaginatively, decided to name the place January River. On discovering that no such river existed the Portuguese decided that the area had no economic potential. The French moved in, but later in the 16th Century the Portuguese realized the error of their ways and defeated the French to re-take the territory.

The original settlement was founded at the foot of the Sugar Loaf Mountain. This is another misnamed feature, apart from the fact that the term mountain somewhat overstates its physical dimensions. The indigenous Tamaio Indians called it Pau-nd-Acuqua, which means a high, pointed, isolated peak. A spot-on description in my opinion. However, the Portuguese thought they had said, 'pau de acucar', meaning sugar loaf. The name stuck, which is probably just as well, because I am sure that future tourists prefer to show off their holiday photos with, "This is me in front of Sugar Loaf," rather than, "This is me in front of a high, pointed, isolated peak."

Rio grew largely on the slave trade, which provided labour for the gold mines, and many more were needed on coffee plantations, because there was an awful lot of coffee in Brazil. The Portuguese Royal Family fled to take up residence in Rio in 1808, to escape the Napoleonic wars. Brazil gained independence from Portugal in 1822, with Rio as the capital city. The concrete statue, 'Christ the Redeemer', the signature of the city, was initially conceived as a commemoration of the centenary of Brazilian independence, to be unveiled in 1922. It finally opened to the public in 1931, but it was worth the nine year wait. The iconic statue stands on the top of the 2,300 feet Corcovado, meaning 'hunchback', the most dynamic plinth in the world.

Blame It On the Bossa Nova

We stayed at the Debret Hotel on Copacabana Beach, and we enjoyed many relaxing hours; people-watching at cafes and bars along the Avenida Atlantic. An endless stream of beautiful promenaders, roller skaters and skateboarder passed along the distinctive black and white tiled, sidewalk. Almost as famous is Ipanema Beach, where everyone is 'tall and tanned and young and lovely...'. The famous song, 'The Girl from Ipanema', recorded by Stan Getz and Astrud Gilberto, sung to the Bossa Nova rhythm, highlighted Brazilian music and beat. This was helped along by Frank Sinatra also recording the song. The lyrics were actually written by Rio de Janeiro's poet laureate, Vinicius de Moraes, who often found his inspiration in a glass of whisky or two (or three). I came across a fantastic quote from him, poetic in its eloquence, in which he described whisky as: 'Man's best friend, like a bottled dog'. Why hasn't a famous Scottish distillery bought the copyright? May I suggest an advertising campaign with the slogan: 'A whisky so smooth, it's the bottled dog's bollocks'. A sure fire winner.

The Rio Carnival has only one serious rival: The New Orleans Mardi Gras. The term 'carnival' is derived from the Portuguese word 'carnevale', which comes from the Latin for 'goodbye to meat', and the celebration began as a pre-Lent observance. The city of Rio was showcased panoramically in the movie 'Moonraker', notably the carnival, and the Sugar Loaf cable car fight between Roger Moore, as James Bond, and Richard Kiel as 'Jaws'.

Preparation for the carnival is a full-time, all-year-round occupation for certain sections of Rio society, and different districts of the Favelas produce their own floats, costumes, samba dances and music. These hillside Favelas have become part of the fabric of the city, as they cling to the surrounding, steep-sided slopes. I believe that tourists can now go on escorted tours, but when we were there in the late seventies this was certainly not an option. I suppose they could be described as being equivalent to South Africa's townships, or the shanty towns of some Caribbean islands. The Favelas were actually started by soldiers returning from a northern war, in 1897. The authorities allowed them to camp temporarily on a hillside in central Rio, while accommodation was arranged for them. This never materialized, and, as with so many things that start off as a temporary arrangement, the camps became permanent. The soldiers built huts; there were 100 in 1904 and some 5,000 by 1933. Today, there are approximately 500 little 'towns', each with its own name.

We were sad that our stay in Rio was coming to an end, as, indeed, was our trip round the world. On the flight home, with Varig Airlines, we reminisced about all the places we had visited, all the sights we had seen, and some fantastic people we had met. We were now looking forward to a traditional Christmas, with family and friends, and we decided to start the celebrations early. We relaxed, sunk into our seats and ordered complimentary drinks from the flight attendant. I put on earphones to listen to some in-flight entertainment. How appropriate that the first song was Frank Sinatra singing, 'It's very nice to go travelling… but it's so much nicer, yes it's so much nicer, to come home'. Lyrics which are very true… until the travel bug bites again. There is no known cure, and a quick glance at my portable time-machine tells me that I will soon be… Emperor of China.

Also by John Meadows

You Did Say Have Another Sausage?

ISBN 9781944156152

18080429R00190

Printed in Great Britain
by Amazon